Michael Jackson: The FBI Found Nothing

by D Francis
and Daniel Francis

TRUT

The FBI Found
NOTHING
H

ISBN-13: 978-0992854874 (DF Books Limited)
ISBN-10: 0992854873
Black and White version.

DF Books Limited
www.13june2005.com

Cover Picture, verdict day headlines, mock newspaper and videographer screen-grab fair use is sought.
This book is produced for educational purposes.

Source of contents and Credit: FBI vault website.
vault.fbi.gov/Michael%20Jackson, others mentioned in this book.

Image Source Credit: Some of the images produced in this book are purchased from royalty free sites. Credit is given to third party sources so far as they are known. Fair use is sought for this educational book.

To the extent that third party sources have been used, fair use is sought. This book has been produced for educational purposes.

Disclaimer: The transcripts might not be verbatim. The transcripts have been transcribed from youtube video footage. The authors are not professional transcribers. Some allowance should be given for transcription difficulties due to audio quality, presentation of the subject, inaudibility of the subject, venue, human error and mishearing. There is no intention to misrepresent a subject and any and all suggestions otherwise will be denied and defended.

No warranty is provided.

E quibus hi vacuas implent sermonibus aures,
Hi narrata ferunt alio: mensuraque sicti
Crescit, et auditis aliquid novus adjicit autor.
Illic Credulitas, illic temerarius Error,
Vanaque Lætitia est, consternatique Timores,
Sedilioque recens, dubioque autore Susurri.

With idle tales this fills our empty ears;
The next reports what from the first he hears;
The rolling fictions grow in strength and size,
Each Author adding to the former lies.
Here vain credulity, with new desires,
Leads us astray, and groundless joy inspires,
The dubious whispers, tumults fresh design'd,
And chilling fears astound the anxious mind.

THURSDAY, NOVEMBER 9, 1710.
The Examiner, Number 14
Rev. Jonathan Swift

Introduction

A pervasive shadow of allegations follows Michael Jackson, even in death.

Allegations that were never substantiated in any court of law.

This book contains primary source material from the FBI vault.

It is hoped that the misconceptions surrounding these released files are dispelled, and that some assistance is provided to the reader in understanding the outcome of the 2005 trial.

There are seven released FBI files. This book is structured to provide a synopsis of each file and thereafter the entire file is reproduced.

It is clear from the contents of the files that **'The FBI Found Nothing.'**

This outcome was after a decade of '*forensic,*' '*strategic*' and '*investigative assistance*' provided to the Santa Barbara District Attorneys office.

Two-thirds of the released files, cited **Michael Jackson** as the **'VICTIM'** of '*threats*' and '*extortion*'. This is an overlooked fact.

Michael Jackson maintained his innocence throughout these investigations.

Facing frenzied media attention, Michael Jackson asked the public not to "*condemn*" him; and to allow him to have his "*day in court,*" where he stated he would be "*acquitted and vindicated when the truth is told.*"

Michael Jackson was acquitted of all charges on **13 June 2005**. Thereafter, the FBI files were administratively closed.

Contents

Table of Contents

Neverland Statement - 22 December 1993

Neverland Statement - 22 December 1993

[...] and fans. I wish to convey my deepest gratitude for your love and support.

I am doing well and I am strong. As you may already know, after my tour ended, I remained out of the country undergoing treatment for a dependency on pain medication. This medication was initially prescribed to ease the excruciating pain that I was suffering after reconstruction surgery on my scalp.

There have been many disgusting statements made recently concerning allegations of improper conduct on my part.

These statements about me are totally false.

As I have maintained from the very beginning, I am hoping for a speedy end to the **horrifying, horrifying** experience to which I have been subjected.

I shall not in this statement respond to all the false allegations that have been made against me, since my lawyers have advised me that this is not the proper forum in which to do that.

I will say that I am **particularly upset** at the handling of this mass matter by the incredible, terrible mass media. At every opportunity, the media has dissected and manipulated these allegations to reach their own conclusions.

I ask all of you to wait to hear the **truth** before you label or condemn me. Don't treat me like a criminal, because **I AM INNOCENT.**

I have been forced to submit to a dehumanizing and humiliating examination by the Santa Barbara County Sheriff's Department and the Los Angeles Police Department earlier this week. They served a search warrant on me, which allowed them to view and photograph my body including my penis, my buttocks, my lower torso, thighs, and any other area that they wanted.

They were supposed to be looking for any discoloration, spotting, blotches or any other evidence of a skin disorder called **VITILIGO** which I have previously spoken about.

The warrant also directed me to cooperate in any examination of my body by their physician to determine the condition of my skin including whether I had **VITILIGO** or any other skin disorder.

The warrant further stated that I had no right to refuse this examination or photographs, and if I failed to cooperate with them they would introduce that refusal at any trial as an indication of my guilt.

It was the most humiliating ordeal of my life... one that no person should ever have to suffer. Even after experiencing the **indignity** of this search, the parties involved were still not satisfied. They wanted to take even more pictures.

It was a nightmare, a horrifying nightmare, but if this is what I have to endure to prove my innocence, my complete innocence, so be it.

Throughout my life I have only tried to help thousands upon thousands of children to live happy lives. It brings tears to my eyes when I see any child that suffers.

I am not guilty of these allegations.

But if I am guilty of anything it is of giving all that I have to give to help children all over the world; it is of loving children of all ages and races, it is of gaining sheer joy from seeing children with their innocent and smiling faces, it is of enjoying through them the childhood that **I missed myself**.

If I am guilty of anything, it is of believing what God said about children:

> *"Suffer little children to come unto me, and forbid them not for this is the Kingdom of Heaven."*

In no way do I think that I am God but **I do try to be God-like in my heart.**

I AM TOTALLY INNOCENT OF ANY WRONGDOING AND I KNOW THESE TERRIBLE ALLEGATIONS WILL ALL BE PROVEN FALSE.

Again, to my friends and fans, thank you very much for all of your support.

Together, we will see this through to the very end.

I love you very much and may God bless you all.

I love you. Good-bye.

Michael Jackson

Live from Neverland Valley

NAACP Image Awards 1994

26th NAACP Image Awards

NAACP Image Awards 1994

The 26th NAACP Image Awards ceremony was held at the Pasadena Civic Auditorium on 05 January 1994.

Michael Jackson delivered a five-minute speech declaring his innocence to a supportive and affectionate audience. Michael Jackson received a standing ovation, and on a number of occasions he had to pause to allow the cheering and applause to subside.

> Hostess [Jasmine Guy]: Hello again I am Jasmine Guy again. And on behalf of all dancers I am proud to present the first Image Award for Choreography in Film or Television.
>
> African American culture has created all styles of dance from the explosive Afro-Caribbean rhythms of Katherine Dunham , to the Cake Walk, to the Charleston, to the dazzling tap dancing of Bill "Bojangles" Robinson, and Sammy Davis, to the fluid moves of Judith Jamison, to the grace of dance theater Harlem, to the show stopping moves of tonight's nominees, and they are: Debbie Allen (The 65th Annual Academy Awards); Michael Peters (What's Love Got To Do With It); Otis Sallid (Malcolm X); Russell Clark (Townsend Television); and Tina Landon and Omar Lopez (for If).
>
> Here to present the very first Image Award for Outstanding Choreography. One of the greatest dancer choreographers in history, last years Entertainer of the Year, the best recording artist in the world, the King of Pop, Rock and Soul: **Mr Michael Jackson**.

[Cheering, applause, and a standing ovation.]

> Michael Jackson: I love you too.
>
> Michael Jackson: Thank you for your warm and generous support, I love you very much. [Applause and cheering.]
>
> Michael Jackson: For decades, the NAACP has stood at the forefront of the struggle for equal justice under the law for all people in our land. They have fought in the lunchrooms of the South, in the hallowed halls of the Supreme Court and the boardrooms of corporate America - for **justice, equality** and the very dignity of all mankind.
>
> Michael Jackson: Members of the NAACP have been jailed and even killed in the noble pursuit of those ideals, upon which our country

was founded. None of these goals is more meaningful for me at this time in my life than the notion that **everyone is presumed to be innocent.** [Loud cheering and applause.]

Michael Jackson: **Everyone is presumed to be innocent and totally-innocent until they are charged with a crime, and then convicted by a jury of their peers.** [Loud applause, cheering and a standing ovation.]

Michael Jackson: I never. I never really took the time to understand the importance of that ideal until now. **Until I became the victim of false allegations.** [Applause and screaming]

Michael Jackson: **And the willingness of others to believe and exploit the worst before they have a chance to hear the TRUTH.**

Audience member: Tell it, Michael.

Michael Jackson: Because...

Audience Member: Speak out Michael. We love you.

Michael Jackson: Oh I love you.

Audience Member: We love you, Michael.

Michael Jackson: I love you more!

Michael Jackson: Because not only, because not only am I presumed to be innocent, **I am innocent.**

Audience: Yes! [Cheering and applause.]

Michael Jackson: And I know the truth will be my salvation. [Applause and cheering.]

Michael Jackson: I have been strengthened in my fight to prove my innocence by my faith in God, and by the knowledge that I am not fighting this battle alone. [Applause]

Michael Jackson: Together, we will see this thing through.

Michael Jackson: I am very proud to be here. [Cheering and applause.]

Michael Jackson: And now it is my distinct honor to announce the recipient of the first **NAACP Image Award for Outstanding Choreography in Film or Television**. The Image Award goes to...

Audience: Debbie Allen.

Michael Jackson: You're right **Debbie Allen**.

Debbie Allen: Thank you.

Debbie Allen: This is indeed a historic moment for many reasons. God be with you Michael; **we are all on your side**. [Cheering, whistling, and applause.]

[Photo: Screengrab.]

Neverland Statement - 30 January 2005

Neverland Statement - 30 January 2005

In the last few weeks, a large amount of ugly, malicious information has been released into the media about me.

Apparently, this information was leaked through transcripts in a grand jury proceeding **where neither my lawyers, nor I, ever appeared.**

The information is disgusting and false.

Years ago, I allowed a family to visit and spend some time at Neverland.

Neverland is my home. I allowed this family into my home because they told me their son was ill with cancer and needed my help.

Through the years, I have helped thousands of children who were ill or in distress.

These events have caused a nightmare for my family, my children and me. I never intend to place myself in so vulnerable a position again.

I love my community and I have great faith in our justice system.

Please keep an open mind and let me have my day in court.

I deserve a fair trial like every other American citizen.

I will be **acquitted** and **vindicated when the truth is told.**

Michael Jackson

FBI Website

FBI Website

"Michael Jackson (1958-2009) was a famous singer and entertainer. Between 1993 and 1994 and separately between 2004 and 2005, Jackson was investigated by California law enforcement agencies for possible child molestation. He was acquitted of all such charges. The FBI provided technical and investigative assistance to these agencies during the cases. The Bureau also investigated threats made against Mr. Jackson and others by an individual who was later imprisoned for these crimes. These investigations occurred between 1992 and 2005."

Source: https://vault.fbi.gov/popular-culture?b_start:int=80

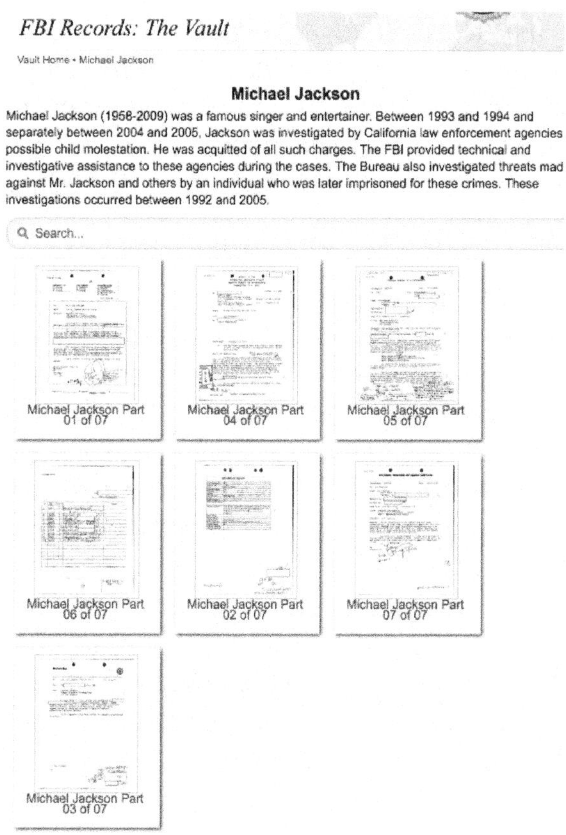

Picture: Screengrab.

On the 22 December 2009 the FBI published the following information:

> *"In response to Freedom of Information Act requests, the Bureau has released its investigative files on the late entertainer Michael Jackson, who died earlier this year.*
>
> *"The records total 333 pages, divided into seven files. They detail the FBI's investigation of a man who threatened to kill Jackson, as well as various forms of assistance to California authorities in two cases involving allegations that Jackson had abused children. It should be emphasized that none of these allegations were ever proven in court.*
>
> *"The files are available on the Freedom of Information Act/Privacy website, but here is a quick rundown of what they contain.*
>
> *"The first file—9A-LA-142276—was opened by the Los Angeles FBI office when it was asked to lead a federal case against a California man already under arrest for sending numerous threatening letters. The man—who falsely claimed to be the son of mobster John Gotti—had staked out Jackson's house and threatened to kill him, the U.S. president, and others. He was ruled incompetent to stand trial and sent to prison for two years.*
>
> *"The second and third files—62D-LA-162715 and 62D-LO-11779—involve the Bureau's support of local law enforcement. In 1993, the Los Angeles and the Santa Barbara Police departments formed a task force to investigate an allegation that Jackson had molested a young boy. FBI field divisions in Los Angeles and New York—as well as Bureau overseas offices in Manila and London—provided assistance in that case. Investigators gathered public records on Jackson, interviewed a potential witness, and followed various other leads. The FBI assisted Los Angeles Police Department detectives who traveled to the Philippines to interview possible witnesses and shared news reports from London about a potential victim. The U.S. Attorney declined to pursue a federal investigation, including a possible violation of the Mann Act (transporting a minor across state lines for immoral purposes), and no charges were filed by the state.*
>
> *"The fourth file—95A-HQ-1148159—concerns a 1995 request by a U.S. Customs agent in Florida that the Bureau examine a VHS videotape connected with Jackson to see if it contained child pornography. Forensic specialists discovered that the tape was a "poor quality third or fourth generation recording" and informed the Customs Service of their findings.*

"In 2003, Jackson was charged by the state of California with molestation and other counts.

"The final three files—62D-LA-236081, 252B-IR-6808, and 305B-LA-239205—detail the Bureau's support to local law enforcement during the ensuing investigation. The first of these files describes an FBI response to a Los Angeles Police Department request to analyze computers and digital media obtained from Jackson's home under court warrant. The second involves a request by the Santa Barbara County District Attorney for help and guidance from behavioral analysts in the FBI's Critical Incident Response Group. In the last of the three files, an FBI agent from Los Angeles traveled to New York to interview a potential witness. The agent found this individual unwilling to cooperate and closed the matter. The case went to court in 2005, and Jackson was acquitted of all charges."

Source: https://archives.fbi.gov/archives/news/stories/2009/december/jackson_122209

This book reproduces the FBI files.

Far from the medias scaremongering portrayal of Michael Jackson as a sexual predator, the documents clearly show that all leads were closed.

It can be concluded without a doubt that the **FBI Found Nothing.**

FBI Website

Chapter One - Press Cuttings

OUTCOMES

Outcomes

In 1993, the London authorities sent press cuttings to their counterparts in Los Angeles.

Legat London advised that they intended to take **no further action** about the information provided.

Outcome: **No further action.**

FD-36 (Rev. 11-17-88)

FBI

TRANSMIT VIA:
- ☐ Teletype
- ☐ Facsimile
- ☒ AIRTEL

PRECEDENCE:
- ☐ Immediate
- ☐ Priority
- ☐ Routine

CLASSIFICATION:
- ☐ TOP SECRET
- ☐ SECRET
- ☐ CONFIDENTIAL
- ☐ UNCLAS E F T O
- ☐ UNCLAS

Date 9/2/93

TO : SAC, LOS ANGELES

FROM : LEGAT, LONDON (62D-LO-11779)

SUBJECT : MICHAEL JACKSON;
ALLEGATION OF CHILD ABUSE;
DOMESTIC POLICE COOPERATION

Enclosed is a letter and its attachments dated September 1993 which was received 9/2/93 from [redacted] [redacted] b7D

The letter provides background information on articles that appeared in the U.K. press concerning a British national who alleges that MICHAEL JACKSON made an indecent telephone call to him during 1979. [redacted] [redacted] b6 b7C

The enclosed information is provided to Los Angeles Division who is requested to provide the information to the appropriate local authorities. [redacted] have advised that they intend to take no action in this matter and is providing the information for information only. b7D

Legat London is taking no further action in this matter.

2-Los Angeles (Enc. 1)
1-London

RID:rkg
(3)

L/T set rkg

Open & Close C-4

62D-LO-11779-1
Searched
Indexed
Serialized
Filed

Approved: ________ Transmitted ________ (Number) (Time) Per ________

THE
PLE
AK

By CHESTER STERN
ne Correspondent

People who witness or me will be given a new em speak out in court reprisals.

Michael Howard is to act l of criminals walking free ms are scared to testify.

rials lence the r — been more ions, quir- have

s, to Party ber,

esses and tities life. t of i no with ds. ority iated ickly where ecure

Protection for court witnesses

transport to take witnesses to and from court.

The controversial rule which forces the prosecution in major trials to disclose full details of their case in advance is also likely to be amended.

And Mr Howard's plans include a law to prevent unscrupulous defence lawyers from tracking down witnesses prepared to give evidence against their clients.

They follow mounting pressure from backbenchers

Continued on Page 2

Strange phone calls from Michael Jackson

SUPERSTAR AND FAN: Michael Jackson with Terry George in 1983

CONTACTING POLICE: Sister LaToya

By DENNA ALLEN and ANDREW CHAPMAN

SUPERSTAR Michael Jackson made an extraordinary sexually explicit transatlantic telephone call to a 13-year-old British schoolboy fan, it was revealed yesterday.

Now details of the allegations made by Terry George are to be handed to Scotland Yard and Los Angeles police investigating the Jackson child sex scandal.

American detectives are also planning to question LaToya Jackson, who has voiced concern about 50 boys visiting the home she shared with younger brother Michael. Last night she instructed her lawyer to contact the Los Angeles Police Department.

Disturbing

Meanwhile, Terry George, now a 28-year-old disc jockey, has spoken for the first time about the disturbing late-night phone call Jackson made to his home when he was just a boy.

The multi-millionaire singer asked Terry, then 13, about sexual activities in graphic terms. At the same time the star described his own intimate physical actions during the conversation.

After the Jackson scandal exploded last week, Terry said: 'I can believe that the

Continued on Page 3

■ JULIE BURCHILL 31 ■ NIGEL DEMPSTER 47 ■ PATRIC WALKER 54 ■ MONEY 71-79

'THE MAIL ON SUNDAY' 29th AUGUST '93

AWAY FROM SCANDAL: Michael Jackson yesterday — marching with Thai Air Force cadets during his Asian tour

Jackson's strange call to British boy

From Page One

allegations are true because of what happened to me. If it hadn't been for that phone call I would never have believed it was possible. But when I first heard the news I immediately felt part of it all.

'I'd only dared tell a handful of my closest friends, because I thought nobody would believe me. At last now they know I was telling the truth about what Michael Jackson said to me.

'He just came straight out with his questions. I just giggled. I felt embarrassed and awkward. I didn't really understand what he was talking about.

'I tried to steer him off the subject and then he asked: "Do you believe I'm doing it now?"

'I said "Are you?" I felt panicky. I was shocked. I tried to talk about something else but he brought it back into the conversation. I was uncomfortable.

'The whole conversation lasted about 15 minutes, but he talked about this intimate sexual act for five minutes or so. Then he said he'd phone me the next day.

'Looking back I could have hung up, but he was a superstar and I was flattered and I didn't want him to stop ringing me.'

The friendship with the Yorkshire boy started as part of Terry's hobby of collecting autographs and interviews with stars. Paul McCartney, Kim Wilde, Cilla Black, Boy George – all share a place in his treasured photo album.

Intimate

With a small tape recorder, – a Christmas presents from his proud parents – Terry would wait at stage doors and inside hotel lobbies hoping to snatch a few words and a photograph.

He had already captured Omar Sharif, but his greatest scoop came in February 1979 when he coaxed an interview from Jackson, then 20, who was performing in Leeds. Terry eavesdropped in the lobby of the Dragonara Hotel listening for details of room numbers from porters and cleaners. One let it slip that the Jackson entourage had taken over the eighth floor.

Terry slipped into the lift and knocked on Jackson's door. The superstar answered and invited him into his suite for an exclusive interview.

The questions were innocent fanzine trivia, but it was a magical 30 minutes for the young boy.

'He spoke to me like a friend,' recalls Terry. 'He made me feel special and at the end of it he asked if we could keep in touch and we swapped telephone numbers and addresses.'

Several days later Terry answered the phone at his home in Leeds. Jackson was on the line calling from his London hotel.

'Hi, it's Michael ... is Terry there?'

Again the conversation was easy and casual as the superstar chatted about the tour. Jackson returned to the US, but more calls followed over the next three months. 'Sometimes he rang in the middle of the night,' says Terry. 'Once my father answered. He boasts that he's spoken to Michael Jackson.'

But then came the call in late spring 1979 that shattered the innocence of the relationship.

And very soon afterwards the calls began to peter out. They came to an abrupt end when Terry's parents phone was cut off because he had run up a £340 bill calling the US. His mother said: 'You've been phoning that Michael Jackson, haven't you?'

Charges

Terry tried calling Jackson several times, reversing the charges from a phone box. When he got through it became clear his superstar friend didn't want to know.

The final rejection came four years later when Terry tried to rekindle their friendship when Jackson came to London again. Terry tracked him down and was even photographed alongside his idol, but now the management were on hand to issue the polite brush-off.

'I felt used because he'd wanted my friendship when I was just a boy. Now I was a young man he just didn't seem to want to know,' says Terry.

SHOCKED: Terry George

'Looking back it was wrong of Michael. The call wasn't from a young teenager, but a grown man.'

Now Terry has sworn an affidavit for the Los Angeles Police Department and is prepared to travel to California to help their Enquiries.

Superintendent Michael Hames, head of the Obscene Publications Squad, said yesterday: 'We will investigate this matter alongside the Los Angeles police.'

what was happening.

They claim fear of threats by Jackson's associates stopped them from talking until now.

The Quindoys are seeking \$500,000 (£330,000) in back pay from the superstar, who celebrates his 35th birthday today.

Mr Quindoy, who is preparing a book about the singer, said: 'Michael is such a big man. I was trying to protect him, but it lingered in my mind that it was a civic duty to tell the truth.'

The initial scandal erupted when a dentist in a custody battle alleged his 13-year-old son had been sexually abused at Jackson's home.

Jackson's staff claimed the man was trying to extort millions of dollars.

A Los Angeles TV station claimed last night that, while denying all allegations, Jackson's staff had offered the father £230,000 to keep quiet but he had refused

Hoping

Meanwhile Detective Bill Dworin, of the Los Angeles police child exploitation unit, said he was hoping to speak to Jackson's elder sister LaToya, who has voiced concern about Michael's boy guests.

'We are aware she might be able to identify other children who have spent time in Michael Jackson's company,' he said.

Visitors to the ranch included Home Alone star Macaulay Culkin, 12, and Australian Wade Robson, 10, who both insist they were not sexually assaulted.

Several former employees rallied to the star's defence. One said Quindoy and LaToya had misinterpreted simple kindness.

And Jamee Ruth Newkirk, a former executive at Jackson's ranch, said: 'I never had evidence of anything mischievous ... if someone spent the night, they had their own bedroom.'

● Pepsi-Cola last night denied Los Angeles newspaper reports that they were investigating Jackson's life with a view to dropping him after a £9 million, ten-year association.

DIANA'S VISION:

I'll make my boy the people's king

DIANA...speaks candidly

PRINCESS DIANA has revealed her vision of a down-to-earth monarchy for the future with William as "the people's king."

She has told close friends how she is determined that William will rule without the "arrogant" views of the Palace.

The Princess has vowed to show her sons how ordinary folk in Britain live and make them "feel in their hearts the people's hopes, joys, problems, fears, ambitions and disappointments."

Diana has even decided not to divorce Charles so that she can shape the princes' personalities and future. Full astonishing story—Pages 4 and 5.

AD PHONE

TH

KO

Brit DJ tells of shock call

By CHARLES YATES and DAVID WOODING

A BRITISH disc jockey has told how Michael Jackson made an obscene phone call to him when he was a star-struck schoolboy.

Terry George was only 13 when he had a bizarre late-night conversation with the superstar — who described how he was fondling himself at the other end of the line.

Terry, now 28, is passing on details of the sex chat to Los Angeles police probing the Jackson child-abuse allegations. He first met the star when, as a schoolboy autograph hunter, he managed to interview him in his home city of Leeds.

They became pals and regularly had transatlantic chats — until in one call Jackson, then 20, asked him in graphic detail about sexual activities.

The millionaire told how he was performing a sex act on himself as they spoke.

Terry said he believes the abuse allegations against Jackson — "because of what happened to me."

CONCERT

His revelations are being relayed to the management entourage of the singer, in Singapore on his world tour.

Yesterday 47,000 fans, including actress Liz Taylor, turned a sell-out concert at Singapore's National Stadium into a huge 35th birthday party for Jacko.

He was driven there in a van, peering from behind curtains with a mask over his nose and mouth.

Terry went on: "If it hadn't been for that call I would never have believed the allegations were possible.

"But when I first heard the news I immediately felt

Continued on Page Seven

Masked . . . Jacko peers from van on way to show yesterday

BINGO + GO FOR £1M GOALS: Page 13

'THE SUN' 30th AUGUST '93

switchboard.

Don't worry about the cost, we'll ring you straight back. The number is:

071 782 4134

JACKO SPOT

FUN park bosses still plan to send needy kids to visit Jacko in California after a charity drive at Lightwater Valley, North Yorks

Tecs hired for Pepsi 'probe'

PEPSI-Cola has hired a [illegible] detective agency to [illegible]igate Jacko, it was c[illegible]ed yesterday.

The soft drinks giant, whose ads are fronted by the star, has told Kroll Associates to "examine Jackson's character", U.S. newspapers say.

Kroll is largely staffed by former CIA officers. One writer said: "If you want someone to dig up the dirt, they are the people." Pepsi denied the probe.

We backo Jacko .. fans in London yesterday

Banner headlines . . . in support of Michael

He's a healer not a feeler

LONDON PROTEST

HUNDREDS of fans marched in London yesterday to sing their support for Michael Jackson.

They waved banners saying: "Michael is a healer not a feeler" and "You'll never Moonwalk alone."

They sang Happy Birthday at the demo near Eros' statue in Piccadilly Circus.

Interior designer Louise Ayre, 21, of Beckenham, Kent, said: "He's innocent. I'm in love with him and these allegations are blackmail."

Chris Rich, 11, from Barnet, North London, said: "If he asked me to go to his ranch Neverland I'd be really happy."

Student Ann Stephenson, 20, of Bedford, said: "The Press is saying the stories have ruined his career, but this demonstration shows we still support him."

Sonya Henson, 21, of Barnet, said: "He'll never be able to go around his fairground rides with kids hanging off him without people raising an eyebrow."

[illegible] said. It was at this meeting that the demands were made. The father repeatedly demanded the money to fund a film project. His demands were refused.

"He said he would accuse Michael of being a child molester if we failed to pay up."

Jacko, pictured above performing in Singapore last night, remained silent throughout the meeting, Pellicano said.

Chandler, 42 — whose son claims the star performed oral sex on him — "stormed out" after an hour.

Later that day, Pellicano claims Chandler's lawyers offered Jacko "a deal" in which the father would receive more than £3million a year over four years.

Horrors

This was also "turned down flat," he said.

"We believe the child-abuse charges stemmed from these meetings," he added. "Mr Jackson adamantly denies all the charges against him."

But last night the source close to Dr Chandler said he was "furious" at Pellicano's claims.

"It is true he tried to reach an out-of-court settlement with the Jackson camp," he said.

"But it was to spare his son the horrors of a massive court case.

"Jackson's side offered Dr Chandler £220,000 to drop the charges. But by then Dr Chandler had reported the matter to authorities.

"He is very upset by Jackson's attempts to discredit him and his son. He absolutely believes Jordy is telling the truth. He acted in the boy's best interests"

Jordy . . . 'abused by star'

The dentist's lawyer Barry Rothman said: "There was no blackmail attempt. We stand by our charges."

Police yesterday revealed they had begun a probe into the alleged blackmail attempt

A spokesman for Los Angeles police said: "Both sides are making charges against each other and we will look at all sides.

"Our inquiries regarding the child sex abuse claims against Mr Jackson are still very active.

"We are talking to dozens of children who have known him."

Littlejohn — Page Six

MY PHONE SEX WITH STAR

Continued from Page One

part of it all. I'd only dared tell a handful of my closest friends, because I thought nobody would believe me. [illegible] last they know I w[illegible] telling the truth about what Michael Jackson said to me."

Terry told a Sunday newspaper: "He just came straight out with his questions.

"I felt embarrassed and awkward. I didn't really understand what he was talking about. I tried to steer him off the subject and he asked, 'Do you believe I'm doing it now?'

"I said, 'Are you?' I felt panicky. I was shocked.

"The whole conversation lasted about 15 minutes and he talked about this intimate sexual act for five minutes or so.

"I could have hung up, but he was a superstar and I was flattered and I didn't want him to stop ringing me."

The pair's friendship started in February 1979 when Terry tracked Jacko to his room at the Dragonara Hotel, where he was staying before a performance.

Over the next three months they spoke several times on the phone — often "in the middle of the night."

Then came the conversation that shattered the relationship.

In 1983 Terry tried to renew the friendship when Jacko was in London. They were pictured together but the star's entourage brushed him away from any further contact.

Terry said: "I felt used because he had wanted my friendship when I was just a boy.

"Now I was a young man he didn't seem to want to know."

The storm surrounding Jacko blew up last week after it was alleged he abused Jordy Schwartz, 13, son of a rich California dentist.

Mates . . . Jackson and Terry George in 1983

Cliff: It's the price of fame

CLIFF Richard has backed Jacko — and says the child-abuse claims are part of the price of fame.

Cliff, 52, told a Christian festival in Corby, Northants: "He's probably the best singer alive and look at what he's going through.

"When you become a public image, you're up for grabs and very, very vulnerable."

NOW READ LATOYA JACKSON'S EXPLOSIVE BOOK: See Pages 16 and 17

Telecommunications Act 1984

Improper use of public telecommunication system.

43.—(1) A person who—

(a) sends, by means of a public telecommunication system, a message or other matter that is grossly offensive or of an indecent, obscene or menacing character; or

(b) sends by those means, for the purpose of causing annoyance, inconvenience or needless anxiety to another, a message that he knows to be false or persistently makes use for that purpose of a public telecommunication system;

shall be guilty of an offence and liable on summary conviction to a fine not exceeding level 3 on the standard scale.

(2) Subsection (1) above does not apply to anything done in the course of providing a cable programme service ~~(within the meaning of Part IV of this Act).~~

NOTE: Amended vide Schedule 5 of the Cable and Broadcasting Act 1984

CLASSIFICATION: **UNCLAS**

OFFICE OF THE LEGAL ATTACHE
AMERICAN EMBASSY
LONDON, ENGLAND

SECURE FAX: [redacted]
NON-SECURE FAX: [redacted]
TELEPHONE: [redacted] **Ext** [redacted]

b2
b6
b7C

Date: 9/2/93

☐ I M M E D I A T E
☒ P R I O R I T Y
☐ R O U T I N E

Number of pages including this page: 20

TO: SAC, LOS ANGELES   File No:

FAX NO:

ATTN:

FROM: LEGAL ATTACHE, LONDON (62D-LO-11779)

ORIGINATOR: DLAT [redacted]   b6 b7C

SUBJECT: MICHAEL JACKSON;
ALLEGATION OF CHILD ABUSE;
DOMESTIC POLICE COOPERATION

SPECIAL NOTES/INSTRUCTIONS: b7D

Attached for Los Angeles is a copy of an airtel dated 9/2/93 and an enclosure letter and attachments from [redacted] [redacted] regarding captioned subject.

The original airtel and attachments are being forwarded via Bureau mail.

62D-LO-11779-2

Searched..........
Indexed..........
Serialized..........
Filed..........

Approved: ______   CLASSIFICATION: **UNCLAS**   **Sent:** 9/3/93

0017 MRI 01368

RR RUCNFB LON

DE FBILA #0018 2941855

ZNR UUUUU

R 211830Z OCT 93

FM FBI LOS ANGELES (62D-LO-11779) (RUC)

TO DIRECTOR FBI/ROUTINE/

LEGAT LONDON/ROUTINE/

BT

UNCLAS

CITE: //3410:C-1//

PASS: FBIHQ, SSA [redacted] FLU II, OLIA; SSA [redacted] b6 b7C

VCMO.

SUBJECT: MICHAEL JACKSON; ALLEGATION OF CHILD ABUSE; DOMESTIC POLICE COOPERATION; OO: LONDON.

RE LEGAT LONDON AIRTEL TO LOS ANGELES, DATED SEPTEMBER 2, 1993.

FOR INFORMATION OF LEGAT LONDON, THE LETTER, DATED SEPTEMBER 1993, TO [redacted], DEPUTY LEGAL ATTACHE, AMERICAN EMBASSY, LONDON, FROM [redacted] b6 b7C b7D

C-1 10/27/93 cms

62D-LO-11779-3

SEARCHED INDEXED
SERIALIZED cms FILED cms

OCT 22 1993

[redacted] ...CHE — London

b6 b7C

PAGE TWO DE FBILA 0018 UNCLAS

[redacted] AND ATTACHED NEWSPAPER ARTICLES REGARDING MICHAEL JACKSON AND BRITISH NATIONAL TERANCE GEORGE WERE FURNISHED TO THE LOS ANGELES POLICE DEPARTMENT (LAPD). THESE ITEMS WERE PROVIDED ON OCTOBER 4, 1993 TO [redacted] OF THE SEXUALLY EXPLOITED CHILDREN'S UNIT OF THE LAPD. FOR INFORMATION OF LEGAT LONDON, LOS ANGELES IS MAINTAINING LIAISON WITH LAPD AND THE SANTA BARBARA SHERIFF'S OFFICE IN THE CONTINUED INVESTIGATION OF MOLESTATION ALLEGATIONS AGAINST MICHAEL JACKSON, UNDER LOS ANGELES FILE 62D-LA-162715.

b6
b7C
b7D

BT

#0018

NNNN

FEDERAL BUREAU OF INVESTIGATION
FOIPA
DELETED PAGE INFORMATION SHEET

No Duplication Fees are charged for Deleted Page Information Sheet(s).

Total Deleted Page(s) ~ 13
Page 4 ~ b6, b7C, b7D
Page 5 ~ b6, b7C, b7D
Page 6 ~ b6, b7C
Page 7 ~ b6, b7C
Page 8 ~ b6, b7C
Page 13 ~ b6, b7C, b7D
Page 14 ~ b6, b7C, b7D
Page 15 ~ b6, b7C, b7D
Page 16 ~ b6, b7C, b7D
Page 17 ~ b6, b7C, b7D
Page 18 ~ b6, b7C, b7D
Page 19 ~ b6, b7C, b7D
Page 20 ~ b6, b7C, b7D

Chapter Two - Computers

OUTCOMES

Outcomes

On 15 January 2004, the Santa Barbara Sheriff's Department requested the assistance of the FBI in processing the computer hard drives and related media.

The request stipulated that the hardware should be sent to the Santa Barbara Sheriff's Office Laboratory for processing due to the sensitive nature of the case.

Sixteen Apple Macintoshes, Windows machines and four DVD's underwent examination and review.

The results of the examinations showed **NO EVIDENCE.**

Outcome: The **case file closed** following Michael Jackson's acquittal on 13 June 2005.

CART SERVICE REQUEST

Service Request ID:	482
Request Date:	1/15/04
UCFN:	62D - LA - 236081
Submitting Agency:	FBI
Requestor:	SA [redacted]
Address:	
City, State Zip:	Santa Maria CA
Phone:	[redacted]
Assign Request to:	LA
Date Analysis Needed:	
Request Description:	Santa Barbara Sheriff's Dept. has requested assistance processing computers and related media relating to the Michael Jackson case. SBSD has requested examiners with [redacted] backgrounds.
Search String:	
Search Location:	
Legal Authority:	Search Warrant
System Information:	Apple Macintosh & Windows machines (stand alone).
SuspectCharged:	No
Accessed Evidence:	
Privileged Information:	

b2 b6 b7C

b2 b7E

b6 b7C

1/15/04

OBA, HQ

1/15/04

16165.wpd

Subm ID# 16165

62D-LA-236081-CART-1

FD-340a (Rev. 11-12-89)

b6
b7C

(Title) Michael Joe Jackson's [redacted] -Victim

DPC

(File No.) 62D-LA-236681-CART

Item	Date Filed	To be returned Yes	To be returned No		Disposition
1A1	4-13-04		X	Case Notes-exams (3/2/04-3/11/04) (15 pgs) Case Notes-exams (3/20/04-3/29/04) (13 pgs)	SM
1A2	4-13-04		X	List of all specimens (3 pages) SM	
1A3	4-13-04		X	Case notes-exams (printed) (4 pages) Case notes-exams (handwritten) (7 pages) SM	
1A4	4-13-04		X	Review of string search/keyword hits (18 pages) SM	
1A5	4-13-04		X	Case notes-exams (7 pages) SM	
1A6	4-13-04		X	FedEx Receipt for DELAR SM	
1A7	4-13-04		X	Case notes-exams (2/12/04-3/5/04) (9 pages) Case notes-exams (3/22/04-4/1/04) (11 pgs)	SM

62D-LA-236681-CART
SM
4/13/04

FD-340 (Rev. 3-8-01)

Universal Case File Number 62D-LA-236081-CART-1A1

Field Office Acquiring Evidence LA

Serial # of Originating Document 12

Date Received 4/5/2004

From [redacted]
(Name of Contributor)

CART HQ
(Address of Contributor)

(City and State)

By [redacted]

b6
b7C

To Be Returned ☐ Yes ☒ No

Receipt Given ☐ Yes ☒ No

Grand Jury Material - Disseminate Only Pursuant to Rule 6 (e)
Federal Rules of Criminal Procedure
☐ Yes ☒ No

Federal Taxpayer Information (FTI)
☐ Yes ☒ No

Title: MICHAEL JOE JACKSON;
[redacted] VICTIM;
DPC

Reference
(Communication Enclosing Material)

Description: ☐ , Original notes re interview of

Case Notes - exams (3/2/04 - 3/11/04) (15 pages)

Case Notes - exams (3/20/04 - 3/29/04) (13 pages)

4-13-04
[initials]

FD-340 (Rev. 3-8-01)

Universal Case File Number 62D-LA-236081-CART-1A2

Field Office Acquiring Evidence LA

Serial # of Originating Document 12

Date Received 4/5/2004

From ______ (Name of Contributor)

CART HQ (Address of Contributor)

(City and State)

By ______

To Be Returned ☐ Yes ☒ No

Receipt Given ☐ Yes ☒ No

b6
b7C

Grand Jury Material - Disseminate Only Pursuant to Rule 6 (e) Federal Rules of Criminal Procedure

☐ Yes ☒ No

Federal Taxpayer Information (FTI)

☐ Yes ☒ No

Title: MICHAEL JOE JACKSON; ______ VICTIM;

DPC

Reference: (Communication Enclosing Material)

Description: ☐ Original notes re interview of

LIST OF ALL SPECIMENS

(3 pages)

4-13-04

62D-LA-236081
LIST OF SPECIMENS

SBSO Item Number	*FBI "Q" Number*	*DE Number*	*Size*		*Comments*
SBSO MX200-05	**QLA1**				
Item 908	QLA1_1	DELA1	1 GB		4 - PB 1400c laptop from bedroom/office
Item 909	QLA1_2	DELA1	30 GB		Apple PB G4 laptop from office
Item 910A	QLA1_3	DELA1	60 GB		Apple PB G4 from office
Item 910B	QLA1_4	DELA1	80 GB		Apple PB G4 from office
Item 912A	QLA1_5	DELA2	80 GB		Apple PB G4 from office
SBSO MX200-02	**QLA2**				
Item 329	QLA2_1	DELA2	30 GB		Apple laptop with projector from suitcase from stairwell closet
Item 336	QLA2_2	DELA3	60 GB		Apple eMac from master den floor area
Item 342	QLA2_3	DELA4	60 GB		iMac from MJJ office desk
Item 347A	QLA2_4	DELA4	40 GB		2 - PB G4 from MJJ bedroom
Item 644	QLA2_5	DELA5	60 GB		Apple PB G4 laptop from upstairs video library bathroom
Item 645	QLA2_6	DELA3	40 GB		Apple laptop from upstairs video library bathroom
Item 911	QLA2_7	DELA5	30 GB		Apple PB G4 from office
Item 347B	QLA2_8	DELA5	20 GB		2 - PB G4 from MJJ bedroom
Item 912B	QLA2_9	DELA7	80 GB		Apple PB G4 from office
SBSOMX200-01	**QLA3**				
Item 308	QLA3_1	DELA4	8 GB		3 - laptop from locked closet in master bedroom
SB Police Dept. Lab HARD DRIVE #22	**QLA4**				
Item 346	QLA4_1	DELA5	2 GB		1 - PB G3 laptop from MJJ bedroom

b2
b7E

62D-LA-236081-CART-1A2

Page 1 of 3
Last printed 4/5/2004 1:29 PM

62D-LA-236081
LIST OF SPECIMENS

DE Number	Contents – FBI Item	Contents – SBSO Item	Comments
DELA12	QLA1_2	909	4 DVDs with copies of graphics files.
DELA13	QLA1_2	909	CD-Summary Results
DELA14	QLA1_3	910A	CD-Summary Results
DELA15	QLA1_4	910B	CD-Summary Results
DELA16	QLA2_8	347B	CD-Summary Results
DELA17	QLA2_5	644	CD-Summary Results
DELA18	QLA2_7	911	CD-Summary Results
DELA19	QLA1_5	912A	CD-Summary Results
DELA20	QLA2_1	329	CD-Summary Results
DELA21	QLA2_2	336	CD-Summary Results
DELA22	QLA2_3	342	CD-Summary Results
DELA23	QLA2_4	347A	CD-Summary Results
DELA24	QLA2_6	645	CD-Summary Results
DELA25	QLA2_9	912B	CD-Summary Results
DELA26	QLA3_1	308	CD-Summary Results
DELA27	QLA4_1	346	CD-Summary Results

Page 3 of 3
Last printed 4/5/2004 1:29 PM

FD-340 (Rev. 3-8-01)

Universal Case File Number 62D-LA-236081-CART-1A3

Field Office Acquiring Evidence LA

Serial # of Originating Document 12

Date Received 4/5/2004

From ____________ (Name of Contributor)

CV - CART (Address of Contributor)

____________ and State)

By ____________

b6
b7C

To Be Returned ☐ Yes ☒ No

Receipt Given ☐ Yes ☒ No

Grand Jury Material - Disseminate Only Pursuant to Rule 6 (e) Federal Rules of Criminal Procedure

☐ Yes ☒ No

Federal Taxpayer Information (FTI)

☐ Yes ☒ No

Title: MICHAEL JOE JACKSON;
____________ - VICTIM;
DPC

Reference: ____________ (Communication Enclosing Material)

Description: ☐ Original notes re interview of

Case notes - exams (printed) (4 pages)
Case notes - exams (handwritten) (7 pages)

4-13-04

FD-340 (Rev. 3-8-01)

Universal Case File Number 62D-LA-236081-CART-1A4

Field Office Acquiring Evidence LA

Serial # of Originating Document 12

Date Received 04/05/2004

From DET. [redacted] (Name of Contributor)

SBSO (Address of Contributor)

(City and State)

By [redacted]

b6
b7C

To Be Returned ☐ Yes ☒ No

Receipt Given ☐ Yes ☒ No

Grand Jury Material - Disseminate Only Pursuant to Rule 6 (e) Federal Rules of Criminal Procedure

☐ Yes ☒ No

Federal Taxpayer Information (FTI)

☐ Yes ☒ No

Title: MICHAEL JOE JACKSON; [redacted] VICTIM; DP

Reference (Communication Enclosing Material)

Description: ☒ Original notes re interview of

Review of string search / Keyword hits (18 pages)

4-13-04

QLA2_9

STRING SEARCH / NOTHING

62D-LA-236081-CART-1A4

1 of 18

QLA1_5

STRING SEARCH / NOTHING

2 of 18

QLA2-1

STRING SEARCH / NOTHING

3 of 18

QLA2_7

STRING SEARCH / NOTHING

7 of 18

QLA2_8

STRING SEARCH / NOTHING

8 of 18

QLA2 _ 6

NOTHING NOTABLE

9 of 18

OLA2-2

b2
b7E

BED

NOTHING

10 of 18

QLA2_5

STRING SEARCHES / NOTHING

11 of 18

QLAI_4

NOTHING

12 of 18

QLA3_1

STRING SEARCHES / NOTHING
EXCEPT AS PREVIOUSLY NOTED -

13 of 18

QLA1_3

STRING SEARCHES / NOTHING

14 of 18

QLA2_3

STRING SEARCHES / NOTHING

15 of 18

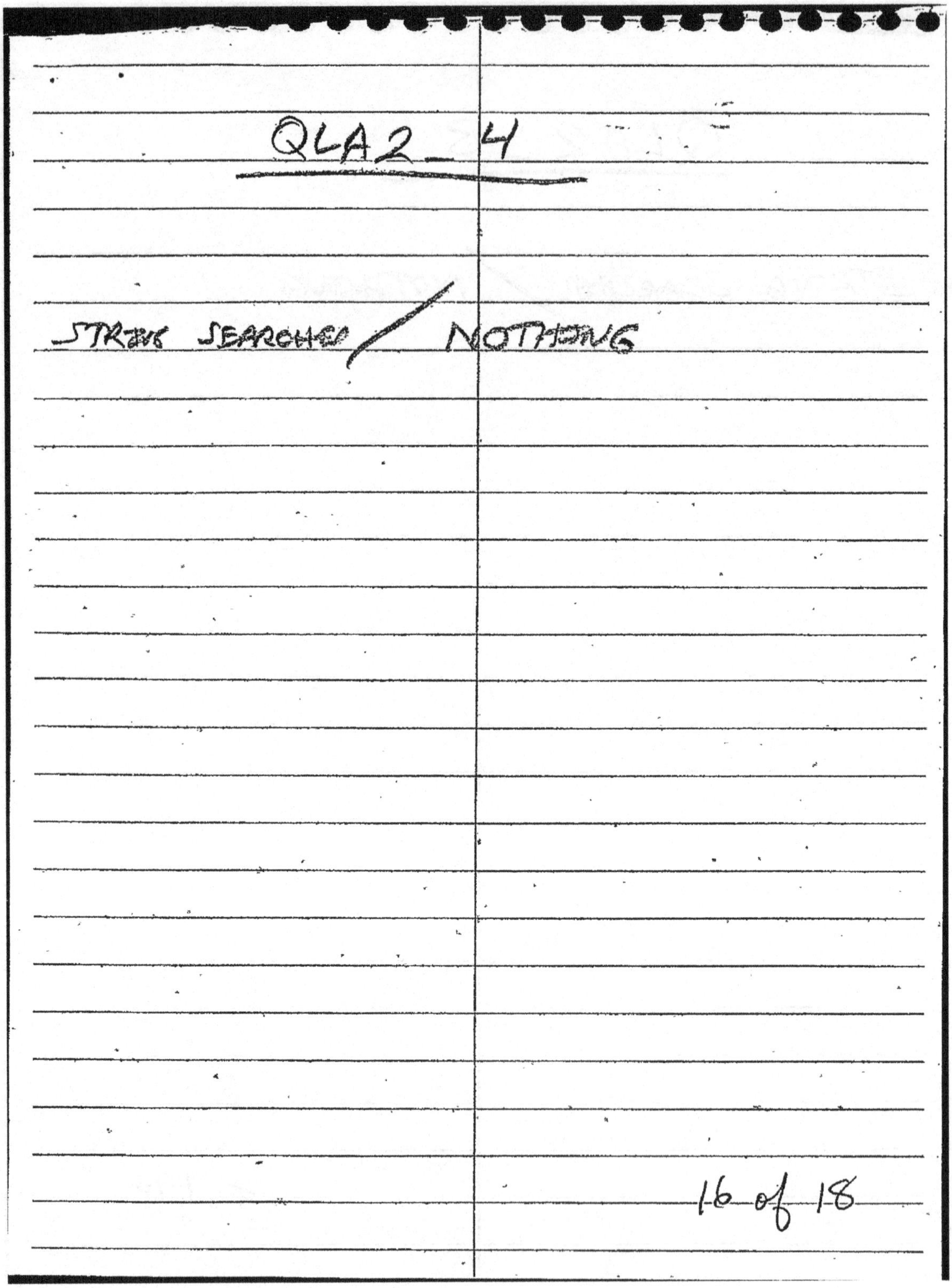
QLA2_4

STRING SEARCHES / NOTHING

16 of 18

QLA4_1

STRING SEARCHES / NOTHING

17 of 18

QLAL 5

NO NOTABLES FILES ON QLA-5

QLA2-1

NO NOTABLES FILES ON QLA2-1

18 of 18

FD-340 (Rev. 3-8-01)

Universal Case File Number 62D-LA-236081-CART-1A5

Field Office Acquiring Evidence LA

Serial # of Originating Document 12

Date Received 4/5/2004

From [redacted] (Name of Contributor)

CART HQ (Address of Contributor)

(City and State)

By [redacted]

b6
b7C

To Be Returned ☐ Yes ☒ No

Receipt Given ☐ Yes ☒ No

Grand Jury Material - Disseminate Only Pursuant to Rule 6 (e) Federal Rules of Criminal Procedure

☐ Yes ☒ No

Federal Taxpayer Information (FTI)

☐ Yes ☒ No

Title: MICHAEL JOE JACKSON; [redacted] VICTIM; DPC

Reference: (Communication Enclosing Material)

Description: ☐ Original notes re interview of

Case notes - exams (7 pages)

4-13-04
SM

FD-340 (Rev. 3-8-01)

Universal Case File Number 62D-LA-236081-CART-1A6

Field Office Acquiring Evidence LA

Serial # of Originating Document 12

Date Received 4/5/2004

From [redacted]

(Name of Contributor)

CART HQ

(Address of Contributor)

[redacted] and State)

By [redacted]

To Be Returned ☐ Yes ☒ No

Receipt Given ☐ Yes ☒ No

b6
b7C

Grand Jury Material - Disseminate Only Pursuant to Rule 6 (e)
Federal Rules of Criminal Procedure

☐ Yes ☒ No

Federal Taxpayer Information (FTI)

☐ Yes ☒ No

Title: MICHAEL JOE JACKSON;
[redacted] - VICTIM;

Reference

(Communication Enclosing Material)

Description: ☒ Original notes re interview of

FedEx Receipt FOR DELA12

4-13-04

DELA12 4 DVDs

FedEx Express USA Airbill

FedEx Tracking Number 844973090960

Form I.D. No. 0200

b2
b6
b7C

Sender's Copy

1 From Please print and press hard.

Date 3/25/04 Sender's FedEx Account Number 1410-2190-7

Sender's Name [redacted] Phone [redacted]

Company FBI/CART

Address ERF BLDG 27958A CART

Dept./Floor/Suite/Room

City QUANTICO State VA ZIP 22135

2 Your Internal Billing Reference First 24 characters will appear on invoice. OPTIONAL

3 To

Recipient's Name FBI Phone [redacted]

Company ATTN: FORENSIC PROGRAMS

Address ERF BLDG #27958A

To "HOLD" at FedEx location, print FedEx address. We cannot deliver to P.O. boxes or P.O. ZIP codes.

Address

Dept./Floor/Suite/Room

City QUANTICO State VA ZIP 22135

Try online shipping at fedex.com

By using this Airbill you agree to the service conditions on the back of this Airbill and in our current Service Guide, including terms that limit our liability.

Questions? Visit our Web site at fedex.com or call 1.800.Go.FedEx® 800.463.3339.

4a Express Package Service Packages up to 150 lbs. Delivery commitment may be later in some areas.

- [X] FedEx Priority Overnight — Next business morning
- [ ] FedEx Standard Overnight — Next business afternoon
- [ ] FedEx First Overnight — Earliest next business morning delivery to select locations
- [ ] FedEx 2Day — Second business day
- [ ] FedEx Express Saver — Third business day

FedEx Envelope rate not available. Minimum charge: One-pound rate

4b Express Freight Service Packages over 150 lbs. Delivery commitment may be later in some areas.

- [ ] FedEx 1Day Freight* — Next business day
- [ ] FedEx 2Day Freight — Second business day
- [ ] FedEx 3Day Freight — Third business day

*Call for Confirmation:

5 Packaging *Declared value limit $500

- [ ] FedEx Envelope*
- [X] FedEx Pak* — Includes FedEx Small Pak, FedEx Large Pak, and FedEx Sturdy Pak
- [ ] Other

6 Special Handling Include FedEx address in Section 3.

- [ ] SATURDAY Delivery — Available ONLY for FedEx Priority Overnight and FedEx 2Day to select ZIP codes
- [ ] HOLD Weekday at FedEx Location — NOT Available for FedEx First Overnight
- [ ] HOLD Saturday at FedEx Location — Available ONLY for FedEx Priority Overnight and FedEx 2Day to select locations

Does this shipment contain dangerous goods? One box must be checked.

- [X] No
- [ ] Yes — As per attached Shipper's Declaration
- [ ] Yes — Shipper's Declaration not required
- [ ] Dry Ice — Dry Ice, 9, UN 1845 ____ x ____ kg

Dangerous Goods (including Dry Ice) cannot be shipped in FedEx packaging.

- [ ] Cargo Aircraft Only

7 Payment Bill to: Enter FedEx Acct. No. or Credit Card No. below.

- [X] Sender — Acct. No. in Section 1 will be billed.
- [ ] Recipient
- [ ] Third Party
- [ ] Credit Card
- [ ] Cash/Check

FedEx Acct. No. Credit Card No. Exp. Date

Total Packages	Total Weight	Total Declared Value†
1	1	$ .00

†Our liability is limited to $100 unless you declare a higher value. See back for details.

FedEx Use Only

8 Release Signature Sign to authorize delivery without obtaining signature.

By signing you authorize us to deliver this shipment without obtaining a signature and agree to indemnify and hold us harmless from any resulting claims.

446

Rev. Date 10/01 • Part #157612 • ©1994–2001 FedEx • PRINTED IN U.S.A. MWI 03

RETAIN THIS COPY FOR YOUR RECORDS.

Terms And Conditions

Definitions On this Airbill, "we," "our," and "us" refer to Federal Express Corporation, its employees, and agents. "You" and "your" refer to the sender, its employees, and agents.

Agreement To Terms By giving us your package to deliver, you agree to all the terms on this Airbill and in our current Service Guide, which is available on request. You also agree to those terms on behalf of any third party with an interest in the package. If there is a conflict between the Service Guide and this Airbill, the Service Guide will control. No one is authorized to change the terms of our Agreement.

Responsibility For Packaging And Completing Airbill You are responsible for adequately packaging your goods and properly filling out this Airbill. If you omit the number of packages and/or weight per package, our billing will be based on our best estimate of the number of packages we received and/or an estimated "default" weight per package as determined by us.

Responsibility For Payment Even if you give us different payment instructions, you will always be primarily responsible for all delivery costs, as well as any cost we incur in either returning your package to you or warehousing it pending disposition.

Limitations On Our Liability And Liabilities Not Assumed

- Our liability in connection with this shipment is limited to the lesser of your actual damages or $100, unless you declare a higher value, pay an additional charge, and document your actual loss in a timely manner. You may pay an additional charge for each additional $100 of declared value. The declared value does not constitute, nor do we provide, cargo liability insurance.
- In any event, we will not be liable for any damage, whether direct, incidental, special, or consequential in excess of the declared value of a shipment, whether or not Federal Express had knowledge that such damages might be incurred including but not limited to loss of income or profits.
- We won't be liable:
  - for your acts or omissions, including but not limited to improper or insufficient packing, securing, marking, or addressing, or those of the recipient or anyone else with an interest in the package.
  - if you or the recipient violates any of the terms of our Agreement.
  - for loss or damage to shipments of prohibited items.
  - for loss, damage, or delay caused by events we cannot control, including but not limited to acts of God, perils of the air, weather conditions, acts of public enemies, war, strikes, civil commotions, or acts of public authorities with actual or apparent authority.

Declared Value Limits

- The highest declared value allowed for a FedEx Envelope and FedEx Pak shipment is $500.
- For other shipments, the highest declared value allowed is $50,000 unless your package contains items of extraordinary value, in which case the highest declared value allowed is $500.
- Items of extraordinary value include shipments containing such items as artwork, jewelry, furs, precious metals, negotiable instruments, and other items listed in our Service Guide.
- You may send more than one package on this Airbill and fill in the total declared value for all packages, not to exceed the $100, $500, or $50,000 per package limit described above. (Example: 5 packages can have a total declared value of up to $250,000.) In that case, our liability is limited to the actual value of the package(s) lost or damaged, but may not exceed the maximum allowable declared value(s) or the total declared value, whichever is less. You are responsible for proving the actual loss or damage.

Filing A Claim YOU MUST MAKE ALL CLAIMS IN WRITING and notify us of your claim within strict time limits set out in the current Service Guide.

You may call our Customer Service department at 1.800.Go.FedEx® 800.463.3339 to report a claim; however, you must still file a timely written claim.

Within 90 days after you notify us of your claim, you must send us all the information you have about it. We aren't obligated to act on any claim until you have paid all transportation charges, and you may not deduct the amount of your claim from those charges.

If the recipient accepts your package without noting any damage on the delivery record, we will assume the package was delivered in good condition. For us to process your claim, you must make the original shipping cartons and packing available for inspection.

Right To Inspect We may, at our option, open and inspect your packages before or after you give them to us to deliver.

Right Of Rejection We reserve the right to reject a shipment when such shipment would be likely to cause delay or damage to other shipments, equipment, or personnel; or if the shipment is prohibited by law; or if the shipment would violate any terms of our Airbill or our current Service Guide.

C.O.D. Services C.O.D. SERVICE IS NOT AVAILABLE WITH THIS AIRBILL. If C.O.D. Service is required, please use a Federal Express C.O.D. Airbill.

Air Transportation Tax Included A federal excise tax when required by the Internal Revenue Code on the air transportation portion of this service, if any, is paid by us.

Money-Back Guarantee In the event of untimely delivery, Federal Express will, at your request and with some limitations, refund or credit all transportation charges. See current Service Guide for more information.

Part #157611/157612 • Rev. 10/01

FD-340 (Rev. 3-8-01)

Universal Case File Number 62D-LA-236081-CART-1A7

Field Office Acquiring Evidence LA

Serial # of Originating Document 12

Date Received 4/5/2004

From [redacted]

(Name of Contributor)

CART HQ

(Address of Contributor)

(City and State)

By [redacted]

b6
b7C

To Be Returned ☐ Yes ☒ No

Receipt Given ☐ Yes ☒ No

Grand Jury Material - Disseminate Only Pursuant to Rule 6 (e) Federal Rules of Criminal Procedure

☐ Yes ☒ No

Federal Taxpayer Information (FTI)

☐ Yes ☒ No

Title: MICHAEL JOE JACKSON;

[redacted] - VICTIM;

DPC

Reference

(Communication Enclosing Material)

Description: ☐ Original notes re interview of

Case notes - exams (2/12/04 – 3/5/04) (9 pages)

Case notes - exams (3/22/04 – 4/1/04) (11 pages)

4-13-04

FD-340 (Rev. 3-8-01)

Universal Case File Number 62D-LA-236081-CART-1A8

Field Office Acquiring Evidence LA

Serial # of Originating Document 12

Date Received 4/5/2004

From [redacted]
(Name of Contributor)

CART - HQ
(Address of Contributor)

(City and State)

By [redacted]

b6
b7C

To Be Returned ☐ Yes ☒ No

Receipt Given ☐ Yes ☒ No

Grand Jury Material - Disseminate Only Pursuant to Rule 6 (e)
Federal Rules of Criminal Procedure
☐ Yes ☒ No

Federal Taxpayer Information (FTI)
☐ Yes ☒ No

Title: MICHAEL JOE JACKSON;
[redacted] VICTIM;
DPC

Reference: (Communication Enclosing Material)

Description: ☐ Original notes re interview of

Case notes - combined, sorted by Specimen number, for CART examiners LL, BAG, WEC, JVK. (51 pages)

4-13-04
BM

FD-302 (Rev. 10-6-95)

- 1 -

FEDERAL BUREAU OF INVESTIGATION

Date of transcription 04/05/2004

Computer Analysis Response Team
Report of Examination

Included herein are the results of a digital forensic examination performed by an FBI Certified Forensic Examiner. This examination has been performed in accordance with CART policies and procedures.

Case Reference: 62D-LA-236081

Specimens: The following evidence was submitted.

Contributor Item Number	FBI Specimen Number	Description
SBSO MX200-05	**QLA1**	
Item 908	QLA1_1	
Item 909	QLA1_2	
Item 910A	QLA1_3	
Item 910B	QLA1_4	
Item 912A	QLA1_5	
SBSO MX200-02	**QLA2**	
Item 329	QLA2_1	
Item 336	QLA2_2	
Item 342	QLA2_3	

b2
b7E

Investigation on 0218-04012004 at Santa Barbara, CA

File # 62D-LA-236081-CART - 2 Date dictated 04/05/2004

by ITS/FE

b6
b7C

This document contains neither recommendations nor conclusions of the FBI. It is the property of the FBI and is loaned to your agency; it and its contents are not to be distributed outside your agency.

FD-302a (Rev. 10-6-95)

62D-LA-236081

Continuation of FD-302 of CART Computer Examination, On 0218-04012004, Page 2

b2
b7E

Contributor Item Number	FBI Specimen Number	Description
Item 347A	QLA2_4	
Item 644	QLA2_5	
Item 645	QLA2_6	
Item 911	QLA2_7	
Item 347B	QLA2_8	
Item 912B	QLA2_9	
SBSOMX200-01	**QLA3**	
Item 308	QLA3_1	
SB Police Dept. Lab HARD DRIVE #22	**QLA4**	
Item 346	QLA4_1	

Request: Per an electronic communication, serial 12, CART Headquarters was requested to examine thirteen Macintosh computers in Santa Barbara, California. The SBSO requested that the examination be conducted at their laboratory in Santa Barbara, due to the sensitive nature of the case. Of note, there were actually sixteen not thirteen.

b2
b7E

Summary of Results:

FD-302a (Rev. 10-6-95)

62D-LA-236081

Continuation of FD-302 of CART Computer Examination, On 0218-04012004, Page 3

Derivative Evidence (DE): The following items were produced as derivative evidence.

DE Number	Contents/Description
DELA1	
DELA2	
DELA3	
DELA4	
DELA5	
DELA6	
DELA7	
DELA8	
DELA9	
DELA10	CD containing summary results for QLA1_1 (first version)
DELA11	CD containing summary results for QLA1_1 (revised per direction of SBSO detective)
DELA12	4 DVDs containing copies of corrupted graphics files from QLA1_2
DELA13	CD containing summary results of QLA1_2
DELA14	CD containing summary results of QLA1_3
DELA15	CD containing summary results of QLA1_4
DELA16	CD containing summary results of QLA2_8
DELA17	CD containing summary results of QLA2_5
DELA18	CD containing summary results of QLA2_7

b2
b7E

FD-302a (Rev. 10-6-95)

62D-LA-236081

Continuation of FD-302 of CART Computer Examination , On 0218-04012004, Page 4

DE Number	Contents/Description
DELA19	CD containing summary results of QLA1_5
DELA20	CD containing summary results of QLA2_1
DELA21	CD containing summary results of QLA2_2
DELA22	CD containing summary results of QLA2_3
DELA23	CD containing summary results of QLA2_4
DELA24	CD containing summary results of QLA2_6
DELA25	CD containing summary results of QLA2_9
DELA26	CD containing summary results of QLA3_1
DELA27	CD containing summary results of QLA4_1

b2
b7E

Examination:

FD-302a (Rev. 10-6-95)

62D-LA-236081

Continuation of FD-302 of CART Computer Examination , On 0218-04012004 , Page 7

b2
b6
b7C
b7E

Disposition: The contributor retains all original specimens and derivative evidence, with the exception DELA12, which will be returned to the contributor by the FBI Investigative Technology Division when the graphics conversion has been completed. CART Headquarters retains no magnetic media copies of original or derivative evidence for this case.

CART ADMINISTRATIVE REVIEW OF CASE FILE

b6
b7C

Examiner Name: [redacted] (lead)

Case ID: UCFN: 62D-LA-236081 Report Date: 4/5/2004

Admin Review Completed By: [redacted] 4/8/2004

Type or Print Official Name *Admin Reviewer's Signature and Date*

Request Documentation

- Is the request for examination documented? (Yes) No
- If additional communications occurred, were they documented? (Yes) No N/A
- If request was discontinued prior to completion, was all documentation up to that point retained, and a final report issued documenting the discontinuation? Yes No (N/A)

Case Notes (If the case was discontinued before the start of the examination, skip this section)

- Are all notes in ink? (with the exception of sketches) (Yes) No
  Note: No obliteration, "whiteout" or eraser permitted).
- Are all corrections made with a single strikeout and initialed by the examiner? Yes No (N/A)
- Do all pages of case notes have UCFN or Case ID? (Yes) No
- Do all pages of case notes have examiner's [and technician's] handwritten initials? (Yes) No
- Do all pages of case notes have page # of total pages? (Yes) No
- Is each procedure dated? (Yes) No
- If procedures are completed by more than one examiner, was each procedure initialed by the examiner [and technician]? (Yes) No N/A
- Is the documentation retained (i.e., 1A envelope)? (Yes) No
- Does the documentation account for total number of pages? (Yes) No

Final Report (i.e., FD302 or Lab Report) contain the following information:

- Are all the fields filled in correctly on the final report? *See EXM-13* (Yes) No
- Does the Final Report contain the following:
  1. Examiner's name? (Yes) No
  2. Examiner's hand written initials on original? (Yes) No
  3. Examiner's Unit? (i.e., CART, NTRCFL) (Yes) No N/A
  4. Examiner's phone number? *(acceptable to be included on EC only)* Yes No (N/A)
  5. UCFN and/or Case ID? (Yes) No
  6. Specimen numbers used to list items? (Yes) No
  7. Evidence control number(s) on evidence list? (Yes) No
  8. Documentation of all processes performed? (Yes) No
  9. Documentation of examination results? (Yes) No
  10. Enclosure count? Yes No (N/A)
  11. Disposition of evidence, derivative evidence and notes statement? (Yes) No N/A

General:

- Has the record been closed in the CART Database? Yes (No)
- Has a peer review been performed and documented? (Yes) No
- If CE is sending out AE report, was the AE report administratively reviewed? (HQ only) Yes No (N/A)

07/16/2003

U.S. Department of Justice

Federal Bureau of Investigation

In Reply, Please Refer to
File No. 62D-LA-236081

11000 Wilshire Blvd #1700
Los Angeles, California 90024
(310) 477-6565
April 5, 2004

Sheriff Jim Anderson
Santa Barbara County Sheriff's Office
4434 Calle Real
Santa Barbara, CA 93110

Attention: Detective [redacted] b6 b7C

RE: MICHAEL JOE JACKSON;
[redacted] - VICTIM;
DPC

Dear Sheriff Anderson:

Enclosed is the Computer Analysis Response Team (CART) report of examination on sixteen Macintosh computer hard drive images related to the captioned case. In accordance with your request, the examination was conducted in the Santa Barbara Sheriff's Office laboratory under the investigative supervision of your detectives.

If you or your staff have any questions about this examination, please contact Special Agent [redacted] telephone [redacted] b2 b6 b7C

Sincerely,

RICHARD T. GARCIA
Assistant Director in Charge

By: [redacted] b6 b7C
Supervisory Senior Resident Agent

SBSO_Ltr.wpd 62D-LA-236081-CART-3

---- Working Copy ---- Page 1

Precedence: PRIORITY Date: 03/29/2004

To: Investigative Technology Attn: [redacted] b6 b7C
Forensic Audio Video Image Analysis Unit

From: Investigative Technology
DES/CART/ERF Annex
Contact: [redacted] b2 b6 b7C

Approved By: [redacted] b6 b7C

Drafted By: [redacted] gjl

Case ID #: 62D-LA-236081 (Pending)
66F-HQ-1422276-Field Ops (None)

Title: MICHAEL JOE JACKSON;
[redacted]-VICTIM; b6 b7C
DPC

COMPUTER ANALYSIS RESPONSE TEAM (CART)
FIELD OPERATIONS AND SUPPORT

Synopsis: CART Examiner [redacted] is forwarding four (4) DVDs, labeled as Derivative Evidence (DE) and containing image files to the Forensic Audio Video Image Analysis Unit (FAVIAU) so they may convert the files to a readable format. b6 b7C

Details: The image files contained on the four (4) DVDs cannot be read by standard graphics viewers. It is requested that FAVIAU convert all graphics files on enclosed media to a form readable by standard graphics viewers. Per previous conversations with FAVIAU personnel, the formats are proprietary, but specialized digital processing can render the files readable by non-proprietary viewers. It is further requested that FAVIAU place results on DVD or CD and ship them back to the address listed below. For questions/further information, contact [redacted] [redacted] b2 b6 b7C

Mailing address for return of evidence and results is:
Santa Barbara County Sheriff's Office
ATTN: Detective [redacted] b6 b7C
4434 Calle Real
Santa Barbara, CA 93110
Phone 805-681-4100

LEAD(s):

Case ID : 62D-LA-236081 Serial : 19
66F-HQ-1422276-FIELD OPS 41
62D-LA-236081-CART 4

---- Working Copy ---- Page 2

Set Lead 1: (Action)

INVESTIGATIVE TECHNOLOGY

AT ERF

Convert all graphics files on enclosed media to a form readable by standard graphics viewers and place results on DVD or CD and ship them back to the address provided.

CC: [redacted]

b6
b7C

---- Working Copy ---- Page 1

Precedence: ROUTINE Date: 06/13/2005

To: Los Angeles

From: Los Angeles
Santa Maria RA
Contact: SA [redacted] b2 b6 b7C

Approved By: [redacted]

Drafted By: [redacted]

Case ID #: 62D-LA-236081 (Closed) b6 b7C

Title: MICHAEL JOE JACKSON;
DOMESTIC POLICE COOPERATION

Synopsis: Close case.

Details: The writer request that the captioned investigation be closed. There are no outstanding leads or evidence items.

164dfw0404

Case ID : 62D-LA-236081 Serial : 57
62D-LA-236081-CART 5

Federal Bureau of Investigation
Los Angeles Field Office
Santa Maria Resident Agency

To: Unit Chief [redacted] CART Unit, Quantico

From: SSRA [redacted]

Date: June 9, 2004

Re: Michael Jackson, aka et al (62D-LA-236081)

b6
b7C

[redacted] Please forward the attached copies of the letter of commendation from the Santa Barbara County Sheriff's Department (SBSD) to both [redacted] and [redacted] As indicated in the letter, [redacted] and [redacted] did a great job. The SBSD appreciates it and our office (Los Angeles and the Santa Maria RA) appreciates what they did for the SBSD on behalf of the FBI. Liaison in this matter has at times been delicate and sensitive. The team contributed significantly to easing those concerns with their good work, professionalism, and discretion. Many thanks to [redacted] and [redacted]

1

62d-LA-236081-6

Sheriff's Department

SANTA BARBARA COUNTY

HEADQUARTERS
P.O. Box 6427 • 4434 Calle Real • Santa Barbara, California 93160
Phone (805) 681-4100 • Fax: (805) 681-4322

JIM ANDERSON
Sheriff-Coroner

KENNETH R. SHEMWELL
Undersheriff

STATIONS

Buellton
140 W. Highway 246
Buellton, CA 93427
Phone (805) 686-8150

Carpinteria
5775 Carpinteria Avenue
Carpinteria, CA 93013
Phone (805) 684-4561

Lompoc
751 Burton Mesa Road
Lompoc, CA 93436
Phone (805) 737-7737

New Cuyama
70 Newsome Street
New Cuyama, CA 93254
Phone (661) 766-2310

Santa Maria
812-A W. Foster Road
Santa Maria, CA 93455
Phone (805) 934-6150

Solvang
1745 Mission Drive
Solvang, CA 93463
Phone (805) 686-5000

Sheriff - Coroner Office
66 South San Antonio Road
Santa Barbara, CA 93110
Phone (805) 681-4146

Main Jail
4436 Calle Real
Santa Barbara, CA 93110
Phone (805) 681-4250

COURT SERVICES

Santa Barbara Division
1122 Santa Barbara Street
Post Office Box 656
Santa Barbara, CA 93102
Phone (805) 568-2900

Santa Maria Division
312-O E. Cook Street
Santa Maria, CA 93455
Phone (805) 346-7430

Lompoc Division
115 Civic Center Plaza
Lompoc, CA 93436
Phone (805) 737-7710

April 27, 2004

Senior Resident Agent
US Department of Justice
11000 Wilshire Blvd #1700
Los Angeles, Ca. 90024

b6
b7C

Regarding: Michael Joe Jackson; [redacted]

Dear Senior Resident Agent [redacted]

On behalf of the Santa Barbara County Sheriff's Department, Criminal Investigations Division, I would like to thank you, Special Agent [redacted] [redacted] and those involved in the Computer Analysis Response Team who worked to diligently examine the Macintosh hard drive images and quickly provided to us a report for the lead detectives involved in the above referenced case (your file 62D-LA-236081).

b6
b7C

Sheriff's Department Detective [redacted] and Detective [redacted] [redacted] worked alongside Agent [redacted] Agent [redacted] and Agent [redacted] stating that your staff are truly experts at what they do. Their assistance in this matter was greatly appreciated.

Sincerely,

Jim Anderson
SHERIFF/ CORONER

Criminal Investigations Division

b6
b7C

JA:MD;jt

LA-236081-6

FEDERAL BUREAU OF INVESTIGATION
FOIPA
DELETED PAGE INFORMATION SHEET

No Duplication Fees are charged for Deleted Page Information Sheet(s).

Total Deleted Page(s) ~ 123
Page 7 ~ b2, b6, b7C, b7E
Page 8 ~ b2, b7E
Page 9 ~ b2, b7E
Page 10 ~ b2, b7E
Page 11 ~ b2, b6, b7C, b7E
Page 12 ~ b2, b6, b7C, b7E
Page 13 ~ b2, b7E
Page 14 ~ b2, b7E
Page 15 ~ b2, b7E
Page 16 ~ b2, b6, b7C, b7E
Page 17 ~ b2, b6, b7C, b7E
Page 18 ~ b2, b6, b7C, b7E
Page 19 ~ b2, b6, b7C, b7E
Page 20 ~ b2, b6, b7C, b7E
Page 21 ~ b2, b6, b7C, b7E
Page 22 ~ b2, b6, b7C, b7E
Page 23 ~ b2, b7E
Page 24 ~ b2, b6, b7C, b7E
Page 25 ~ b2, b6, b7C, b7E
Page 26 ~ b2, b6, b7C, b7E
Page 27 ~ b2, b7E
Page 28 ~ b2, b7E
Page 29 ~ b2, b6, b7C, b7E
Page 30 ~ b2, b7E
Page 31 ~ b2, b7E
Page 32 ~ b2, b6, b7C, b7E
Page 33 ~ b2, b6, b7C, b7E
Page 34 ~ b2, b7E
Page 39 ~ b2, b6, b7C, b7E
Page 40 ~ b2, b7E
Page 41 ~ b2, b6, b7C, b7E
Page 42 ~ b2, b6, b7C, b7E
Page 43 ~ b2, b7E
Page 44 ~ b2, b7E
Page 45 ~ b2, b7E
Page 46 ~ b2, b7E
Page 47 ~ b2, b7E
Page 48 ~ b2, b6, b7C, b7E
Page 49 ~ b2, b6, b7C, b7E
Page 52 ~ b2, b7E
Page 55 ~ b2, b6, b7C, b7E
Page 56 ~ b2, b7E
Page 57 ~ b2, b6, b7C, b7E
Page 71 ~ b2, b6, b7C, b7E

Page 72 ~ b2, b6, b7C, b7E
Page 73 ~ b2, b6, b7C, b7E
Page 74 ~ b2, b6, b7C, b7E
Page 75 ~ b2, b6, b7C, b7E
Page 76 ~ b2, b6, b7C, b7E
Page 77 ~ b2, b7E
Page 82 ~ b2, b6, b7C, b7E
Page 83 ~ b2, b6, b7C, b7E
Page 84 ~ b2, b6, b7C, b7E
Page 85 ~ b2, b6, b7C, b7E
Page 86 ~ b2, b6, b7C, b7E
Page 87 ~ b2, b6, b7C, b7E
Page 88 ~ b2, b6, b7C, b7E
Page 89 ~ b2, b6, b7C, b7E
Page 90 ~ b2, b6, b7C, b7E
Page 91 ~ b2, b6, b7C, b7E
Page 92 ~ b2, b6, b7C, b7E
Page 93 ~ b2, b7E
Page 94 ~ b2, b7E
Page 95 ~ b2, b7E
Page 96 ~ b2, b6, b7C, b7E
Page 97 ~ b2, b6, b7C, b7E
Page 98 ~ b2, b6, b7C, b7E
Page 99 ~ b2, b6, b7C, b7E
Page 100 ~ b2, b6, b7C, b7E
Page 101 ~ b2, b6, b7C, b7E
Page 103 ~ b2, b6, b7C, b7E
Page 104 ~ b2, b6, b7C, b7E
Page 105 ~ b2, b6, b7C, b7E
Page 106 ~ b2, b6, b7C, b7E
Page 107 ~ b2, b6, b7C, b7E
Page 108 ~ b2, b6, b7C, b7E
Page 109 ~ b2, b6, b7C, b7E
Page 110 ~ b2, b6, b7C, b7E
Page 111 ~ b2, b6, b7C, b7E
Page 112 ~ b2, b6, b7C, b7E
Page 113 ~ b2, b6, b7C, b7E
Page 114 ~ b2, b6, b7C, b7E
Page 115 ~ b2, b6, b7C, b7E
Page 116 ~ b2, b6, b7C, b7E
Page 117 ~ b2, b6, b7C, b7E
Page 118 ~ b2, b6, b7C, b7E
Page 119 ~ b2, b6, b7C, b7E
Page 120 ~ b2, b6, b7C, b7E
Page 121 ~ b2, b7E
Page 122 ~ b2, b6, b7C, b7E
Page 123 ~ b2, b6, b7C, b7E
Page 124 ~ b2, b7E
Page 125 ~ b2, b6, b7C, b7E
Page 126 ~ b2, b7E
Page 127 ~ b2, b6, b7C, b7E

Page 128 ~ b2, b6, b7C, b7E
Page 129 ~ b2, b6, b7C, b7E
Page 130 ~ b2, b6, b7C, b7E
Page 131 ~ b2, b6, b7C, b7E
Page 132 ~ b2, b6, b7C, b7E
Page 133 ~ b2, b6, b7C, b7E
Page 134 ~ b2, b6, b7C, b7E
Page 135 ~ b2, b6, b7C, b7E
Page 136 ~ b2, b6, b7C, b7E
Page 137 ~ b2, b6, b7C, b7E
Page 138 ~ b2, b7E
Page 139 ~ b2, b6, b7C, b7E
Page 140 ~ b2, b6, b7C, b7E
Page 141 ~ b2, b6, b7C, b7E
Page 142 ~ b2, b7E
Page 143 ~ b2, b6, b7C, b7E
Page 144 ~ b2, b6, b7C, b7E
Page 145 ~ b2, b6, b7C, b7E
Page 146 ~ b2, b6, b7C, b7E
Page 147 ~ b2, b6, b7C, b7E
Page 148 ~ b2, b6, b7C, b7E
Page 149 ~ b2, b6, b7C, b7E
Page 150 ~ b2, b7E
Page 151 ~ b2, b7E
Page 152 ~ b2, b6, b7C, b7E
Page 153 ~ b2, b6, b7C, b7E
Page 158 ~ b2, b7E
Page 159 ~ b2, b6, b7C, b7E

Chapter Three - Closed Leads

OUTCOMES

Outcomes

This FBI file consists of certified copies of Michael Jackson's driving license, press cuttings, redacted notes, a doodle and details of travel arrangements. It also includes jotted down words such as *"extortion,"* *"send money,"* *"30K"*, *"5K"*, *"male chimp,"* *"what truths?"* and a blank page.

Mann Act:

The LAPD contacted the FBI. They wanted to know if the FBI would pursue a federal prosecution under the Mann Act.

Outcome: **No action.**

Manila Investigation:

The LAPD telephoned the FBI to inform them that two investigators were traveling to Manila to interview Michael Jackson's former employees.

Legat Manila provided the FBI with newspaper articles for their information. The Philippine Daily Inquirer dated 23 September 1993, stated,

> *"The couple [were] claiming Jackson owed them $283,000 in overtime pay."*

Outcome: **No action.**

Canadian Investigation:

This investigation included locating and interviewing a social worker based in Canada.

A couple who work in child services heard noises through a train cabin wall and reported it to the train conductor.

Outcome: **No action.**

New York Investigation:

LAPD requested assistance to ascertain if Michael Jackson was the subject of a restraining order.

The FBI searched the New York City Supreme Courts computerized and manual records. **Nothing found.**

Outcome: **No action.**

Alleged "Mexican Boys" Investigation:

The LAPD called the FBI.

An author contacted the LAPD. The author was writing a book about the allegations against Michael Jackson. He informed the LAPD that there was an alleged FBI covered-up involving two Mexican boys.

The FBI searched both manual and automated indices, **no references found.**

Outcome: **No records** of a Mexican Boys Investigation. **No records** of any allegations involving Michael Jackson and Mexican boys. **Nothing Found.**

> *"No outstanding leads remain for the Los Angeles Office in this matter. This file will be placed in the closed status."*

Outcome: Nothing found.

Memorandum

To : SAC, LOS ANGELES (62D-LA-NEW) Date 9/16/93

From : SA [redacted] (C-1) (P)

Subject: MICHAEL JACKSON;
DOMESTIC POLICE COOPERATION;
OO: LOS ANGELES

b6
b7C

On September 7, 1993, writer was contacted by [redacted] [redacted] Los Angeles Police Department (LAPD), Child Sexual Abuse Section, (213) 485-2883. He requested assistance from the Federal Bureau of Investigation (FBI), in their investigation of child molestation allegation against entertainer, Michael Jackson.

It is requested that this matter be opened and assigned to writer.

1 - Los Angeles

(1)

62D-LA-162715-1

O&A 62D OO:LA 9/16/93

9-16-93

1*

INDEXED FILED

1993

FBI — LOS ANGELES

[redacted] b6 b7C

FD-340a (Rev. 10-3-77)

(Title) Michael Jackson

(File No.) 62D-LA-162715

Item	Date Filed	To be returned Yes	No		Disposition
1	1/31/94			– CDL – Michael Jackson	
2	"			– Investigative notes	
3	"			– DMV records – [redacted]	

b6
b7C

62D LA-162715-1A

CB

FD-340 (Rev. 4-2-85)

Field File No. 62D-LA-162715-1A1

Serial # of Originating Document ________

OO and File No. ________

Date Received 9/30/93

From DMV - Sacramento
(Name of Contributor)

____
(Address of Contributor)

By [redacted] b6 b7C

To Be Returned ☐ Yes ☐ No Receipt Given ☐ Yes ☐ No

Grand Jury Material - Disseminate Only Pursuant to Rule 6(e), Federal Rules of Criminal Procedure ☐ Yes ☐ No

Title:

Reference: ________
(Communication Enclosing Material)

Description: ☐ Original notes re interview of
CDL - Michael Jackson

```
TP
DATE:09-30-93*TIME:13:04*
MATCHED ON:*L/N*F/N* MI* BD
DMV RECORD FOR LAW ENFORCEMENT USE ONLY
DL/NO:N8685798*B/D:08-29-58*NAME:JACKSON MICHAEL JOE*
RES/ADDR: AS OF 08-11-89:10969 WILSHIRE BLVD STE 2206 LOS ANGELES 90024*
OTH/ADDR AS OF 07-05-89:10960 WILSHIRE BLVD 2206 LOS ANGELES *
IDENTIFYING INFORMATION:
SEX:MALE*HAIR:BLACK*EYES:BRN*HT:5-09*WT:120*
LIC/ISS:09-06-85*EXP/BD:97*RBM2*CLASS:C NON-COMMERCIAL*
LATEST APP:
DL TYPE:RENEWAL*ISS/DATE: 09-06-85*OFFICE: LSA*BATES:199*
LICENSE STATUS:
  VALID*
DEPARTMENTAL ACTIONS:
NONE
CONVICTIONS:
NONE
FAILURES TO APPEAR:
NONE
ACCIDENTS:
DATE       LOCATION                  VEH LIC   REPORT NO     FR CASE NO
04-21-91   SANTA BARBARA 071191 2KXZ777   97604512992   91 02 28071
END                       PARTY FOUND MOST AT FAULT

UTPUT MSG 023        FROM CL20 FOR FBI1      09/30/93 13:05
```

```
BFD                    CERTIFIED DRIVER'S LICENSE REQUEST
ENTER DESTINATION:   C/DDL0
FROM: LOS ANGELES POLICE DEPARTMENT -  FBI LOS ANGELES___________________________
REQ CERTIFIED COPY OF DL44/ALL AVAILABLE:  PHOTOS X SIGNATURES _ THUMB PRINTS _
          CDL#           CASE#              CDL#         CASE
          N8685798       88A___             ________     ______
          ________       ______             ________     ______
          ________       ______             ________     ______
COMMENTS: ____________________________________________________________________
______________________________________________________________________________
REFER TO: SA [          ]_____  SERIAL# 00000  DIV. FBI  PHONE 310 4776565
ADD: 11000 _ WILSHIRE BLVD__ CITY: LOS ANGELES____ STATE: CA  ZIP: 90024
                                                                        b6
                                                                        b7C

BFD-00, INPUT ACCEPTED, MESSAGE BEING ROUTED
INPUT MSG  073
                                          09/30/93 14:27 NO MSGS WAITING
```

APPLICATION FOR DRIVERS LICENSE OR IDENTIFICATION CARD

IF YOU ARE APPLYING FOR THE FIRST TIME, YOU MUST PRESENT EVIDENCE OF YOUR BIRTH DATE, SUCH A CERTIFICATE (certified copy or original) OR OTHER LEGAL DOCUMENT ACCEPTABLE TO THE DEPARTMENT

Check what you are applying for (NOTE: Your thumbprint will be required.)

☒ Driver's License ☐ Instruction Permit

☒ Duplicate Driver's License—License was: ☐ Lost ☐ Stolen ☐ Mutilated ☐ Destroyed

Identification Card: ☐ Regu ☐ Senio (age

Class: ☒ 3 (Basic License) ☐ 4 (Motorcycle) ☐ 1 ☐ 2

(An explanation of classes of driver's licenses is found in the California Driver's Handbook.) N8685798

PART I—MUST BE COMPLETED BY ALL APPLICANTS

PLEASE PRINT CAREFULLY IN INK

Calif. Driver's License No. or Calif. I.D. Card No. (if any):

Full Name: MICHAEL JOE JACKSON (FIRST / MIDDLE / LAST)

Mailing Address: 4641 Hayvenhurst No.

City: Los Angeles Zip code 91316

Sex: M Color hair: BLK Color eyes: BRN

Height: 5'9" Weight: 120 Birthdate: 8 29 58 (MONTH DAY YEAR)

(Enter residence address if different from mailing address.)

Residence address

City Zip code

Have you applied for a California Driver's License, Instruction Permit, or California Identification Card within the past 12 months? (If yes, please circle which one.) Yes

Have you ever had a California Driver's License? Yes

Have you ever had a California Identification Card? Yes

If yes to any of the above, print year of expiration

Have you applied for a license or California Identification Card under a former or different name (including maiden name) within the past seven (7) years? Yes

If yes, print name

PART II—MUST BE COMPLETED BY DRIVER'S LICENSE OR INSTRUCTION PERMIT APPLICANTS

Are you wearing contact lenses? Yes ☐ No ☐

THE ANSWER TO ITEM (1) BELOW IS FOR THE CONFIDENTIAL USE OF THE DEPARTMENT OF MOTOR VEHICLES

(2) Have you had your driving privilege or a license canceled, refused, suspended or revoked, within the past seven (7) years? Yes

If yes, briefly explain

(3) Have you held a driver's license in another state or country within the past three (3) years? Yes

If yes, indicate where and number (STATE OR COUNTRY)

If yes, when did or will license expire?

PART III—MUST BE COMPLETED BY ALL APPLICANTS

I hereby certify, under penalty of perjury, that all statements on this application are true, and that my birth date is as shown on this application. (Perjury is punishable by imprisonment, fine or both.)

Executed at (CITY) (STATE) on (DATE) X (SIGNATURE OF APPLICANT)

PLEASE TAKE THIS COMPLETED FORM WITH ANY DRIVER'S LICENSE OR IDENTIFICATION CARD YOU M AND THE FEE TO THE DRIVER'S LICENSE TYPIST.

PART IV—MUST BE COMPLETED IF DRIVER'S LICENSE OR INSTRUCTION PERMIT APPLICANT IS U YEARS OF AGE

Before an application for a driver's license can be accepted for a minor, signatures accepting liability for the minor are required. This form can be completed by the minor and signed by required persons prior to visiting the local DMV office.

AND

Your Certificate of Completion of Driver Education, Driver Training, or Certificate of Simultaneous Enrollment in Driver Education and Training.

ACCEPTANCE OF LIABILITY

Executed at (CITY) (STATE) on (DATE)

The signatory certifies under penalty of perjury that:

1. He/she is over the age of 18 and is a resident of the State of California.
2. He/she has full custody of and consents to the issuance of an original or duplicate driver's license to the applicant named herein, and
3. He/she assumes the liability specified in Sections 17707 thru 17710 of the Vehicle Code.
4. All statements made on this form are true and correct.

SIGNATURES

(If only one person has custody, that person should write "*custody*" before signing.)

X X

Address (STREET) Address (STREET)

(CITY) (CITY)

Phone Phone

lential information deleted per section 1808.5 C.V.C. and
ir Credit Reporting Act.

State of California
DEPARTMENT OF MOTOR VEHICLES
Division of Headquarters Operations

I hereby certify that the document to which this is affixed is a true copy of the records of the Department of Motor Vehicles

Motor Vehicle File No. N868 5798

Date 10-6-93 Signed J. Kind

In accordance with Section 1813 CVC, the above employee of the Division of Headquarters Operations has been authorized to prepare under seal and certify copies of records of this Division.

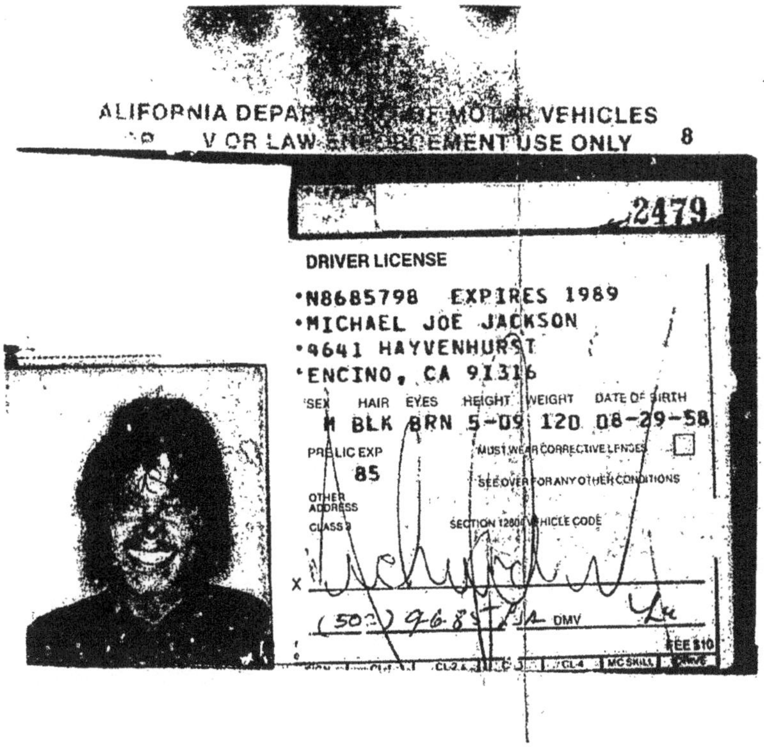

ALIFORNIA DEPA[illegible] MOTOR VEHICLES
[illegible] V OR LAW ENFORCEMENT USE ONLY 8

2479

DRIVER LICENSE

•N8685798 EXPIRES 1989
•MICHAEL JOE JACKSON
•4641 HAYVENHURST
•ENCINO, CA 91316

SEX	HAIR	EYES	HEIGHT	WEIGHT	DATE OF BIRTH
M	BLK	BRN	5-09	120	08-29-58

PRE LIC EXP
85

MUST WEAR CORRECTIVE LENSES

SEE OVER FOR ANY OTHER CONDITIONS

OTHER ADDRESS

CLASS 3

SECTION 12804 VEHICLE CODE

X

(503) 9685[illegible] DMV

FEE $10

State of California
DEPARTMENT OF MOTOR VEHICLES
Division of Headquarters Operations

I hereby certify that the document to which this is affixed is a true copy of the records of the Department of Motor Vehicles

Motor Vehicle File No. N8685798

Date 10-6-93 Signed [signature]

In accordance with Section 1813 CVC, the above employee of the Division of Headquarters Operations has been authorized to prepare under seal and certify copies of records of this Division

FD-340 (Rev. 4-2-85)

Field File No. 62D-LA-162715/A2

Serial # of Originating Document ______

OO and File No. ______

Date Received ______

From ______
(Name of Contributor)

______
(Address of Contributor)

______ [redacted] ate)

By ______ [redacted] b6 b7C
(Name of Special Agent)

To Be Returned ☐ Yes ☐ No Receipt Given ☐ Yes ☐ No

Grand Jury Material - Disseminate Only Pursuant to Rule 6(e), Federal Rules of Criminal Procedure ☐ Yes ☐ No

Title:

Reference: ______
(Communication Enclosing Material)

Description: ☐ Original notes re interview of

______

Investigative Notes

b6
b7C
b7D

— NO Knowledge of

NO rumor

Restraining order - Michael J.

b6
b7C

(restraining order) → NY City

b6
b7C

Michael Joe Jackson

D-3-(8-29-58)

(10-9-69)

b6
b7C

American on Line

123

1A

b6
b7C

3-5-93 → (Phil.) → Two Round Trip To Phil.

Flew and

- Sent - Letter - Compensated

disclose

British press - European

b6
b7C

Wednesday / (Backwash - Extortion)

INS

INS

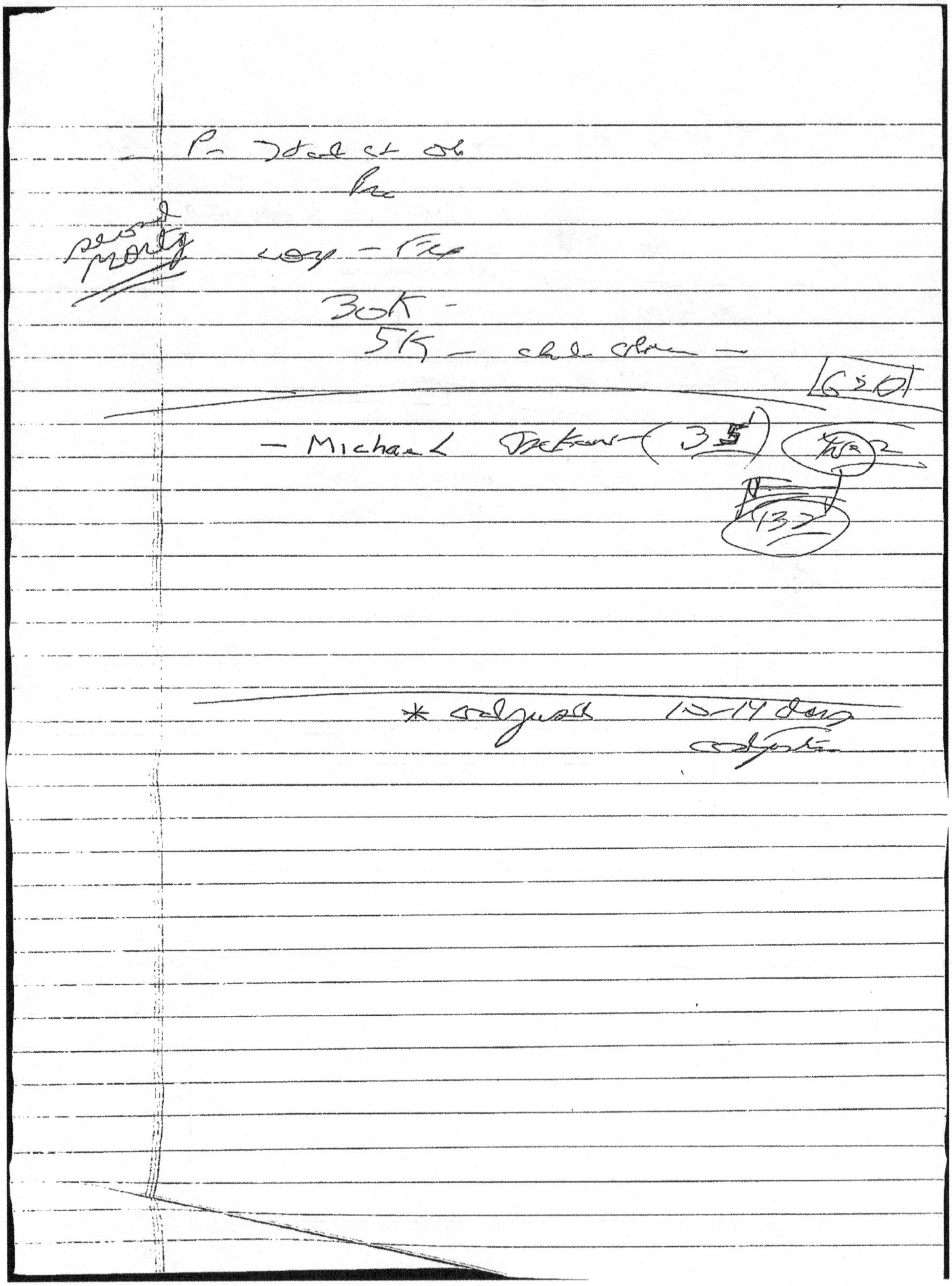

second mortg

30K -

5K -

- Michael [illegible] (35)

– 2/9/92 – → sends Toys to Australia

– Shipping → documents.

b6
b7C

– on Sale in

— Not near him.

Not same contact.

Male chimp.

b6
b7C

Chimp — Male chimp.

8-9-90

didn't sign.

8-30-90 -

High turnover rate

10:10 AM DA's office

DA's office.

Present, Gil Garcetti.

213 965-1562

b6
b7C

lead investigation.

8/17 ... LAPD

b6
b7C
b7D

What's Truth?

8/17/93 –

8/17/93 –

FD-340 (Rev. 4-2-86)

Field File No. 62D-LA-162715-1A3

Serial # of Originating Document ______

OO and File No. LA

Date Received 10-26-93

From DMV- [redacted]

(Name of Contributor)

b6
b7C

______

(Address of Contributor)

______

By [redacted]

(Name of Special Agent)

To Be Returned ☐ Yes ☐ No Receipt Given ☐ Yes ☐ No

Grand Jury Material - Disseminate Only Pursuant to Rule 6(e), Federal Rules of Criminal Procedure ☐ Yes ☐ No

Title:

Reference: ______

(Communication Enclosing Material)

Description: ☐ Original notes re interview of

DMV [redacted]

b6
b7C

SAC NOTES

To: SAC, LOS ANGELES (62D-LA-162715)

MSL RV From: SSA [redacted] b6 b7C

Subject: MICHAEL JACKSON;

DOMESTIC POLICE COOPERATION;
OO: LOS ANGELES

On September 7, 1993, [redacted] Los Angeles Police Department, Sexually Exploited Child Unit telephonically contacted SA [redacted] inquiring if the FBI would be interested in working a possible federal violation against Jackson concerning the transportation of a minor across state lines for immoral purposes, (MANN ACT). He advised that a meeting was scheduled on 9/10/93 at 10:00 AM at the office of the Los Angeles District Attorney, 310 West Temple, 17th Floor. b6 b7C

On Sept 7, 1993, SA [redacted] contacted AUSA Patricia Donahue, (213) 894-0640 asking if she would like to attend the meeting. On September 8, 1993, AUSA Donahue advised that she checked with her front office and they had made the decision that the United States Attorney was not interested in prosecuting Michael Jackson for a violation of the Mann Act. She also indicated she would not be attending the meeting at the District Attorney's Office. b6 b7C

On September 8, 1993, SSA [redacted] FBIHQ, VCMO, was advised of the scheduled meeting and concurred that the FBI could assist the Los Angeles Police Department and the Santa Barbara Sheriff's Office, under a Domestic Police Cooperation matter.

On September 10, 1993, a meeting was held at the Los Angeles County District Attorney's conference room. In attendance were Gil Garcetti, the District Attorney; Lauren Weis, Acting Head Deputy, Sexual Crimes and Child Abuse Division; Willaim Hodgman, Deputy District Attorney, and investigators from the Los Angeles Police Department and Santa Barbara County Sheriff's Office.

1 - SAC PARSONS
1 - SENIOR ASAC MORLEY
1 - ASAC ADAMSKI
1 - ASAC IDEN
1 - ASAC PARKER
1 - ASAC THORNTON
1 - ASAC CURRAN
1 - SSA [redacted] b6 b7C
1 - 62D-LA-162715
SLS/sls
(9)

62D LA-162715-2

All in attendance were briefed of the investigation to date. The United States Attorney's position of not pursuing a federal investigation was expressed to the group. SA [redacted] offered the assistance of the FBI in covering leads that may develop under a Domestic Police Cooperation classification.

On September 16, 1993, [redacted] LAPD telephonically contacted SA [redacted] to advise that two investigators from their task force would be travelling to Manila to interview two prior domestic employees of the Santa Barbara residence of Michael Jackson. Contact will be made to Legat Manila to advise of the travel of the investigators and their purpose in Manila. Other leads are anticipated to Legat Ottawa to request local authorities to locate and interview a social worker in Canada who may have corroborating information of misconduct by Michael Jackson.

b6
b7C

Additionally, allegations of Illegal Interception of Communications violations was reported to the FBI on September 16, 1993 by the Los Angeles County District Attorney. ASAC Parker and SSA [redacted], have been notified. A meeting will be held at the District Attorney's Office on September 17, 1993, at 8:30 AM.

Sep 17 5 07 PM '93

0046 MRI 00325

PP RUCNFB FBILA

DE MAN #0002 2601237

ZNR UUUUU

P 170616Z SEP 93

FM LEGAT MANILA (62D-LA-162715) (P)

TO DIRECTOR FBI/PRIORITY/

FBI LOS ANGELES/PRIORITY/

BT

UNCLAS

CITE: //5480:MH246.260//

PASS: FBIHQ, SSA [redacted] FLU 11, OLIA; FBI LOS ANGELES - SA [redacted] b6 b7C

SUBJECT: MICHAEL JACKSON (SINGER/ENTERTAINER); DOMESTIC POLICE COOPERATION; OO: LOS ANGELES.

REFERENCE TELEPHONE CALL OF FBI LOS ANGELES SPECIAL AGENT (SA) [redacted] TO ASSISTANT LEGAL ATTACHE (ALAT) [redacted] AT LEGAL ATTACHE OFFICE (LEGAT) MANILA ON 9/17/93. b6 b7C

IN REFERENCE TELEPHONE CALL, SA [redacted] INFORMED ALAT [redacted] THAT [redacted] LOS ANGELES POLICE

62D-LA-162715-3

SEARCHED ___ INDEXED ___
SERIALIZED ___ FILED ___
SEP 17 1993
...ELES

TELETYPE

copy to [redacted] b6 b7C

PAGE TWO DE MAN 0002 UNCLAS

DEPARTMENT (LAPD) AND [redacted] SANTA BARBARA SHERIFF'S OFFICE (SBSO), PLAN TO TRAVEL TO MANILA, PHILIPPINES, ARRIVING THE EVENING OF 9/21/93, FOR THE PURPOSE OF INTERVIEWING [redacted] AND [redacted] CONCERNING THEIR KNOWLEDGE OF ACCUSATIONS AGAINST MICHAEL JACKSON OF SEXUAL ABUSE OF YOUNG BOYS. b6 b7C

HOTEL RESERVATIONS HAVE BEEN MADE FOR [redacted] AND [redacted] AT THE MANILA DIAMOND HOTEL, ROXAS BOULEVARD CORNER, DR. J. QUINTOS STREET, ERMITA, MANILA, PHILIPPINES, TELEPHONE NUMBER 011-632-536-2211, WITH CONFIRMATION NUMBERS FOR [redacted] AND [redacted] AS 5791 AND 5790 RESPECTIVELY.

LEGAT MANILA IS MAKING ARRANGEMENTS FOR AN OFFICIAL EMBASSY VEHICLE WITH DRIVER/EXPEDITER TO MEET THE DETECTIVES UPON ARRIVAL AT THE NINOY AQUINO INTERNATIONAL AIRPORT TO TRANSPORT THEM TO THEIR HOTEL.

LEGAT IS BRIEFING ACTING CHARGE D'AFFAIRES AND THE REGIONAL SECURITY OFFICER AT THE U.S. EMBASSY, MANILA, PHILIPPINES.

LEGAT HAS ESTABLISHED CONTACT WITH ATTORNEY [redacted] WHO IS REPRESENTING [redacted] HE IS MAKING ARRANGEMENTS FOR INTERVIEWS TO BE CONDUCTED WITH [redacted] AT HIS LAW OFFICE ON WEDNESDAY, 9/22/93. b6 b7C

PAGE THREE DE MAN 0002 UNCLAS

LEGAT MANILA WILL ALSO BRIEF [redacted] [redacted] [redacted] MAY WANT TO HAVE A REPRESENTATIVE PARTICIPATE IN THE INTERVIEWS.

b6
b7C
b7D

BT

#0002

NNNN

FD-36 (Rev. 8-29-85)

FBI

TRANSMIT VIA:	PRECEDENCE:	CLASSIFICATION:
[X] Teletype	[ ] Immediate	[ ] TOP SECRET
[ ] Facsimile	[X] Priority	[ ] SECRET
[ ] AIRTEL	[ ] Routine	[ ] CONFIDENTIAL
		[ ] UNCLAS E F T O
		[X] UNCLAS

Date 9/17/93

FM FBI LOS ANGELES (62D-LA-162715) (P)

TO DIRECTOR FBI/PRIORITY/

LEGAT MANILA/PRIORITY/

BT

UNCLAS

CITE: //3410:C-1//

PASS: FBIHQ, SSA [redacted] VCMO; SSA [redacted] FLU II, ~~ELU2~~,

OLIA; LEGAT MANILA, ALAT [redacted]

SUBJECT: MICHAEL JACKSON, SINGER/ENTERTAINER; DOMESTIC POLICE COOPERATION; OO: LOS ANGELES.

b6
b7C

REFERENCE LEGAT MANILA TELETYPE TO DIRECTOR DATED SEPTEMBER 17, 1993 AND TELEPHONE CALL OF FBI LOS ANGELES SA [redacted] TO ASSISTANT LEGAL ATTACHE (ALAT) [redacted] [redacted] AT LEGAL ATTACHE OFFICE, LEGAT MANILA, ON SEPTEMBER 17, 1993.

Corrected ISM

SEARCHED
INDEXED
SERIALIZED
FILED

Approved: CJP/plm   Original filename: ISM001W.260

Time Received: Telprep filename: ISM00180.260

MRI/JULIAN DATE: 105/261   ISN: 30

FOX DATE & TIME OF ACCEPTANCE: 0318

62D-LA-162715-4

^PAGE 2 62D-LA-162715 UNCLAS

ON SEPTEMBER 17, 1993, A TASK FORCE MEETING WAS HELD AT THE LOS ANGELES COUNTY DISTRICT ATTORNEY'S OFFICE REGARDING THE MICHAEL JACKSON INVESTIGATION. THE TASK FORCE WAS ADVISED OF THE ARRANGEMENTS MADE BY LEGAT MANILA CONCERNING HOTEL ACCOMMODATIONS AND TRANSPORTATION FROM THE AIRPORT TO THE HOTEL. [redacted] LOS ANGELES POLICE DEPARTMENT (LAPD), ADVISED THAT [redacted] SANTA BARBARA SHERIFF'S OFFICE (SBSO), HAD THROUGH THEIR TRAVEL AGENCY MADE RESERVATIONS AT THE HYATT HOTEL, 702 ROXAS BOULEVARD, PASAY, MANILA, PHILIPPINES, TELEPHONE NUMBER 011-6328331334.

b6
b7C

[redacted] REQUESTS THAT THE RESERVATIONS FOR THE MANILA DIAMOND HOTEL BE CANCELLED.

LAUREN WEIS, ACTING HEAD DEPUTY, SEXUAL CRIMES AND CHILD ABUSE DIVISION, FOR THE LOS ANGELES COUNTY DISTRICT ATTORNEY'S OFFICE INQUIRED WHETHER OR NOT LEGAT MANILA, OR THROUGH THE UNITED STATES EMBASSY IN MANILA, could provide A STENOGRAPHER ~~COULD BE PROVIDED~~ TO TAKE SHORTHAND DURING THE INTERVIEW WITH THE [redacted] WHICH IS SCHEDULED ON SEPTEMBER 22, 1993.

^PAGE 3 62D-LA-162715 UNCLAS

[redacted] AND [redacted] WERE ADVISED THAT AN EMBASSY VEHICLE WITH DRIVER/EXPEDITER WILL MEET THEM AT THE INTERNATIONAL AIRPORT TO TRANSPORT THEM TO THEIR HOTEL. LOS ANGELES FIELD OFFICE APPRECIATES THE COURTESY EXTENDED TO THE INVESTIGATORS IN THIS MATTER. b6 b7C

~~BT~~

~~Leads~~

Legat Manila: at Manila, PI; will advise Los Angeles if a stenographer will be provided.

BT

0045 MRI 00165

PP FBILA

DE FBILA #0030 2610338

ZNR UUUUU

P 180314Z SEP 93

FM FBI LOS ANGELES (62D-LA-162715) (P)

TO DIRECTOR FBI/PRIORITY/

LEGAT MANILA/PRIORITY/

BT

UNCLAS

CITE: //3410:C-1//

PASS: FBIHQ, SSA [redacted] VCMO; SSA [redacted] FLU II,

OLIA; LEGAT MANILA, ALAT [redacted]

SUBJECT: MICHAEL JACKSON, SINGER/ENTERTAINER; DOMESTIC POLICE COOPERATION; OO: LOS ANGELES. b6 b7C

REFERENCE LEGAT MANILA TELETYPE TO DIRECTOR DATED SEPTEMBER 17, 1993 AND TELEPHONE CALL OF FBI LOS ANGELES SA [redacted] TO ASSISTANT LEGAL ATTACHE (ALAT) [redacted] [redacted] AT LEGAL ATTACHE OFFICE, LEGAT MANILA, ON SEPTEMBER 17, 1993.

TELETYPE

62D LA-162715-4

SEARCHED________

INDEXED________

SERIALIZED________

FILED________

[redacted] b6 b7C

PAGE TWO DE PHILA 0030 UNCLAS

ON SEPTEMBER 17, 1993, A TASK FORCE MEETING WAS HELD AT THE LOS ANGELES COUNTY DISTRICT ATTORNEY S OFFICE REGARDING THE MICHAEL JACKSON INVESTIGATION. THE TASK FORCE WAS ADVISED OF THE ARRANGEMENTS MADE BY LEGAT MANILA CONCERNING HOTEL ACCOMMODATIONS AND TRANSPORTATION FROM THE AIRPORT TO THE HOTEL. [redacted] LOS ANGELES POLICE DEPARTMENT (LAPD), ADVISED THAT [redacted] SANTA BARBARA SHERIFF S OFFICE (SBSO), HAD THROUGH THEIR TRAVEL AGENCY MADE RESERVATIONS AT THE HYATT HOTEL, 702 ROXAS BOULEVARD, PASAY, MANILA, PHILIPPINES, TELEPHONE NUMBER 011-6328331334.

[redacted] REQUESTS THAT THE RESERVATIONS FOR THE MANILA DIAMOND HOTEL BE CANCELLED.

b6
b7C

LAUREN WEIS, ACTING HEAD DEPUTY, SEXUAL CRIMES AND CHILD ABUSE DIVISION, FOR THE LOS ANGELES COUNTY DISTRICT ATTORNEY S OFFICE INQUIRED WHETHER OR NOT LEGAT MANILA, OR THROUGH THE UNITED STATES EMBASSY IN MANILA, COULD PROVIDE A STENOGRAPHER TO TAKE SHORTHAND DURING THE INTERVIEW WITH THE [redacted] WHICH IS SCHEDULED ON SEPTEMBER 22, 1993.

[redacted] AND [redacted] WERE ADVISED THAT AN EMBASSY VEHICLE WITH DRIVER/EXPEDITER WILL MEET THEM AT THE

PAGE THREE DE FBILA 0030 UNCLAS

INTERNATIONAL AIRPORT TO TRANSPORT THEM TO THEIR HOTEL. LOS ANGELES FIELD OFFICE APPRECIATES THE COURTESY EXTENDED TO THE INVESTIGATORS IN THIS MATTER.

LEGAT MANILA AT MANILA, PHILIPPINES, WILL ADVISE LOS ANGELES IF A STENOGRAPHER WILL BE PROVIDED.

BT

#0030

NNNN

SEP 24 5 50 PM '93

0038 MRI 00366

RR RUCNFB FBILA

DE MAN #0004 2671240

ZNR UUUUU

R 240650Z SEP 93

FM LEGAT MANILA (62D-LA-162715) (RUC)

TO DIRECTOR FBI/ROUTINE/

FBI LOS ANGELES/ROUTINE/

BT

UNCLAS

CITE: //5480:MH252.266//

PASS: FBIHQ, SSA [redacted] FLU II, OLIA; SSA [redacted]

VCMO; FBI LOS ANGELES, SA [redacted]

SUBJECT: MICHAEL JACKSON, SINGER/ENTERTAINER; DOMESTIC POLICE COOPERATION; OO: LOS ANGELES.

REFERENCE LOS ANGELES TELETYPE DATED 9/18/93. b6 b7C

[redacted] LOS ANGELES POLICE DEPARTMENT (LAPD), AND [redacted] SANTA BARBARA SHERIFF'S OFFICE (SBSO), ARRIVED IN MANILA THE EVENING OF 9/21/93 AND CONDUCTED INTERVIEWS WITH [redacted] ON 9/22/93 AND 9/23/93.

SEARCHED INDEXED SERIALIZED FILED

SEP 24 1993

FBI — LOS ANGELES

TELETYPE

62D-LA-162715-5

PAGE TWO DE MAN 0004 UNCLAS

LEGAT MANILA SET UP THE INTERVIEWS THROUGH [redacted] LAWYER AND ACCOMPANIED THE OFFICERS TO THE FIRST INTERVIEW TO ENSURE THAT THERE WERE NO PROBLEMS. b6 b7C

[redacted] b6 b7C b7D

[redacted] AND [redacted] DEPARTED MANILA THE MORNING OF 9/24/93. b6 b7C

IN A TELEPHONE CONVERSATION PRIOR TO THEIR DEPARTURE, [redacted] AND [redacted] EXPRESSED APPRECIATION TO LEGAT AND SAID THEY FELT THEY HAD BEEN SUCCESSFUL IN THEIR INTERVIEWS WITH [redacted] b6 b7C

LEGAT MANILA CONSIDERS THIS CASE RUC.

BT

#0004

NNNN

FD-36 (Rev. 11-17-88)

FBI

TRANSMIT VIA:
- [ ] Teletype
- [ ] Facsimile
- [X] AIRTEL

PRECEDENCE:
- [ ] Immediate
- [ ] Priority
- [ ] Routine

CLASSIFICATION:
- [ ] TOP SECRET
- [ ] SECRET
- [ ] CONFIDENTIAL
- [ ] UNCLAS E F T O
- [ ] UNCLAS

Date 9/2/93

TO : SAC, LOS ANGELES

FROM : LEGAT, LONDON (62D-LO-11779)

SUBJECT : MICHAEL JACKSON;
ALLEGATION OF CHILD ABUSE;
DOMESTIC POLICE COOPERATION

Enclosed is a letter and its attachments dated September 1993 which was received 9/2/93 from [redacted] [redacted] b7D

The letter provides background information on articles that appeared in the U.K. press concerning a British national who alleges that MICHAEL JACKSON made an indecent telephone call to him during 1979. [redacted] [redacted] b6 b7C

The enclosed information is provided to Los Angeles Division who is requested to provide the information to the appropriate local authorities. [redacted] have advised that they intend to take no action in this matter and is providing the information for information only. b7D

Legat London is taking no further action in this matter.

2-Los Angeles (Enc. 1)
1-London

RID:rkg
(3)

O&A 9/30/93

62D-LA-162715-7

assign to [redacted]

SEARCHED S/S
INDEXED
SERIALIZED
FILED

b6 b7C b7

Approved: ______ Transmitted ______ (Number) (Time) Per ______

Routing Slip
FD-4 (Rev. 8-8-89)

Date 9/27/93

To: XXXXXXXXXXFBI, LOS ANGELES
Att.: SA [redacted]

FILE # 62D-LA-162715

Title b6 b7C

- [ ] SAC
- [ ] ASAC
- [ ] Supv.
- [ ] Agent
- [ ] OSM
- [ ] Rotor #
- [ ] Steno
- [ ] Typist
- [ ] M

Room

RE: ATTACHED NEWSPAPER ARTICLES

- [ ] Acknowledge
- [ ] Assign [ ] Reassign
- [ ] Bring file
- [ ] Call me
- [ ] Correct
- [ ] Deadline
- [ ] Delinquent
- [ ] Discontinue
- [ ] Expedite
- [ ] File
- [ ] For Information
- [ ] Handle
- [ ] Initial & return
- [ ] Leads need attention
- [ ] Mark for indexing
- [ ] Open case
- [ ] Prepare lead cards
- [ ] Prepare tickler
- [ ] Recharge file [ ] serial
- [ ]
- [ ] Send to
- [ ] Return assignment card
- [ ] Return file [ ] serial
- [ ]
- [ ] Return with action taken
- [ ] Return with explanation
- [ ] Search and return
- [ ] See me
- [ ] Type

b6
b7C

Referencing the recent visit of LAPD and SBSO Detectives to Legat Manila, to interview [redacted]

Legat Manila is enclosing the attached newspaper articles for information of SA [redacted]

62D-LA-162715-8

SEARCHED
SERIALIZED
SERIALIZED
FILED

1993

XXX [redacted] /ALAT Manila

See reverse side

Office LEGAT MANILA

★U.S. Government Printing Office: 1989-241-706/08027

The Philippine Star
Sep 23, 1993

PAGE 8

US detectives question Filipino couple on Jackson child abuse

MANILA (UPI) — Two California detectives investigating child molestation allegations against Michael Jackson met Wednesday with a Philippine couple who claims the megastar fondled young boys.

The detectives, one from Los Angeles, the other from Santa Barbara, began meeting Wednesday afternoon with Mariano Quindoy and his wife, Faye. The Philippine couple managed Jackson's Neverland Valley home from 1988 to 1990.

"As the media already knows, we are here to talk to the Quindoys," said Sgt. Deborah Linden, deputy sheriff at the Santa Barbara County Sheriff's Department. "We are not here to comment on the investigation," she added during a break in the meeting at a downtown law office.

Jackson has been haunted for weeks by allegations he sexually abused a 13-year-old boy. The boy has filed a civil suit against the 35-year-old singer in Los Angeles. No criminal charges have so far been filed against Jackson.

The singer's representatives have branded the allegations part of a failed plot to extort $20 million from Jackson, currently on a world tour promoting his latest album, "Dangerous." Family and friends have rushed to his defense, insisting the allegations could not be true.

Quindoy, a 59-year-old Philippine lawyer who left Jackson's ranch due to disagreements with other staff and a pay dispute, claimed he saw the singer fondle young boys on at least two occasions.

He and his wife said they had "reason to believe" the 13-year-old's allegations against Jackson, although the alleged incident occurred long after they had left the singer's employ.

Appearing relaxed and accompanied by three lawyers, Quindoy reiterated Wednesday that he was willing to testify if the case went to court. He declined to say whether the two detectives had requested his testimony.

Linden and Los Angeles police detective Fred Sicard arrived in Manila Tuesday night and are scheduled to remain in the Philippines until at least Saturday. They declined to comment on their planned activities during the week.

Mr. Quindoy plans to write a book about what he allegedly saw during his employment at the Neverland resort. He has denied his allegations could be designed to stoke interest in the manuscript.

Los Angeles police detectives Federico Sicard and Deborah Ellen Linder arrive at the Ninoy Aquino International Airport Tuesday night and were met by US Embassy officials, who refused to comment on the purpose of their visit here. However, initial reports indicated they were to interview Filipino couple Mark and Faye Quindoy about their statements regarding the child abuse case against pop superstar Michael Jackson. STAR photo by RICKY ALEGRE

Philippine Daily Inquirer Sept 23, 1993

CHILD ABUSE RAPS

Pinoy couple quizzed on Jackson

TWO American detectives yesterday began questioning two Filipino former aides to Michael Jackson about allegations the American superstar sexually molested a 13-year-old boy in his California mansion.

"We cannot comment on the interview or the investigation," detective Federico Sicard told reporters before a private meeting with Filipino lawyer Mark Quindoy and his wife Faye in Makati.

"We have to maintain our integrity on the investigation," said Sicard, a member of the Child Abuse unit of the Los Angeles Police Department's Juvenile Division.

Quindoy expressed willingness to testify in a US court about "abnormalities" that, he said, he witnessed while he and his wife worked for Jackson at his Neverland Valley ranch from 1988 to 1990.

Quindoy, 59, who has accused Jackson of indecently assaulting the youth, declined to comment when asked if the California detectives told him they wanted the couple to give evidence in Los Angeles.

In an earlier talk with newsmen, Quindoy said all the evidence he has to prove his claim was in a diary where he listed down the names and addresses of children and former Jackson employees who he said were willing to corroborate charges of sexual abuse against the superstar.

Jackson has denied the accusations and says he is the target of a $20-million blackmail attempt.

Anthony Pellicano, a private detective working for Jackson, confirmed the Quindoys were employed at Neverland ranch but said they were "failed extortionists trying to resurrect themselves."

The couple are claiming Jack-

See PINOY, P. 10

JACKSON

Pinoy . . . (From page 1)

son owed them $283,000 in overtime pay.

A US embassy official attended the meeting along with Santa Barbara deputy sheriff Deborah Linden.

In a press conference last week, Quindoy said he saw Jackson engaging in "abnormalities that would constitute pedophilia and sexual molestation" on some of the young boys brought to Neverland.

"He (Jackson) is a gay. He is a homosexual. There's no question about that," said Quindoy, who worked as manager of Jackson's estate from May, 1988, to August, 1990.

The American detectives arrived in Manila Tuesday night and met with National Bureau of Investigation (NBI) Director Epimaco Velasco yesterday morning.

About 100,000 fans turned out on Tuesday to see Jackson in Tel Aviv, the latest stop on his "Dangerous" world tour. *With Reuter report*

SEP-03-1993 17:59 FROM LEGAL ATTACHE LONDON TO P.01

CLASSIFICATION: UNCLAS

OFFICE OF THE LEGAL ATTACHE
AMERICAN EMBASSY
LONDON, ENGLAND

SECURE FAX: [redacted]
NON-SECURE FAX: [redacted]
TELEPHONE: [redacted] Ext [redacted]

b2
b6
b7C

Date: 9/2/93

☐ IMMEDIATE
☒ PRIORITY
☐ ROUTINE

Number of pages including this page: 20

TO: SAC, LOS ANGELES File No:

C-1

FAX NO:

ATTN:

FACSIMILE

FROM: LEGAL ATTACHE, LONDON (62D-LO-11779) REC. 9-3-93 1052

ORIGINATOR: DLAT [redacted] INT. DATE TIME b6 b7C

SUBJECT: MICHAEL JACKSON; ALLEGATION OF CHILD ABUSE; DOMESTIC POLICE COOPERATION

SENT INT. DATE TIME

SPECIAL NOTES/INSTRUCTIONS:

Attached for Los Angeles is a copy of an airtel dated 9/2/93 and an enclosure letter and attachments from [redacted] [redacted] regarding captioned subject. b7D

1

The original airtel and attachments are being forwarded via Bureau mail.

FEDERAL BUREAU OF INVESTIGATION

SPECIAL AGENT

11000 WILSHIRE BLVD., #1700 (310) 477-6565
LOS ANGELES, CA 90024 (310) 996-______

b6
b7C

62D LA-162715-9
~~62D-LO-11779~~

SEARCHED INDEXED
SERIALIZED FILED
1993
FBI - LOS ANGELES

Approved: CLASSIFICATION: UNCLAS Sent

b2
b6
b7C

SEP-03-1993 10:02 P.001

FBI

TRANSMIT VIA:
- [ ] Teletype
- [ ] Facsimile
- [X] AIRTEL

PRECEDENCE:
- [ ] Immediate
- [ ] Priority
- [ ] Routine

CLASSIFICATION:
- [ ] TOP SECRET
- [ ] SECRET
- [ ] CONFIDENTIAL
- [ ] UNCLAS E F T O
- [ ] UNCLAS

Date 9/2/93

TO : SAC, LOS ANGELES

FROM : LEGAT, LONDON (62D-LO-11779)

SUBJECT : MICHAEL JACKSON;
ALLEGATION OF CHILD ABUSE;
DOMESTIC POLICE COOPERATION

Enclosed is a letter and its attachments dated September 1993 which was received 9/2/93 from [redacted] b7D

The letter provides background information on articles that appeared in the U.K. press concerning a British national who alleges that MICHAEL JACKSON made an indecent telephone call to him during 1979. [redacted] b6 b7C

The enclosed information is provided to Los Angeles Division who is requested to provide the information to the appropriate local authorities. [redacted] have advised that they intend to take no action in this matter and is providing the information for information only. b7D

Legat London is taking no further action in this matter.

2-Los Angeles (Enc. 1)
1-London

RID:rkg
(3)

Approved: ______ Transmitted ______ (Number) (Time) Per ______

SEP-03-1993 10:00 FROM LEGAL ATTACHE LONDON TO P.06

THE
PLE
AK

By CHESTER STERN
...e Correspondent

...eople who witness or ...me will be given a new ...em speak out in court ...reprisals.

... Michael Howard is to act ...d of criminals walking free ...ms are scared to testify.

Protection for court witnesses

transport to take witnesses to and from court.

The controversial rule which forces the prosecution in major trials to disclose full details of their case in advance is also likely to be amended.

And Mr Howard's plans include a law to prevent unscrupulous defence lawyers from tracking down witnesses prepared to give evidence against their clients.

They follow mounting pressure from backbenchers

Continued on Page 2

Strange phone calls from Michael Jackson

SUPERSTAR AND FAN: Michael Jackson with Terry George in 1983

CONTACTING POLICE: Sister LaToya

By DENNA ALLEN and ANDREW CHAPMAN

SUPERSTAR Michael Jackson made an extraordinary sexually explicit transatlantic telephone call to a 13-year-old British schoolboy fan, it was revealed yesterday.

Now details of the allegations made by Terry George are to be handed to Scotland Yard and Los Angeles police investigating the Jackson child sex scandal.

American detectives are also planning to question LaToya Jackson, who has voiced concern about 50 boys visiting the home she shared with younger brother Michael. Last night she instructed her lawyer to contact the Los Angeles Police Department.

Disturbing

Meanwhile, Terry George, now a 28-year-old disc jockey, has spoken for the first time about the disturbing late-night phone call Jackson made to his home when he was just a boy.

The multi-millionaire singer asked Terry, then 13, about sexual activities in graphic terms. At the same time the star described his own intimate physical actions during the conversation.

After the Jackson scandal exploded last week, Terry said: 'I can believe that the

Continued on Page 3

JULIE BURCHILL 31 ■ NIGEL DEMPSTER 47 ■ PATRIC WALKER 54 ■ MONEY 71-79

'The Mail on Sunday' 29th August '93

SEP-03-1993 10:06 P.006

b2
b6
b7C

AWAY FROM SCANDAL: Michael Jackson yesterday — marching with Thai Air Force cadets during his Asian tour

Jackson's strange call to British boy

...Page One

...tions are true ...e of what happened ... If it hadn't been ...t phone call I would have believed it was ...e. But when I first ... the news I ...iately felt part of it

...only dared tell a ...l of my closest ..., because I thought ... would believe me. ... now they know I ...elling the truth ... what Michael ... said to me.

...just came straight ...th his questions. I ...giggled. I felt ...assed and awkward. ... really understand ... he was talking

...ed to steer him off ...bject and then he "Do you believe I'm ... now?"

...d "Are you?" I felt ... I was shocked. I ... to talk about ...ing else but he ... it back into the ...sation. I was ...ortable.

...whole conversation ...about 15 minutes, ... talked about this ... sexual act for five minutes or so. Then he said he'd phone me the next day.

'Looking back I could have hung up, but he was a superstar and I was flattered and I didn't want him to stop ringing me.'

The friendship with the Yorkshire boy started as part of Terry's hobby of collecting autographs and interviews with stars. Paul McCartney, Kim Wilde, Cilla Black, Boy George — all share a place in his treasured photo album.

Intimate

With a small tape recorder, — a Christmas presents from his proud parents — Terry would wait at stage doors and inside hotel lobbies hoping to snatch a few words and a photograph.

He had already captured Omar Sharif, but his greatest scoop came in February 1979 when he coaxed an interview from Jackson, then 20, who was performing in Leeds. Terry eavesdropped in the lobby of the Dragonara Hotel listening for details of room numbers from porters and cleaners. One let it slip that the Jackson entourage had taken over the eighth floor.

Terry slipped into the lift and knocked on Jackson's door. The superstar answered and invited him into his suite for an exclusive interview.

The questions were innocent fanzine trivia, but it was a magical 30 minutes for the young boy.

'He spoke to me like a friend,' recalls Terry. 'He made me feel special and at the end of it he asked if we could keep in touch and we swapped telephone numbers and addresses.'

Several days later Terry answered the phone at his home in Leeds. Jackson was on the line calling from his London hotel.

'Hi, it's Michael ... is Terry there?'

Again the conversation was easy and casual as the superstar chatted about the tour. Jackson returned to the US, but more calls followed over the next three months. 'Sometimes he rang in the middle of the night,' says Terry. 'Once my father answered. He boasts that he's spoken to Michael Jackson.'

But then came the call in late spring 1979 that shattered the innocence of the relationship.

And very soon afterwards the calls began to peter out. They came to an abrupt end when Terry's parents phone was cut off because he had run up a £340 bill calling the US. His mother said: 'You've been phoning that Michael Jackson, haven't you?'

Charges

Terry tried calling Jackson several times, reversing the charges from a phone box. When he got through it became clear his superstar friend didn't want to know.

The final rejection came four years later when Terry tried to rekindle their friendship when Jackson came to London again. Terry tracked him down and was even photographed alongside his idol, but now the management were on hand to issue the polite brush-off.

'I felt used because he'd wanted my friendship when I was just a boy. Now I was a young man he just didn't seem to want to know,' says Terry.

SHOCKED: Terry George

'Looking back it was wrong of Michael. The call wasn't from a young teenager, but a grown man.'

Now Terry has sworn an affidavit for the Los Angeles Police Department and is prepared to travel to California to help their Enquiries.

Superintendent Michael Hames, head of the Obscene Publications Squad, said yesterday: 'We will investigate this matter alongside the Los Angeles police.'

...jobs because they did not like what was happening.

They claim fear of threats by Jackson's associates stopped them from talking until now.

The Quindoys are seeking $500,000 (£330,000) in back pay from the superstar, who celebrates his 35th birthday today.

Mr Quindoy, who is preparing a book about the singer, said: 'Michael is such a big man. I was trying to protect him, but it lingered in my mind that it was a civic duty to tell the truth.'

The initial scandal erupted when a dentist in a custody battle alleged his 13-year-old son had been sexually abused at Jackson's home.

Jackson's staff claimed the man was trying to extort millions of dollars.

A Los Angeles TV station claimed last night that, while denying all allegations, Jackson's staff had offered the father £230,000 to keep quiet but he had refused

Hoping

Meanwhile Detective Bill Dworin, of the Los Angeles police child exploitation unit, said he was hoping to speak to Jackson's elder sister LaToya, who has voiced concern about Michael's boy guests.

'We are aware she might be able to identify other children who have spent time in Michael Jackson's company,' he said.

Visitors to the ranch included Home Alone star Macaulay Culkin, 12, and Australian Wade Robson, 10, who both insist they were not sexually assaulted.

Several former employees rallied to the star's defence. One said Quindoy and LaToya had misinterpreted simple kindness.

And James Ruth Newkirk, a former executive at Jackson's ranch, said: 'I never had evidence of anything mischievous ... if someone spent the night, they had their own bedroom.'

● Pepsi-Cola last night denied Los Angeles newspaper reports that they were investigating Jackson's life with a view to dropping him after a £9 million, ten-year association.

SEP-03-1993 10:03 FROM LEGAL ATTACHE LONDON TO P.08

DIANA...speaks candidly

DIANA'S VISION:

I'll make my boy the people's king

PRINCESS DIANA has revealed her vision of a down-to-earth monarchy for the future with William as "the people's king."

She has told close friends how she is determined that William will rule without the "arrogant" views of the Palace.

The Princess has vowed to show her sons how ordinary folk in Britain live and make them "feel in their hearts the people's hopes, joys, problems, fears, ambitions and disappointments."

Diana has even decided not to divorce Charles so that she can shape the princes' personalities and future. Full astonishing story—Pages 4 and 5.

AD PHONE TH KO

Brit DJ tells of shock call

By CHARLES YATES and DAVID WOODING

A BRITISH disc jockey has told how Michael Jackson made an obscene phone call to him when he was a star-struck schoolboy.

Terry George was only 13 when he had a bizarre late-night conversation with the superstar — who described how he was fondling himself at the other end of the line.

Terry, now 28, is passing on details of the sex chat to Los Angeles police probing the Jackson child-abuse allegations. He first met the star when, as a schoolboy autograph hunter, he managed to interview him in his home city of Leeds.

They became pals and regularly had transatlantic chats — until in one call Jackson, then 20, asked him in graphic detail about sexual activities.

The millionaire told how he was performing a sex act on himself as they spoke.

Terry said he believes the abuse allegations against Jackson — "because of what happened to me."

CONCERT

His revelations are being relayed to the management entourage of the singer, in Singapore on his world tour.

Yesterday 47,000 fans, including actress Liz Taylor, turned a sell-out concert at Singapore's National Stadium into a huge 35th birthday party for Jacko.

He was driven there in a van, peering from behind curtains with a mask over his nose and mouth.

Terry went on: "If it hadn't been for that call I would never have believed the allegations were possible.

"But when I first heard the news I immediately felt

Continued on Page Seven

Masked . . . Jacko peers from van on way to show yesterday

BINGO + GO FOR £1M GOALS: Page 13

'THE SUN' 30th AUGUST '93

SEP-03-1993 10:08 P.008

b2
b6
b7C

SEP-03-1993 10:04 FROM LE[...] ATTACHE LONDON TO P.09

do not ring our main switchboard.

Don't worry about the cost, we'll ring you straight back. The number is:

071 782 4134

JACKO SPOT

FUN park bosses still plan to send needy kids to visit Jacko in California after a charity drive at Lightwater Valley, North Yorks.

Tecs hired for Pepsi 'probe'

PEPSI-Cola has hired a top detective agency to investigate Jacko, it was claimed yesterday.

The soft drinks giant, whose ads are fronted by the star, has told Kroll Associates to "examine Jackson's character", US newspapers say.

Kroll is largely staffed by former CIA officers. One writer said: "If you want someone to dig up the dirt, they are the people." Pepsi denied the probe.

We backo Jacko . . . fans in London yesterday

Banner headlines . . . in support of Michael

He's a healer not a feeler

LONDON PROTEST

HUNDREDS of fans marched in London yesterday to sing their support for Michael Jackson.

They waved banners saying: "Michael is a healer not a feeler" and "You'll never Moonwalk alone."

They sang Happy Birthday at the demo near Eros' statue in Piccadilly Circus.

Interior designer Louise Ayis, 21, of Beckenham, Kent, said: "He's innocent. I'm in love with him and these allegations are blackmail."

Chris Rich, 11, from Barnet, North London, said: "If he asked me to go to his ranch Neverland I'd be really happy."

Student Ann Stephenson, 20, of Bedford, said: "The Press is saying the stories have ruined his career, but this demonstration shows we still support him."

Sonya Henson, 27, of Barnet, said: "He'll never be able to go around his fairground rides with kids hanging off him without people raising an eyebrow."

to drop the charges.

Pellicano said: "It was at this meeting that the demands were made. The father repeatedly demanded the money to fund a film project. His demands were refused.

"He said he would accuse Michael of being a child molester if we failed to pay up."

Jacko, pictured above performing in Singapore last night, remained silent throughout the meeting, Pellicano said.

Chandler, 42 — whose son claims the star performed oral sex on him — "stormed out" after an hour.

Later that day, Pellicano claims Chandler's lawyers offered Jacko "a deal" in which the father would receive more than £3million a year over four years.

Horrors

This was also "turned down flat," he said.

"We believe the child-abuse charges stemmed from these meetings," he added. "Mr Jackson adamantly denies all the charges against him."

But last night the source close to Dr Chandler said he was "furious" at Pellicano's claims.

"It is true he tried to reach an out-of-court

Jordy . . . 'abused by star'

settlement with the Jackson camp," he said.

"But it was to spare his son the horrors of a massive court case.

"Jackson's side offered Dr Chandler £220,000 to drop the charges. But by then Dr Chandler had reported the matter to authorities.

"He is very upset by Jackson's attempts to discredit him and his son. He absolutely believes Jordy is telling the truth. He acted in the boy's best interests."

The dentist's lawyer Barry Rothman said: "There was no blackmail attempt. We stand by our charges."

Police yesterday revealed they had begun a probe into the alleged blackmail attempt.

A spokesman for Los Angeles police said: "Both sides are making charges against each other and we will look at all sides.

"Our inquiries regarding the child sex abuse claims against Mr Jackson are still very active.

"We are talking to dozens of children who have known him."

Littlejohn — Page Six

MY PHONE SEX WITH STAR

Continued from Page One

part of it all. I'd only dared tell a handful of my closest friends, because I thought nobody would believe me.

"At last they know I was telling the truth about what Michael Jackson said to me."

Terry told a Sunday newspaper: "He just came straight out with his questions.

"I felt embarrassed and awkward. I didn't really understand what he was talking about. I tried to steer him off the subject and he asked, 'Do you believe I'm doing it now?'

"I said, 'Are you?' I felt panicky. I was shocked.

"The whole conversation lasted about 15 minutes and he talked about this intimate sexual act for five minutes or so.

"I could have hung up, but he was a superstar and I was flattered and I didn't want him to stop ringing me."

The pair's friendship started in February 1979 when Terry tracked Jacko to his room at the Dragonara Hotel, where he was staying before a performance.

Over the next three months they spoke several times on the phone — often "in the middle of the night."

Then came the conversation that shattered the relationship.

In 1983 Terry tried to renew the friendship when Jacko was in London. They were pictured together but the star's entourage brushed him away from any further contact.

Terry said: "I felt used because he had wanted my friendship when I was just a boy.

"Now I was a young man he didn't seem to want to know."

The storm surrounding Jacko blew up last week after it was alleged he abused Jordy Schwartz, 13, son of a rich California dentist.

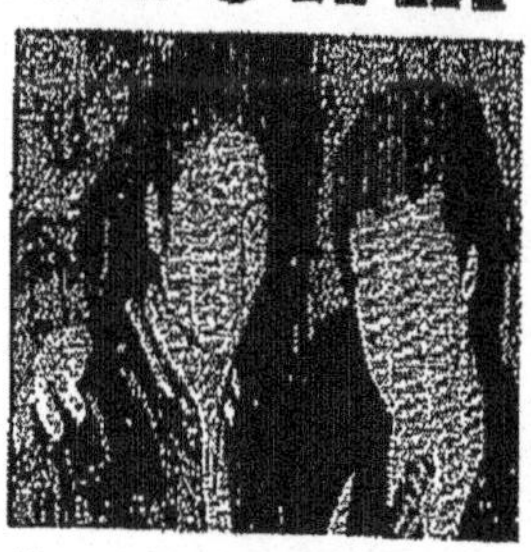

Mates . . . Jackson and Terry George in 1983

Cliff: It's the price of fame

CLIFF Richard has backed Jacko — and says the child-abuse claims are part of the price of fame.

Cliff, 52, told a Christian festival in Corby, Northants: "He's probably the best singer alive and look at what he's going through.

"When you become a public image, you're up for grabs and very, very vulnerable."

NOW READ LATOYA JACKSON'S EXPLOSIVE BOOK: See Pages 16 and 17

SEP-03-1993 10:09 P.009

b2
b6
b7C

SEP-03-1993 10:11 FROM LE[redacted] ATTACHE LONDON TO [redacted] P.18

Telecommunications Act 1984

Improper use of public telecommunication system.

43.—(1) A person who—

(*a*) sends, by means of a public telecommunication system, a message or other matter that is grossly offensive or of an indecent, obscene or menacing character; or

(*b*) sends by those means, for the purpose of causing annoyance, inconvenience or needless anxiety to another, a message that he knows to be false or persistently makes use for that purpose of a public telecommunication system,

shall be guilty of an offence and liable on summary conviction to a fine not exceeding level 3 on the standard scale.

(2) Subsection (1) above does not apply to anything done in the course of providing a cable programme service ~~(within the meaning of Part IV of this Act).~~

NOTE: Amended vide Schedule 5 of the Cable and Broadcasting Act 1984

SEP-03-1993 10:15

TOTAL P.18
P.018

b2
b6
b7C

FD-36 (Rev. 8-29-85)

FBI

TRANSMIT VIA:	PRECEDENCE:	CLASSIFICATION:
☒ Teletype	☐ Immediate	☐ TOP SECRET
☐ Facsimile	☒ Priority	☐ SECRET
☐ AIRTEL	☐ Routine	☐ CONFIDENTIAL
		☐ UNCLAS E F T O
		☒ UNCLAS

Date 10/13/93

FM FBI LOS ANGELES (62D-LA-162715) (P)

TO DIRECTOR FBI/ROUTINE/

FBI NEW YORK/PRIORITY/

BT

UNCLAS

CITE: //3410:C-1//

PASS: FBIHQ, SSA [redacted] VCMO UNIT. b6 b7C

SUBJECT: MICHAEL JACKSON (SINGER/ENTERTAINER); DOMESTIC POLICE COOPERATION; OO: LOS ANGELES.

FOR INFORMATION OF NEW YORK, THE LOS ANGELES OFFICE IS ASSISTING THE LOS ANGELES POLICE DEPARTMENT (LAPD) AND SANTA BARBARA SHERIFF'S OFFICE (SBSO) IN THEIR INVESTIGATION INTO MOLESTATION CHARGES AGAINST MICHAEL JACKSON. THE TASK FORCE FORMED TO INVESTIGATE THESE ALLEGATIONS HAS INFORMATION THAT [redacted] b6 b7C

[redacted] HAVE FILED A RESTRAINING ORDER

SEARCHED
INDEXED
SERIALIZED
FILED

SLS/jak

Approved: [signature] Original filename: JAK001W.286

Time Received: Telprep filename: JAK001S0.286

MRI/JULIAN DATE: 131/287 ISN: 17

FOX DATE & TIME OF ACCEPTANCE: 0219

62D-LA-162715-10

^PAGE 2 (62D-LA-162715) UNCLAS

AGAINST MICHAEL JACKSON ORDERING JACKSON TO STAY AWAY FROM [redacted] THE LAPD REQUESTED THAT THE FBI ATTEMPT TO DETERMINE IF A RESTRAINING ORDER WAS FILED [redacted] AGAINST MICHAEL JACKSON WHOSE TRUE NAME IS MICHAEL JOE JACKSON, DATE OF BIRTH AUGUST 29, 1958.

THE IDENTITY OF THE COURT WHERE THE RESTRAINING ORDER WOULD HAVE BEEN FILED IS UNKNOWN, HOWEVER, AS PROVIDED ABOVE, THE LAST KNOWN ADDRESS FOR [redacted] WAS [redacted] [redacted]

b6
b7C

NEW YORK AT NEW YORK, NEW YORK: WILL DETERMINE IF A RESTRAINING ORDER HAS BEEN FILED [redacted] AGAINST MICHAEL JACKSON.

BT

OCT 13 9 28 PM '93

0019 MRI 00131

PP FBILA

DE FBILA #0017 2870244

ZNR UUUUU

P 140169Z OCT 93

FM FBI LOS ANGELES (62D-LA-162715) (P)

TO DIRECTOR FBI/ROUTINE/

FBI NEW YORK/PRIORITY/

BT

UNCLAS

CITE: //3410:C-1//

PASS: FBIHQ, SSA [redacted] VCMO UNIT. b6 b7C

SUBJECT: MICHAEL JACKSON (SINGER/ENTERTAINER); DOMESTIC POLICE COOPERATION; OO: LOS ANGELES.

FOR INFORMATION OF NEW YORK, THE LOS ANGELES OFFICE IS ASSISTING THE LOS ANGELES POLICE DEPARTMENT (LAPD) AND SANTA BARBARA SHERIFF'S OFFICE (SBSO) IN THEIR INVESTIGATION INTO MOLESTATION CHARGES AGAINST MICHAEL JACKSON. THE TASK FORCE FORMED TO INVESTIGATE THESE ALLEGATIONS HAS INFORMATION THAT

[redacted] b6 b7C

62D-LA-162715-10

SEARCHED________
INDEXED________
SERIALIZED________
FILED________

TELETYPE

[redacted] b6 b7C

PAGE TWO DE FBILA 0017 UNCLAS

[redacted] HAVE FILED A RESTRAINING ORDER AGAINST MICHAEL JACKSON ORDERING JACKSON TO STAY AWAY FROM [redacted] THE LAPD REQUESTED THAT THE FBI ATTEMPT TO DETERMINE IF A RESTRAINING ORDER WAS FILED [redacted] AGAINST MICHAEL JACKSON WHOSE TRUE NAME IS MICHAEL JOE JACKSON, DATE OF BIRTH AUGUST 29, 1958.

THE IDENTITY OF THE COURT WHERE THE RESTRAINING ORDER WOULD HAVE BEEN FILED IS UNKNOWN, HOWEVER, AS PROVIDED ABOVE, THE LAST KNOWN ADDRESS FOR [redacted] WAS [redacted] [redacted]

b6
b7C

NEW YORK AT NEW YORK, NEW YORK: WILL DETERMINE IF A RESTRAINING ORDER HAS BEEN FILED [redacted] AGAINST MICHAEL JACKSON.

BT

#0017

NNNN

FD-36 (Rev. 8-29-85)

FBI

b6
b7C

TRANSMIT VIA:
- [X] Teletype
- [ ] Facsimile
- [ ] AIRTEL

PRECEDENCE:
- [ ] Immediate
- [ ] Priority
- [X] Routine

CLASSIFICATION:
- [ ] TOP SECRET
- [ ] SECRET
- [ ] CONFIDENTIAL
- [ ] UNCLAS E F T O
- [X] UNCLAS

Date 10/19/93

FM FBI LOS ANGELES (62D-LO-11779) (RUC)

TO DIRECTOR FBI/ROUTINE/

LEGAT LONDON/ROUTINE/

BT

UNCLAS

CITE: //3410:C-1//

PASS: FBIHQ, SSA [redacted] FLU II, OLIA; SSA [redacted] b6 b7C

VCMO.

SUBJECT: MICHAEL JACKSON; ALLEGATION OF CHILD ABUSE; DOMESTIC POLICE COOPERATION; OO: LONDON.

RE LEGAT LONDON AIRTEL TO LOS ANGELES, DATED SEPTEMBER 2, 1993.

FOR INFORMATION OF LEGAT LONDON, THE LETTER, DATED SEPTEMBER 1993, TO [redacted] DEPUTY LEGAL ATTACHE, AMERICAN EMBASSY, LONDON, FROM [redacted] b6 b7C b7D

SEARCHED 62D-LO-11779-11
INDEXED
SERIALIZED
FILED

SLS/jak

Approved: ______ Original filename: JAK004W.292

Time Received: ______ Telprep filename: JAK004SD.292

MRI/JULIAN DATE: 1368/294 ISN: 18

FOX DATE & TIME OF ACCEPTANCE: 10/21/93 (11 28 A) @ 1831 R.N.

^PAGE 2 (62D-LO-11779) UNCLAS

[redacted], AND ATTACHED NEWSPAPER ARTICLES REGARDING MICHAEL JACKSON AND BRITISH NATIONAL TERANCE GEORGE WERE FURNISHED TO THE LOS ANGELES POLICE DEPARTMENT (LAPD). THESE ITEMS WERE ~~FURNISHED~~ Provided ON OCTOBER 4, 1993 TO [redacted] [redacted] OF THE SEXUALLY EXPLOITED CHILDREN'S UNIT OF THE LAPD. FOR INFORMATION OF LEGAT LONDON, LOS ANGELES IS MAINTAINING LIAISON WITH LAPD AND THE SANTA BARBARA SHERIFF'S OFFICE IN THE CONTINUED INVESTIGATION OF MOLESTATION ALLEGATIONS AGAINST MICHAEL JACKSON, UNDER LOS ANGELES FILE 62D-LA-162715.

b7D
b6
b7C

BT

OCT 21 12 24 PM '93

0046 MRI 01368

RR FBILA

DE FBILA #0018 2941845

ZNR UUUUU

R 211830Z OCT 93

FM FBI LOS ANGELES (62D-LO-11779) (RUC)

TO DIRECTOR FBI/ROUTINE/

LEGAT LONDON/ROUTINE/

BT

UNCLAS

CITE: //3410:C-1//

PASS: FBIHQ, SSA [redacted] FLU II, OLIA; SSA [redacted] b6 b7C

VCMO.

SUBJECT: MICHAEL JACKSON; ALLEGATION OF CHILD ABUSE; DOMESTIC POLICE COOPERATION; OO: LONDON.

RE LEGAT LONDON AIRTEL TO LOS ANGELES, DATED SEPTEMBER 2, 1993.

FOR INFORMATION OF LEGAT LONDON, THE LETTER, DATED SEPTEMBER 1993, TO [redacted] DEPUTY LEGAL ATTACHE, AMERICAN EMBASSY, LONDON, FROM [redacted] b6 b7C b7D

SEARCHED
INDEXED b6 b7C
SERIALIZED

TELETYPE

62D14-162715-11

FD-36 (Rev. 11-17-88)

FBI

TRANSMIT VIA:	PRECEDENCE:	CLASSIFICATION:
☐ Teletype	☐ Immediate	☐ TOP SECRET
☐ Facsimile	☐ Priority	☐ SECRET
☒ AIRTEL	☐ Routine	☐ CONFIDENTIAL
		☐ UNCLAS E F T O
		☐ UNCLAS

Date 10/22/93

TO : SAC, LOS ANGELES (62D-LA-162715)

FROM : ADIC, NEW YORK (62D-LA-R162715) (RUC) (C-9)

SUBJECT : MICHAEL JACKSON
DOMESTIC POLICE COOPERATION;
OO:LOS ANGELES

On 10/19/93 I.A. [redacted] conducted a search of the records of New York City Supreme court. This search was an attempt to locate a restraining order against Michael Jackson. Computerized and manual searches were conducted with negative results.

b6
b7C

62D-LA-162715-12

2-Los Angeles
1-New York
1-Supv
VDJ/vdj
(4)

Approved: ______ Transmitted ______ (Number) (Time) Per ______

Memorandum

To : SAC, LOS ANGELES (62D-LA-162715) (P) Date 12/28/93

From : SA [redacted] (C-1). b6 b7C

Subject: MICHAEL JOE JACKSON;
DOMESTIC POLICE COOPERATION;
OO: LOS ANGELES

On December 27, 1993, writer received a telephone call from [redacted] Los Angeles Police Department Sexual Exploitation of Children (SEOC). He advised that he had been contacted [redacted] has been writing a book about Michael Jackson concerning allegations of sexual molestations of children. [redacted] advised that [redacted] told [redacted] that he had information that the Federal Bureau of Investigation (FBI) in 1985 or 1986, investigated allegations against Jackson for reportedly molesting two Mexican boys. [redacted] further advised that the Los Angeles FBI Special Agent who investigated the incident was an Hispanic Agent. The SAC, who [redacted] referred to as the one who was Mormon, did not pursue the allegations because Jackson was to receive an honor at the White House from the President. According to [redacted] the investigation was covered up. b6 b7C

[redacted] advised he was providing this information to writer in the event inquiries were received by the FBI Los Angeles Office. b6 b7C

Writer searched indices, both manual and automated for any reference to above mentioned investigation. No references were found.

(1)- Los Angeles

SLS/sls

(1)

62D-LA-162715-13

SEARCHED INDEXED SERIALIZED FILED

1994

FBI — LOS ANGELES

b6 b7C

70-3.11.20 (4/92)

Tape No. 3

STATEMENT FORM

Page 1 of ___

Wit. No.

DR No.

Name	[redacted]	Date/Time of Interview 8-24-93 1500	Location of Interview JUV Telephonic
Resid. Add.		City 8-24-93 1500	Zip Code	Phone
Bus. Add.		City	Zip Code	Phone

Sex	Desc.	Hair	Eyes	Hgt.	Wgt.	DOB	Age	Drivers Lic. No./Other ID	State
M									

Interviewing [redacted] | Serial No(s) | Division

b6
b7C

Other Person(s) Present

Statements: Use third person. Include who, what, where, when, why and how.

[redacted] called [redacted] now working for [redacted] - 10 mo ago [redacted] got restraining order for Jackson in NY

Staple Optional Photo Here

62D-LA-162715-14

For additional space, use reverse

70-3.11.20 (4/92)

Type No. 2

Wit. No.

STATEMENT FORM

Page 1 of ____ b6 b7C

DR No.

Name	Date/Time of Interview	Location of Interview
	8-24-93 1330	JUV DIV Telephonic

Res. Add.	City	Zip Code

Bus. Add.	City	Zip Code

Sex	Desc.	Hair	Eyes	Hgt.	Wgt.	DOB	Age	Drivers Lic. No./Other ID	State
F									

Interviewing Officer(s)	Serial No(s)	Division

Other Person(s) Present

Statements: Use third person. Include who, what, where, when, why and how.

P/R called from Toronto Canada. She & husband works in children services

On Sat - 3-7-92 they took train from Chicago to Grand Canyon. Train continued to CA. They had a compartment on car that Jackson had four compartments.

Jackson had a M/B JUV 12/13 with him along with adult staff. Boy was ID'd as Michael's "cousin"

Jackson was very ~~[illegible]~~ possessive of boy

At night P/R heard questionable noises through wall.

She was concerned enough to notify the conductor of her suspisions.

Staple Optional Photo Here

For additional space, use reverse

Memorandum

To : SAC, LOS ANGELES (62D-LA-162715) Date 1/08/94

From : SA [redacted] (C-1) (P) b6 b7C

Subject: MICHAEL JACKSON;
DOMESTIC POLICE COOPERATION;
OO: LOS ANGELES

For information of the file, the attached search warrant with affidavit, was provided by [redacted] Los Angeles Police Department. Because of the sensitivity of this investigation, it is requested that this serial not be duplicated or disseminated. b6 b7C

CONFIDENTIAL

PLEASE DO NOT DUPLICATE

1 - Los Angeles (62D-LA-162715)

(1)

62D-LA-162715-15

1*

Memorandum

To : SAC, LOS ANGELES (62D-LA-162715) Date 8/08/94

From : SA [redacted] (C-1) (C)

b6
b7C

Subject: MICHAEL JACKSON;
DOMESTIC POLICE COOPERATION;
OO: LOS ANGELES

For information of the file, on this date, writer contacted [redacted] Los Angeles Police Department to enquire of the status of the investigation. [redacted] advised that the Los Angeles County District Attorney's Office was still in the process of deciding whether or not to file charges against Jackson.

b6
b7C

No outstanding leads remain for the Los Angeles Office in this matter. This file will be placed in a closed status.

1 - Los Angeles (62D-LA-162715)

(1)

8/10/94

C-4

8/10/94

62D-LA-162715-16

1994

1*

FEDERAL BUREAU OF INVESTIGATION
FOIPA
DELETED PAGE INFORMATION SHEET

No Duplication Fees are charged for Deleted Page Information Sheet(s).

Total Deleted Page(s) ~ 95
Page 21 ~ b6, b7C, b7D
Page 22 ~ b6, b7C, b7D
Page 23 ~ b6, b7C, b7D
Page 24 ~ b6, b7C, b7D
Page 25 ~ b6, b7C, b7D
Page 26 ~ b6, b7C, b7D
Page 27 ~ b6, b7C, b7D
Page 28 ~ b6, b7C, b7D
Page 29 ~ b6, b7C, b7D
Page 31 ~ b6, b7C
Page 32 ~ b6, b7C
Page 33 ~ b6, b7C
Page 34 ~ b6, b7C
Page 35 ~ b6, b7C
Page 36 ~ b6, b7C
Page 37 ~ b6, b7C
Page 38 ~ b6, b7C
Page 53 ~ Duplicate
Page 54 ~ Duplicate
Page 55 ~ Duplicate
Page 56 ~ Duplicate
Page 57 ~ Duplicate
Page 58 ~ Duplicate
Page 59 ~ Duplicate
Page 60 ~ Duplicate
Page 61 ~ Duplicate
Page 62 ~ Duplicate
Page 63 ~ Duplicate
Page 64 ~ Duplicate
Page 65 ~ Duplicate
Page 66 ~ Duplicate
Page 67 ~ Duplicate
Page 68 ~ Duplicate
Page 69 ~ Duplicate
Page 70 ~ Duplicate
Page 79 ~ b2, b6, b7C, b7D
Page 80 ~ b2, b6, b7C, b7D
Page 81 ~ b6, b7C
Page 86 ~ b2, b6, b7C, b7D
Page 87 ~ b2, b6, b7C, b7D
Page 88 ~ b2, b6, b7C, b7D
Page 89 ~ b2, b6, b7C, b7D
Page 90 ~ b2, b6, b7C, b7D
Page 91 ~ b2, b6, b7C, b7D

Page 92 ~ b2, b6, b7C, b7D
Page 93 ~ b2, b6, b7C, b7D
Page 102 ~ Duplicate
Page 108 ~ Duplicate
Page 109 ~ Duplicate
Page 110 ~ b6, b7C, b7D
Page 111 ~ b6, b7C, b7D
Page 112 ~ b6, b7C, b7D
Page 113 ~ b6, b7C, b7D
Page 114 ~ b6, b7C, b7D
Page 115 ~ b6, b7C, b7D
Page 116 ~ b6, b7C, b7D
Page 117 ~ b6, b7C, b7D
Page 118 ~ b6, b7C, b7D
Page 119 ~ b6, b7C, b7D
Page 120 ~ b6, b7C, b7D
Page 121 ~ b6, b7C, b7D
Page 123 ~ b6, b7C, b7D
Page 124 ~ b6, b7C, b7D
Page 125 ~ b6, b7C, b7D
Page 126 ~ b6, b7C, b7D
Page 127 ~ b6, b7C, b7D
Page 128 ~ b6, b7C, b7D
Page 129 ~ b6, b7C, b7D
Page 130 ~ b6, b7C, b7D
Page 131 ~ b6, b7C, b7D
Page 132 ~ b6, b7C, b7D
Page 133 ~ b6, b7C, b7D
Page 134 ~ b6, b7C, b7D
Page 135 ~ b6, b7C, b7D
Page 136 ~ b6, b7C, b7D
Page 137 ~ b6, b7C, b7D
Page 138 ~ b6, b7C, b7D
Page 139 ~ b6, b7C, b7D
Page 140 ~ b6, b7C, b7D
Page 141 ~ b6, b7C, b7D
Page 142 ~ b6, b7C, b7D
Page 143 ~ b6, b7C, b7D
Page 144 ~ b6, b7C, b7D
Page 145 ~ b6, b7C, b7D
Page 146 ~ b6, b7C, b7D
Page 147 ~ b6, b7C, b7D
Page 148 ~ b6, b7C, b7D
Page 149 ~ b6, b7C, b7D
Page 150 ~ b6, b7C, b7D
Page 151 ~ b6, b7C, b7D
Page 152 ~ b6, b7C, b7D
Page 153 ~ b6, b7C, b7D
Page 154 ~ b6, b7C, b7D
Page 155 ~ b6, b7C, b7D
Page 156 ~ b6, b7C, b7D

Chapter Four - VHS Tape

OUTCOMES

Outcomes

The FBI received a VHS tape on 23 October 1995 from the U.S. Customs Service.

No evidence that the VHS tape ever belonged to Michael Jackson.

The tape was examined and found to be *"poor quality or fourth generation recording."*

No evidence that the tape contained illegal material. **Nothing found.**

Outcome: **Nothing found.**

8-558 (Rev. 8-5-91)

1 - [redacted] 315 b6 b7C
1 -

REPORT OF THE
INFORMATION RESOURCES DIVISION
FEDERAL BUREAU OF INVESTIGATION
WASHINGTON, D. C. 20535

January 24, 1997 b6 b7C

To: [redacted]
Special Agent
United States Customs Service
U.S. Department of the Treasury
Suite 300
100 South Dixie Highway
West Palm Beach, Florida 33401

FBI File No. 95A-HQ-1148159

Lab No. 51024020 E QE

Reference: Letter dated October 20, 1995

Your No. WPO7QS95WP0012

Re: [redacted] SUBJECT; b6 b7C
CHILD PORNOGRAPHY

Specimens received: October 23, 1995

Q1 One VHS video cassette tape with "Tozai" label marked in part "Michael Jackson's Neverland Favorites An All Boy Anthology"

Result of examination: 95A-HQ-1148159-2

A physical and electronic examination of Q1 revealed that it is a poor quality third or fourth generation recording. The Q1 recording contains linear audio and real-time mistracking through the entire tape. The recorder used to make the most recent copy apparently was not functioning properly, resulting in the mistracking anomoly. Numerous stop/start transitions were observed but the nature of these observed transitions suggest that they were produced during one of the previous recordings, not during the latest recording.

[redacted] conducted the video authenticity examination. b6 b7C

Q1 was returned to your office on November 25, 1996, via Federal Express.

MAILED JAN 21 1997 ERF, QT

NH/kas (5)

MAIL ROOM ☑

This Report Is Furnished For Official Use Only

8-259 (Rev. 8-5-91)

RECORDED
10/30/95
et

FEDERAL BUREAU OF INVESTIGATION
UNITED STATES DEPARTMENT OF JUSTICE

video processing

b6
b7C

Work Sheet

b6
b7C

To: [redacted]
Special Agent
United States Customs Service
U. S. Department of the Treasury
Suite 300
100 South Dixie Highway
West Palm Beach, Florida 33401

FBI File No.

Lab No. 51024020 E XX

Reference: Letter dated October 20, 1995

Your No. WPO7QS95WP0012

Re: [redacted] - SUBJECT;
CHILD PORNOGRAPHY

b6
b7C

Specimens received: October 23, 1995

Q1

Transferred [redacted] on 6/13/96 230 P

b6
b7C

REGISTERED MAIL
Rec'd in a sealed
R 305 165 407
box 10/23/95 2:10p

51024020 E

VIDEO ANALYSIS WORKSHEET

Lab. No. 51024020 E QE   Specimen(s) (Q1)   Date 6/26/96

Bufile No. 95A-HQ-1148159   Agency U.S. CUSTOMS, WEST PALM BEACH, FLA.

TAPE FORMAT	RECORD MODE	DISPLAY	ERASE TAB	AUDIO SIGNAL	AUDIO CHARACTERISTICS
☑ VHS	☑ REAL TIME SLP	☑ COLOR	☑ REC'D OUT	☐ NONE	TONES -
☐ S-VHS	☐ TIME LAPSE	☐ B & W	☐ REC'D IN - RBM*	☑ FULL TK MONAURAL	DIST. -
☐ BETA / BETACAM	☐ STILL VIDEO	☐ DATE	☐ REC'D LEFT	☐ HALF TK MONAURA	N/F PARTY -
☐ S-BETA	TV STANDARD	☐ TIME	☐ REC'D RT - SBM*	☐ STEREO	CONV. PROB.-
☐ 8mm	☑ NTSC	☐ QUAD	☐	☐ LINEAR	MODULATION -
☐ HD-8mm	☐ PAL	☐	☐	☐ Hi-Fi	NOISE-LO ___ HI ___ WB ___
☐ U-MATIC	☐ SECAM	☐	☐	☐	SIG/NOISE -
☐ M-II	☐ ORIGINAL AT LEAST 3 OR 4		*RBM = Removed By Me		INTELL. -
☐ RL to RL	☑ COPY - No. of Switch Points SETS		*SBM = Switched Left By Me		

Physical Char. (Tape/Housing): NO SIGNS OF WEAR OR ABUSE

Audio/Video Signal Char: POOR QUALITY VIDEO, SMEARED COLORS, POOR RESOLUTION, NOISE BARS FROM MISTRACKING THROUGHOUT TAPE

Specimen Description: Q1 – ONE VHS VIDEO CASSETTE TAPE WITH TOZAI LABEL MKD IN PT "MICHAEL JACKSON'S NEVERLAND FAVORITES AN ALL BOY VIDEO ANTHOLOGY"

SET UP:

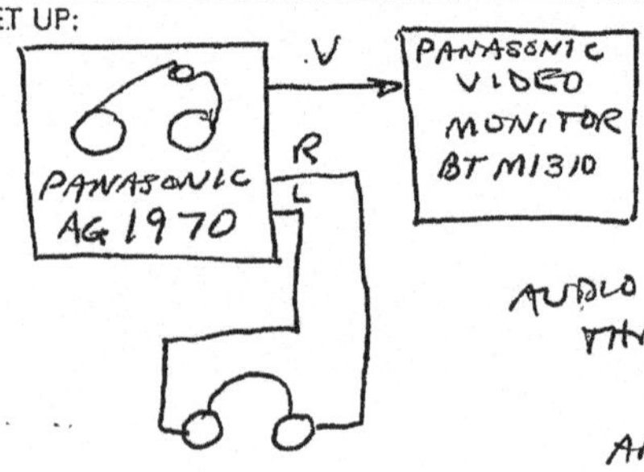

AUDIO IS LINEAR THROUGHOUT

PULL-DOWN MOIRE COLORS, AT SEVERAL POINTS, BUT MOIRE IS WASHED OUT AND BLURRED, INDICATING THAT IT WAS COPIED IN TO TAPE FROM PREVIOUS XFER

RECORD EVENTS DO NOT APPEAR TO HAVE BEEN MADE ON Q1 – MISTRACKING IS REAL-TIME AND CAN BE ADJUSTED, ~~THOUGH NOT CORRECTED~~

APPEARS TO BE STRAIGHT THROUGH RECORDING OF PREVIOUS MATERIAL, MULTIPLE SW PTS AND DISTORTED DI-HEDRAL MAKE IT DIFFICULT TO DETERMINE WHAT GENERATION IT IS, BUT COULD BE A COPY OF A COPY OF A COPY (DEPENDING ON NATURE OF ORIGINAL) (3RD OR 4TH GEN)

Video Tape Copies/Prints

NONE

STOP/START TRANSITIONS APPEAR TO HAVE BEEN MADE DURING ONE OF THE PREVIOUS RECORDINGS – NOT THE LATEST

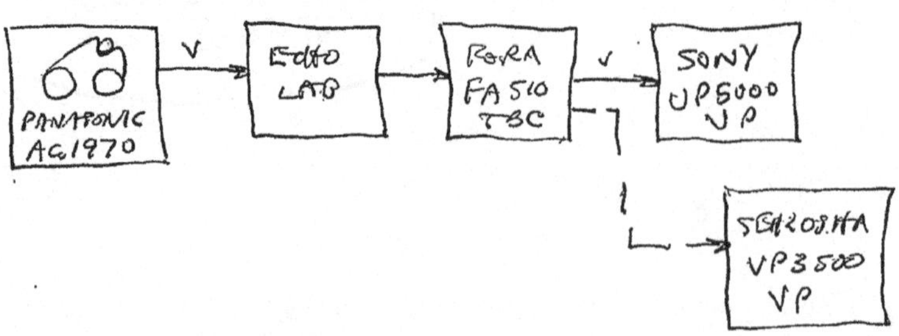

ILL
SAND

SONY
Print paper

8-291 (Rev. 1-6-93)
Evidence Shipping
FEDERAL BUREAU OF INVESTIGATION
BLDG 27958A
QUANTICO, VA. 22135

Date: NOVEMBER 25, 1996

Re: [redacted] SUBJECT; CHILD PORNOGRAPHY

b6
b7C

To:
SA [redacted]
UNITED STATES CUSTOMS SERVICE
U.S. DEPT. OF TREASURY
SUITE 300
100 SOUTH DIXIE HIGHWAY
WEST PALM BEACH, FLORIDA ~~33400~~ 33401

Phone: (407) 659-4606

Invoice of Contents

Description of Contents:

ONE VHS VIDEO CASSETTE TAPE (Q1)
ONE 4 1/2" x 6 1/2" SONY VIDEO PRINT (From Q1 vertical interval showing typical head swithing marks)

(Multi generation copy of poor quality with some program transitions all of which seem to be previously copied into Q1 - that is Q1 appears to be direct copy of all the program material)

FBI File# 95A-HQ-1148159

LAB# 51024020 E QE

Your# WP07QS95WP0012

Return to [redacted] b6 b7C

Engineering Section

Ext. 6667

Shipping# ______

EVIDENCE EVIDENCE EVIDENCE
PRIORITY HANDLING REQUESTED.
UPON RECEIPT, DELIVER TO
CASE AGENT, OR CASE SUPVR.

Shipping Methods

☐ Registered Mail/Return Receipt Requested

☐ Overnight Security Signature Service

☐ Other ______

Packaged by ______
Signature

☐ Hand Delivered ______ Date ______

All items listed above are contained in this package. ______
Signature Written

ORIGINATOR'S COPY

8-291 (Rev. 1-6-93)
Evidence Shipping
FEDERAL BUREAU OF INVESTIGATION
BLDG 27958A
QUANTICO, VA. 22135

79

Date: NOVEMBER 25, 1996

Re: [redacted] SUBJECT; CHILD PORNOGRAPHY

b6
b7C

To:
SA [redacted]
UNITED STATES CUSTOMS SERVICE
U.S. DEPT. OF TREASURY
SUITE 300
100 SOUTH DIXIE HIGHWAY
WEST PALM BEACH, FLORIDA ~~33400~~ 33401

Phone: (407) 659-4606

Invoice of Contents

Description of Contents:

ONE VHS VIDEO CASSETTE TAPE (Q1)
ONE 4 1/2" x 6 1/2" SONY VIDEO PRINT (From Q1 vertical interval showing typical head swithing marks)

(Multi generation copy of poor quality with some program transitions all of which seem to be previously copied into Q1 - that is Q1 appears to be direct copy of all the program material)

FBI File# 95A-HQ-1148159
LAB# 51024020 E QE
Your# WP07QS95WP0012
Return to [redacted] b6 b7C
Engineering Section
Ext. 6667

Shipping# 2555898265

EVIDENCE EVIDENCE EVIDENCE
PRIORITY HANDLING REQUESTED.
UPON RECEIPT, DELIVER TO
CASE AGENT, OR CASE SUPVR.

Shipping Methods

- [ ] Registered Mail/Return Receipt Requested
- [ ] Overnight Security Signature Service
- [ ] Other

Packaged by [redacted]
Signature

b6
b7C

- [ ] Hand Delivered ________ Date ________

All items listed above are contained in this package. ________
Signature Written

79

ORIGINATOR'S COPY

FEDERAL BUREAU OF INVESTIGATION
FOIPA
DELETED PAGE INFORMATION SHEET

No Duplication Fees are charged for Deleted Page Information Sheet(s).

Total Deleted Page(s) ~ 4
Page 3 ~ Referral/Direct
Page 4 ~ Referral/Direct
Page 11 ~ Referral/Direct
Page 13 ~ Referral/Direct

Chapter Five - FBI Notes

OUTCOMES

Outcomes

This file consists of detailed FBI's reports and summaries.

They outline the numerous consultations held with a range of experts. They show a stream of requests for assistance and a plea for the FBI to consider Federal proceedings against Michael Jackson.

Note dated 01 March 2004
This note states that on 27 February 2004, the Assistant District Attorney, Richard Zonen (of the Santa Barbara County District Attorney's office) requested the FBI's assistance '*to develop a prosecutive strategy and to provide forensic guidance.*'

Due to the volume and sensitivity of the case, ADA Zonen requested an on-site review of all the evidence at the Santa Barbara DA's Office on 08-09 March 2004.

Because of the existing gag order, access to the file was limited. Permission was granted for an agent to attend Santa Barbara, to provide a report and also to attend a follow-up meeting.

The follow-up meeting occurred at the FBI headquarters in Quantico on 17-18 March 2004. These dates were scheduled ahead of the commencement of the grand jury hearing.

Urgent Report dated 28 April 2004
This note states that the FBI provided the following assistance:
- Computer Analysis Response Team (CART);
- Field-work;
- Support provided to SBSD and the Santa Barbara County District Attorney's Office and
- Technical Surveillance Counter Measures (TSCM).

The Santa Barbara County District Attorney's Office requested assistance from the Behavioral Sciences Unit (BSU) at Quantico:
- '*Prosecutive Strategy*', and
- '*Threats and suspected computer intrusions*' were referred to the FBI Ventura-CA.

The grand jury indicted Michael Jackson. Although the indictment was under seal, the FBI presumed it was similar to the complaint filed on 18 December 2003.

The report stated that the Santa Maria Police Department was concerned about crowd size, international media coverage and the possibility that the criminal proceedings would be a soft target for terrorism.

The FBI however, asserted that there was no intelligence which indicated that the court proceedings would be a target for terrorism.

Michael Jackson's protection detail consisted of retired LAPD officers.

On 18 November 2003, the Santa Barbara County Sheriff's Department executed a search warrant at Michael Jackson's Neverland Ranch in Santa Ynez, California.

Additional locations searched included:
- A private investigator's office in Beverly Hills, and
- The West Hills, ***"business premises of an individual who filmed***

the victims making coerced statements supportive of Jackson." *

Note dated 26 July 2004
This note recorded the consultation held at the Critical Incident Response Group (CIRG) / Behavioural Analysis Unit (BAU) on 21-22 June 2004.

The Santa Barbara District Attorney's office requested further assistance.

The note continued that the Quantico consultation involved:
- Discussing '*Prosecutive Strategies and potential Expert Testimony*'
- Representatives from the National Centre for the Analysis of Violent Crime (NCAVA)
- Representatives from the Crimes Against Children's Unit (CACU)
- Representatives from the Innocent Images National Initiative (IINI)
- Victim Witness unit
- Computer Analysis Response Team (CART)
- FBI Lab
- Department of Justice and Obscenity Section (CEOS)

During the consultation, the Santa Barbara County District Attorney's Office sought further assistance, and they produced a list:

> *"...A number of related and collateral investigative issues, some of which potential rise to the level of the Federal Violations, in the New York and Miami Division so as well as the Los Angeles Division. It was the opinion of SDDA's Zonen and Auchincloss that if the FBI could investigate these allegations, it could lead to additional and corroborative evidence that would enhance the successful prosecution of their case.*
>
> *"SDDA's Zonen and Auchincloss were informed that CIRG does not set investigative leads for other divisions; however, CIRG would notify Los Angeles Division of the request for investigative assistance and potential federal allegations. Los Angeles Division is requested to review the aforementioned SBCDAO request and coordinate future investigative efforts as deemed appropriate."*

Note dated 26 July 2004
This note from the CIRG to the Los Angeles Division stated the

leads that required action:

Lead 1 - Los Angeles - an FBI agent to take over liaison role between CIRG / BAU and the Santa Barbara County District Attorney's Office to continue '*consultation on Prosecutive Strategies and Expert Testimony*'
Lead 2 - Los Angeles - '*to discuss further requests for assistance*'
Lead 3 - Criminal Investigation - For CACU and IINI

Note dated 10 August 2004
This FBI note from the Los Angeles Division to CIRG provided a summary:

- On 15 July 2004, the FBI agent met with SDDAs Ron Zonen and Gordon Auchincloss '*to discuss investigative issues requiring FBI assistance and potential Federal Violations.*'

- '*Leads referred to New York and Miami Divisions.*'

Note dated 05 April 2005
This note updated the file.

27 February 2004, SDDA Ron Zonen requested NCAVC / BAU111 to '*provide Prosecutive Strategies.*'
[BAU111, Behavioral Analysis Unit 3 or 111 investigates crimes against children.]

22 March [2004] and 23 March 2004, two FBI agents had '*an on-site consultation*' with SDDA Zonen at the Santa Barbara office.

21 June 2004 - 22 June 2004 SDDAs Zonen and Auchincloss traveled to the FBI headquarters at Quantico to meet members of the CIRG / BAU111 to discuss:

- '*Prosecutive Strategies*'
- '*Interview Strategies*'
- '*Expert Testimony*'

Other attendees mentioned:
- Representatives from the Crimes Against Children Unit (CACU)
- Representatives from the Innocent Images National Initiative (IINI)
- Victim Witness Unit
- Computer Analysis Response Team (CART)

- FBI Laboratory
- National Centre for the Analysis of Violent Crime - Los Angeles Coordinator
- Department of Justice Child Exploitation and Obscenity Section (CEOS).

During the discussion, regarding the '*caption investigation and potential federal violations*' a Special Agent was assigned to SBCDA.

Members of the NCAVC / BAU111 had consulted with several agencies regarding an interview with an alleged 1993 accuser.

On 30 September 2004 the NCAVC / BAU111 submitted a report about the '*interview strategies they had disseminated to the FBI agents*' and the '*State and Federal Prosecutive Strategies*' that were discussed during the consultations.

On 16 November 2004, an FBI agent met with SDDA Zonen in Santa Barbara to discuss the prosecution's request for '*Expert Testimony.*'

On 19-20 January 2005, an FBI agent, **a retired FBI** agent and SDDA Zonen reviewed portions of the evidence, the collections of sexually explicit images in magazines and books. There were numerous additional telephone consultations with SDDA Zonen regarding 'Prosecutive Strategies and Expert Testimony'.

The final paragraph of the 05 April 2005 note states that from the beginning of the trial onwards, members of the NCAVC / BAU111 and the **retired FBI agent** continued to consult with the DA's office on various case strategies.

The prosecution notified the **retired FBI agent** that he might be required to attend court as an expert or a rebuttal witness.

Note dated 10 February 2005
This note provided a further update after the trial had commenced.

It stated that on 30 July 2004, a Special Agent had taken over the liaison role. The requested assistance was complete, and the **lead closed.**

A Special Agent and a **retired Special Agent** provided further

Behavioral Analysis and the **lead closed.**

Note dated 29 June 2005
The final note. This note records that **Michael Jackson was acquitted.**

Outcome: **The case administratively closed.**

[* The FBI note stated that *"the victims ma[de]* ***coerced*** *statements supportive of Jackson."*

Far from looking ***'coerced'*** the Arvizo family appeared willing, candid, and animated participants.

It would seem from observing the Youtube footage, that they wanted to clarify the Gavin-Michael Jackson section of the Bashir documentary.

They seemed engaged in the process and enthusiastic.

Janet Arvizo suggested to the videographer that he should take a close-up shot of her holding her son's hand.

She said,

> ***" Wait, wait you know how this Bashir. Hey, you know how Bashir zoomed in on him holding hands, do that the same thing..."***

Gavin Arvizo interrupted;

> ***"'Cos you know..."***

Janet continued,

> ***" Because, because that's what a mother does with a son or a father does with a son... you know, and they tried to make it out to seen, to be something wrong and dirty."***

The Arvizo family talked over each other excitedly.

They seemed genuinely appreciative of the positive impact Michael Jackson had on their lives, which was in stark contrast to their experience of others, who they said judged them because of their socioeconomic status.

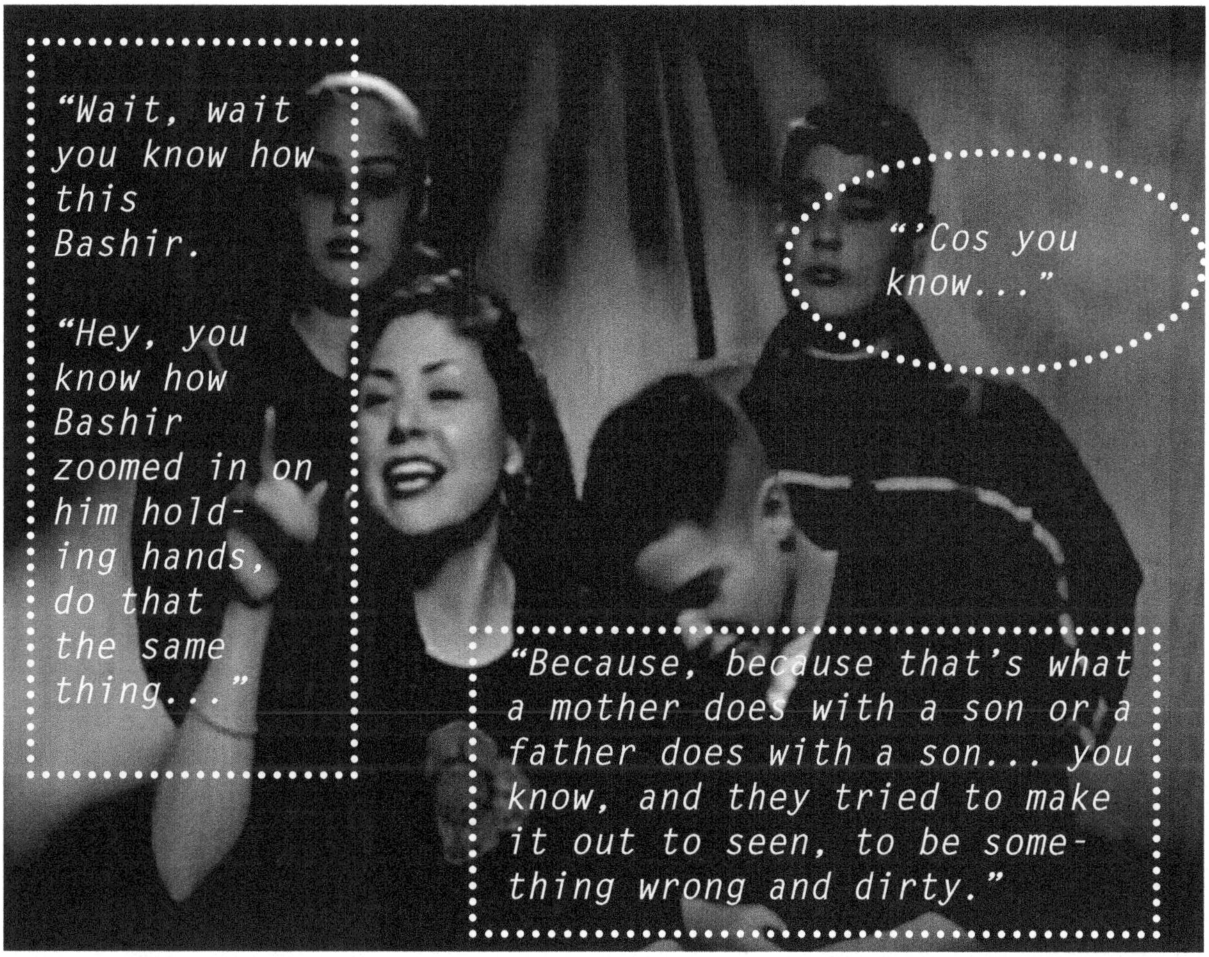

Photo: Screengrab with text overlay.

MAR-01-2004 15:32 [redacted] P.02/04 b2 b6 b7C

(Rev. 01-31-2003)

FEDERAL BUREAU OF INVESTIGATION

Precedence: ROUTINE **Date:** 03/01/2004

To: CIRG **Attn:** NCAVC/BAU-3
UC [redacted]
SSA [redacted] b6 b7C

From: Los Angeles
A-1/Riverside RA
Contact: SA [redacted] b2 b6 b7C

Approved By: [redacted]

Drafted By: [redacted] akn *akn* b6 b7C

Case ID #: 252B-IR-C5363 (Pending)

Title: NEW CASE REQUEST;
CHILD MOLESTATION;
LOS ANGELES

Synopsis: To request that new 252B case be opened and assigned to SSA [redacted]

Administrative: Ref telcalls between SSA [redacted] and SA [redacted] b6 b7C

Details: On 02/27/2004, Assistant District Attorney Rich Zonen, Santa Barbara County District Attorney's Office contacted SA [redacted] to request the assistance of the NCAVC/BAU-3 to develop a prosecutive strategy and to provide forensic guidance regarding a high profile child molestation investigation. It is requested that the NCAVC BAU-3 open and assign a case, which should be captioned as follows:

CHILD MOLESTATION INVESTIGATION;
SANTA BARBARA DISTRICT ATTORNEYS OFFICE;
SANTA BARBARA, CALIFORNIA

In light of the sensitive nature of the investigation, no case specific details are being provided within this communication.

Due to the sheer volume of evidence in this matter and the fact that all evidence in this matter is under seal, ADA Zonen requests that SSA [redacted] travel to California and conduct an on-site review of all evidence in this matter on 3/8-9/2004 at the Santa Barbara DA's Office. ADA Zonen would like to follow up SSA [redacted] on-site review of evidence by traveling to b6 b7C

252B-IR-6808-1

SAC TIDWELL
JKF ASAC PEDEGOR
Rec'd 3/3/04
[redacted] 3/10/04 - Please provide review and CIRG guidance in this request
O&A Rec'd 3/9/04 10
06lakn01.ec

[redacted] PER OUR DISCUSSION:
· SEND EC TO LA & REQUEST THEY TRAVEL TO NCAVC W/REPRESENTATIVE SAMPLE OF EVIDENTIARY MATERIAL
· CONVENE MULTI-DISC. CONSULTATION BOARD, TO INCLUDE IINI
· ASSIGN AS APPROPRIATE
JKF 3/4/04

MAR-01-2004 15:32 [redacted] P.03/04 b6 b7C

To: CIRG From: [redacted]s Angeles
Re: 252B-IR-C5363, 03/01/2004

Quantico, Virginia for further consultation with the NCAVC/BAU-3 on 03/17-18/2004. ADA Zonen has requested the above dates in light of an upcoming grand jury proceeding in this matter.

2

MAR-01-2004 15:32 [redacted] P.04/04

b2
b6
b7C

To: CIRG From: [redacted]s Angeles
Re: 252B-IR-C5363[redacted]03/01/2004

LEAD(s):

Set Lead 1: (Action)

CIRG

AT NCAVC, VIRGINIA

NCAVC is requested to open and assign case as listed in details of this communication.

♦♦

3

TOTAL P.04

(Rev. 01-31-2003)

FEDERAL BUREAU OF INVESTIGATION

Precedence: ROUTINE Date: 03/09/2004

To: Los Angeles Attn: Squad A-1/Riverside RA
SSA [redacted]
SA [redacted] b6 b7C

From: CIRG
NCAVC/BAU III [redacted]
Contact: SSA [redacted] b2 b6 b7C

Approved By: Fedarcyk Janice K JKF

Drafted By: [redacted] jt JN b6 b7C

Case ID #: 252B-IR-6808 (Pending) - 2

Title: CHANGED
Michael Jackson;
Minor Children - Victims;
SEOC;
Investigative and Prosecutive Strategies
Santa Barbara District Attorney's Office
Santa Barbara, California

Synopsis: To request travel by SA [redacted] to: 1) Santa Barbara, California to meet with Assistant District Attorney (ADA) Richard Zonen and 2) NCAVC with members of the Santa Barbara County Investigation and Prosecution Teams for consultation on above captioned matter. b6 b7C

Previous Title: Title marked "Changed" to reflect Subject's Name. Title previously carried as "CHILD MOLESTATION INVESTIGATION; SANTA BARBARA DISTRICT ATTORNEY'S OFFICE; S."ANTA BARBARA, CALIFORNIA.

Administrative: In as much as this case is under a gag order issued by the Santa Barbara County Court, ACS access to this file should be limited.

Details: Request is hereby made that SA [redacted] travel to Santa Barbara County District Attorney's Office to meet with ADA Richard Zonen to review evidence in above captioned matter and advise of information and materials required for a consultation at NCAVC scheduled for 3/22-23/2004. SA [redacted] [redacted] is requested to advise NCAVC of the results of her meeting with ADA Zonen. It is further requested that SA [redacted] b6 b7C

Received 3/16/04 10

To: Los Angeles From: CIRG
Re: 252B-IR-6808, 03/09/2004

accompany the Investigation and Prosecution Team from Santa Barbara County to the NCAVC for this consultation. SA [redacted] [redacted] is authorized to use CIRG TR# 14DV041401 for her travel to both Santa Barbara and the NCAVC. b6 b7C

2

To: Los Angeles From: CIRG
Re: 252B-IR-6808, 03/09/2004

LEAD(s):

Set Lead 1: (Action)

LOS ANGELES

AT SANTA BARBARA, CALIFORNIA

Authorize travel by SA [redacted] to: 1)Santa Barbara, California to meet with Assistant District Attorney (ADA) Richard Zonen and 2)NCAVC with members of the Santa Barbara County Investigation and Prosecution Teams for consultation on above captioned matter. b6 b7C

♦♦

3

FEDARCYK
A SAC ~~DEVECCHIO~~ JKF
UC [redacted] b6 b7C

Jan -
pls tell me they got the wrong unit on p 2.

Urgent Report

Date: April 28, 2004

To: The Director
AD Grant D. Ashley
AD Jana D. Monroe
DAD J. Stephen Tidwell
DAD Keith L. Lourdeau
Section Chief Charles Gregorski
Unit Chief [redacted]
SSA [redacted]
SSA [redacted] b6 b7C
Special Events Management Unit, CTD
CT Watch

From: SSRA [redacted]
Santa Maria Resident Agency
Los Angeles

For further information contact:
SSRA [redacted]
Santa Maria RA, Los Angeles
[redacted], Nextel [redacted] b2 b6 b7C

PLS ENSURE SSRA [redacted] IS AWARE THAT NCAVC, BAU-III, IS FURNISHING SUPPORT NOT BSU. THANKS! JAN ☺

Preparer of Urgent Report:
SSRA [redacted]
Santa Maria RA, Los Angeles
[redacted] Nextel [redacted]

Subject: MICHAEL JOE JACKSON
DPC
62D-LA-236081;

MICHAEL JOE JACKSON;
COURT PROCEEDING;
SANTA MARIA COURTHOUSE;
SANTA MARIA, CA
CT Preparedness - SPECIAL EVENTS
300A-LA-236475

5/3/04 vy file

C/A: SA [redacted] SMRA, [redacted] b2 b6 b7C

Recent Developments:

CART assistance has been provided to the Santa Barbara County Sheriff's Department (SBSD) in support of this investigation and the field work at Santa Barbara in that effort has been completed. Technical Surveillance Countermeasures (TSCM) assistance has been provided to the SBSD and the Santa Barbara County District Attorney's Office (SBCDAO). The SBCDAO

5/6/04 file vy JTL Done 5/4/04 SSA [redacted] pls handle per ASAC instructions b6 b7C
252B-LR-6808-3

has also requested and is receiving assistance from the Behavioral Sciences Unit at Quantico regarding prosecutive strategy. The SBSD and SBCDAO are referring matters involving threats and suspected computer intrusions to the FBI (Ventura RA).

Michael Joe Jackson was indicted by a Santa Barbara County Grand Jury on April 21, 2004. The indictment was sealed, but it is presumed the charges in the indictment are similar to the child molestation charges in the complaint filed against Jackson on December 18, 2003.

Jackson will be arraigned at the Santa Barbara County Courthouse in the city of Santa Maria on Friday morning, April 30, 2004. The Santa Maria Police Department (SMPD), SBSD, and the California Highway Patrol will handle security for the event, with mutual aid assistance from other area law enforcement agencies. At least 90 local officers will be assigned to work the event. Approximately 1,200 spectators, including protesters, are expected to be present. Worldwide media coverage is again expected.

The Santa Maria RA will have a limited presence in the law enforcement command center during this event to monitor any developments that may fall within FBI jurisdiction and to provide any additional support or resources needed by local law enforcement. The SMPD previously requested FBI involvement based on the belief that the Jackson court proceedings could represent a soft target for terrorism due to the worldwide media coverage the case is receiving.

There is no intelligence indicating a threat of a terrorist act targeting this event. The Nation of Islam, represented by its security unit Fruits of Islam, was present during the prior court appearance by Jackson, but will reportedly not be present for this court appearance. Jackson's security is reportedly being provided by a Los Angeles area private security firm (staffed by retired LAPD officers). However [redacted] [redacted] a known New Black Panther Party member, was observed to be present in the crowd during Jackson's first court appearance and was attired in black BDUs (NFI). b6 b7C

Background:

On 11/18/2003, the Santa Barbara County Sheriff's Department (SBSD) executed a search warrant at Michael Jackson's Neverland Ranch in Santa Ynez, California [northern Santa Barbara County, in the territory of the Santa Maria Resident Agency (SMRA), Los Angeles Field Office]. The search was for evidence in support of child molestation allegations against Jackson. The alleged victims are 13-year-old [redacted] and his 12-year-old brother, [redacted] Additional locations b6 b7C searched were a private investigator's office in Beverly Hills, Ca., and the West Hills, Ca., business premises of an individual who filmed the victims making coerced statements supportive of Jackson.

On 11/19/2003, a Ramey warrant was issued for Jackson's arrest, charging multiple counts of child molestation [California Penal Code 288(a)]. Bail was recommended to be set at $3 million. Jackson surrendered himself to the custody of the SBSD on 11/20/2003 and was booked into the Santa Barbara County Jail on the arrest warrant. Jackson posted bail, surrendered his passport, and was thereafter released. Jackson was formally charged the week of 12/15/2003 and was arraigned on those charges 1/16/2004.

(Rev. 01-31-2003)

SantaBarbaraECO3.wpd

FEDERAL BUREAU OF INVESTIGATION

Precedence: ROUTINE **Date:** 07/26/2004

To: Los Angeles **Attn:** SAC James M. Sheehan
SSRA [redacted]
Santa Maria RA

b6
b7C

FBIHQ CACU - UC [redacted]
IINI - UC

From: CIRG
NCAVC/BAU III
Contact: SSA [redacted]

b2
b6
b7C

Approved By: Fedarcyk Janice K

Drafted By: [redacted] jtg

b6
b7C

Case ID #: 252B-IR-6808 (Pending) -4

Title: CHANGED
Michael Jackson;
Minor Children - Victims;
SEOC;
Investigative and Prosecutive Strategies
Santa Barbara District Attorney's Office
Santa Barbara, California

Synopsis: To memorialize the consultation held at Critical Incident Response Group (CIRG)/ Behavioral Analysis Unit (BAU) with Santa Barbara County Prosecution Team and to notify Santa Maria RA of further assistance requested by Santa Barbara District Attorney's Office related to above captioned matter.

Administrative: In as much as this case is under a gag order issued by the Santa Barbara County Court, ACS access to this file has been limited.

Details: On 6/21-22/2004 Senior Deputy District Attorneys (SDDA) Ron Zonen and Gordon Auchincloss from the Santa Barbara County District Attorney's Office traveled to Quantico, VA and met with members of CIRG/BAU-III for the purposes of discussing Prosecutive Strategies and potential Expert Testimony. NCAVC

To: Los Angeles From: CIRG
Re: 252B-IR-6808, 07/26/2004

Coordinator SA [redacted] represented the Los Angeles Division for this consultation. Also present for this consultation were representatives from Crimes Against Children's Unit (CACU), Innocent Images National Initiative (IINI), Victim Witness Unit, Computer Analysis Response Team (CART), FBI Lab, and the Department of Justice Child Exploitation and Obscenity Section (CEOS). b6 b7C

During the course of this consultation further requests for assistance were made by the Santa Barbara County District Attorney's Office (SBCDAO). In addition they produced a list containing a number of related and collateral investigative issues, some of which potentially rise to the level of Federal Violations, in the New York and Miami Divisions as well as the Los Angeles Division. It was the opinion of SDDA's Zonen and Auchincloss that if the FBI could investigate these allegations, it could lead to additional and corroborative evidence that would enhance the successful prosecution of their case.

SDDA's Zonen and Auchincloss were informed that CIRG does not set investigative leads for other divisions, however, CIRG would notify Los Angeles Division of the request for investigative assistance and potential federal allegations. Los Angeles Division is requested to review the aforementioned SBCDAO request and coordinate future investigative efforts as deemed appropriate.

In as mush as SA [redacted] is on extended TDY to FBIHQ, CIRG requests that SA [redacted] be assigned in her absence as NCAVC Coordinator in this case. b6 b7C

2

To: Los Angeles From: CIRG
Re: 252B-IR-6808, 07/26/2004

LEAD(s):

Set Lead 1: (Action)

LOS ANGELES

AT LOS ANGELES, CALIFORNIA

Request SA [redacted] to take over liaison role (in SA [redacted] absence) between CIRG/BAU and Santa Barbara County District Attorney's Office for the purposes of continuing consultation on Prosecutive Strategies and Expert Testimony. b6 b7C

Set Lead 2: (Action)

LOS ANGELES

AT SANTA MARIA, CALIFORNIA

Request contact be made with Senior Deputy District Attorney Ron Zonen (805)568-2426, to discuss further requests for assistance from Santa Barbara County District Attorney's Office.

Set Lead 3: (Info)

CRIMINAL INVESTIGATIVE

AT WASHINGTON, DC

For information of CACU and IINI.

♦♦

3

(Rev. 01-31-2003)

FEDERAL BUREAU OF INVESTIGATION

Precedence: ROUTINE **Date:** 08/10/2004

To: CIRG **Attn:** SSA [redacted] b6 b7C

From: Los Angeles
Santa Maria RA
Contact: SA [redacted] b2 b6 b7C

Approved By: [redacted]

Drafted By: [redacted] b6 b7C

Case ID #: 252B-IR-6808 (Pending) - 5

Title: Michael Jackson;
Minor Children - Victim;
SEOC;
Investigative and Prosecutive Strategies
Santa Barbara District Attorney's Office
Santa Barbara, CA

Synopsis: Cover lead requesting follow up with Senior District Attorney, Ron Zonen, Santa Barbara County District Attorney's Office.

Details: On 07/15/2004, writer met with Senior Deputy District Attorneys (SDDA) Ron Zonen and Gordon Auchincloss to discuss investigative issues requiring FBI assistance and potential Federal Violations.

As a result of the meeting, leads were sent to New York and Miami Divisions.

Los Angeles considers this lead covered.

To: CIRG From: [redacted]s Angeles
Re: 252B-IR-6808, 08/10/2004

LEAD(s):

Set Lead 1: (Info)

CIRG

AT QUANTICO , VIRGINIA

Read and clear.

222dfw04.04
♦♦

2

(Rev. 01-31-2003)

FEDERAL BUREAU OF INVESTIGATION

Precedence: ROUTINE **Date:** 04/05/2005

To: CIRG

From: CIRG
NCAVC/BAU III [redacted]
Contact: SA [redacted] b2 b6 b7C

Approved By: [redacted]

Drafted By: [redacted] tah b6 b7C

Case ID #: 252B-IR-68083-6 (Pending)

Title: Michael Jackson;
Minor Children - Victim;
SEOC;
Investigative and Prosecutive Strategies
Santa Barbara District Attorney's Office
Santa Barbara, California

Synopsis: To update case file.

Details: In February 27, 2004, Senior Deputy District Attorney (SDDA) Ron Zonen, Santa Barbara County District Attorney's Office (SBCDA) requested NCAVC/BAU III provide Prosecutive Strategies for the above captioned case. On March 22, 2005 and March 23, 2004, Supervisory Special Agent (SSA) SA [redacted] and SA [redacted] [redacted] provided an on-site consultation with the SDDA Zonen at the SBCDA's Office. On June 21, 2004 to June 22, 2004, SDDA Zonen and SDDA Gordon Auchincloss traveled to Quantico, Virginia to meet with members of the CIRG/BAU III, to further discuss Prosecutive Strategies, Interview Strategies and Expert Testimony. Also present during the meeting were representatives from Crimes Against Children Unit (CACU), Innocent Images National Initiative (IINI), Victim Witness Unit, Computer Analysis Response Team (CART), FBI Laboratory, Los Angeles NCAVC Coordinator, and the Department of Justice Child Exploitation and Obscenity Section (CEOS). b6 b7C

During the discussions involving the evidence in the above captioned investigation and the potential federal violations that might apply in the case, a Special Agent was assigned to assist the SBCDA. SA [redacted] Santa Maria Resident Agency initially opened up a 62D Police Cooperation case and subsequently a 305 matter to address the investigative demands. Members of NCAVC/BAU III, consulted with the Office of Victim Assistance, CEOS, FBI Agents from Los Angeles, Santa Maria and New York b6 b7C

File 5/3/05

Uploaded 4/22/05

regarding interview strategies for a victim who alleged that Michael Jackson had sexually abused him in 1993. On September 30, 2004, NCAVC/BAU III submitted a report regarding the interview strategies they disseminated to the FBI Agents. Additionally, state and federal Prosecutive Strategies were discussed during the course of the consultations.

On November 16, 2004, SSA [redacted] NCAVC/BAU III met with SDDA Zonen in Santa Barbara to discuss the prosecution's request for Expert Testimony from NCAVC/BAU III. Also present was SA [redacted] from the Santa Maria RA.

On January 19, 2005 and January 20, 2005, SSA [redacted] and retired FBI SSA [redacted] met with SDDA Zonen, SBCDA, to review portions of the evidence obtained during the investigation of Jackson, including the collection of sexually explicit images in magazines, and books. NCAVC/BAU III engaged in numerous additional telephone consultations with SDDA Zonen regarding Prosecutive Strategies and Expert Testimony. b6 b7C

Since prior to the beginning of the trial, members of the NCAVC/BAU III, in addition to retired FBI SSA [redacted] have continued to consult with the SBCDA on various case strategies. Recently, retired FBI SSA [redacted] was informed by SDDA Zonen that he may still request Expert Testimony from the NCAVC/BAU III during the course of the trial as a witness or as a rebuttal witness.

◆◆

2

---- Working Copy ---- Page 1

Precedence: ROUTINE Date: 02/10/2005

To: Los Angeles

From: Los Angeles
A-3
Contact: SA [redacted] b2 b6 b7C

Approved By: [redacted]

Drafted By: [redacted] tah b6 b7C

Case ID #: 252B-IR-6808 (Pending)

Title: Michael Jackson;
Minor Children - Victims;
SEOC;
Investigative and Prosecutive Strategies
Santa Barbara District Attorney's Office
Santa Barbara, California

Synopsis: Lead covered.

Reference:
252B-IR-6808 Serial 4

Details: On July 30, 2004, Special Agent [redacted] was requested to take over liaison role between CIRG/BAU, and the Santa Barbara (SB) County District Attorney's Office. Since the investigation leads were disseminated to the FBI-Santa Maria Resident Agency, SA [redacted] made contact with SA [redacted] regarding their assistance in the investigation. SA [redacted] completed the requested assistance and has submitted an EC closing the lead, serial number 5. Supervisory Special Agent [redacted] and retired Special Agent [redacted] met with the SB County District Attorney's Office and provided further behavioral analysis for the investigation per their request. No further assistance has been requested from FBI-LA NCAVC program. Therefore, this lead is considered covered. b6 b7C

Case ID : 252B-IR-6808 Serial : 7

(Rev. 01-31-2003)

FEDERAL BUREAU OF INVESTIGATION

Precedence: ROUTINE **Date:** 06/29/2005

To: CIRG

From: CIRG
BAU 3
Contact: SSA [redacted]

Approved By: [redacted]

Drafted By: [redacted]

b6
b7C

Case ID #: 252B-IR-6808 (Closed); 8

Title: Michael Jackson;
Minor Children - Victim;
SEOC;
Investigative and Prosecutive Strategies
Santa Barbara District Attorney's Office
Santa Barbara, California

Synopsis: To administratively close case.

Details: On June 14, 2005, the above captioned subject, Michael Jackson, was acquitted of all charges brought against him by the Santa Barbara District Attorney's Office. Due to the completion of the case, no further assistance will be required of the Behavioral Analysis Unit - 3 (BAU), Crimes Against Children. Therefore, it is requested that the above captioned case be administratively closed.

♦♦

Uploaded 7/6/05
VG

Chapter Six - Victim

OUTCOMES

This file represents the bulk of the FBI files released in December 2009.

It contains:

- Several handwritten and typed photocopied letters from a New York man
- Updating FBI records on the trial of the man
- Some press cuttings
- Handwriting samples and
- Fourteen photographs of the Jackson Family compound (developed at a local shopping center).

Michael Jackson was identified as the **CAPTION VICTIM.**

In the Complaint Form dated 29 June 1992, the '*Character of*

Case' stated the nature of the case under investigation,

'EXTORTION - THREATENING LETTERS.'

Michael Jackson was identified as the **'VICTIM'**.

Reuters put the released files into context:

> *"The FBI on Tuesday released hundreds of previously sealed documents related to Michael Jackson, most of them about a 1992 investigation of a man who threatened to kill the pop star and then - U.S. President George H.W. Bush."*

Extracts of the letters follow:

18 May 1992
In a letter addressed to the Daily News dated 18 May 1992:

> *"...And if the chain of command doesn't work I will resort to violence, to bring attention to my problem. I'll commit mass murder at a Michael Jackson concert if necessary, in an attempt to murder Michael, then you will have to deal with my problem in the public eye.*
>
> *"...With Michael Jackson and John Gotti it is about financial compensation, I told you what will happen to John if he doesn't pay up, Michael I will personally attempt to kill if he doesn't pay me my money..."*

21 May 1992 the man wrote:

> *"I decided that because nobody is taking me serious, and I can't handle my state of mind, that I am going to Washington D.C. to threaten to kill the President of the United States George Bush.*
>
> *"If they do not arrest me or solve my problem Im gonna attempt to kill President George Bush..."*

The letter concluded with:

> *"P.S. I Dear [sic.] you to call this a bluff."*

In a typed letter dated 18 May 1992,

"My interest is that half of Michael's estate is mines, my proof is if he doesn't pay up im going after him."

The man was initially arrested on the White House grounds on 22 May 1992 and then released. He was arrested in June 1992 at the Jackson compound.

22 June 1992
As evidence in support of their case, the FBI took fourteen color photos of the Jackson residence at 4641 Hayvenhurst Avenue, Encino, California.

Contemporaneous Press comments:
The news at the time represented only a few inches, not headline news.

The LA Times reported in October 1992:

"A New York man charged with stalking pop singer Janet Jackson is mentally unfit to stand trial.

"U.S. District Court Judge Andrew Hauk determined that [...], 33 is not competent to stand trial based on a psychological evaluation submitted by his attorney. Prosecutors also agreed that [...] is mentally unfit to stand trial.

"[...] Faced a one-count federal indictment charging him with sending 40 threatening letters to the 26-year old singer that allegedly contained threats against her, her boyfriend, her brother Michael, movie director John Singleton and President Bush. The federal charges carry a maximum 20-year prison term."

The LA Times on 13 July 1993, reported that a man was:

"...Initially ... charged with four counts of sending threatening letters, including two to [Janet] Jackson, one to her boyfriend, Rene Elizondo, and other to director John Singleton who worked with her on the soon-to-be-released film 'Poetic Justice.'"

The article stated that in 1993 Mr Jones pleaded guilty to one count involving a threat to Rene Elizondo and that he received a two-year sentence.

In an article headed '*Obsessed Janet Jackson Fan Now faces*

Federal Charges' dated 23 July 1992, Josh Meyer a Times staff writer wrote:

> ***"Four years ago, Michael Jackson was the victim of a woman who claimed to be his spouse, made threats against him and loitered outside the same Encino compound. She too was arrested several times, once at 3 am after scaling a five-foot fence into the compound's backyard toting a champagne bottle."***

In an article in the Los Angeles Magazine in March 2000, Michael Jackson's former lawyer Jay Lavely said,

> ***"The amount [of celebrity stalking] that's publicly known, is the tip of the iceberg."***

2009 Press Reporting:
The news coverage following the release of the FBI files in December 2009, six months after Michael Jackson's death, did not afford Michael Jackson any sympathy.

Generally, anything remotely associated with Michael Jackson results in repeated opinionated-infotainment commentary. **But not when he was identified as THE VICTIM.**

199 pages of previously unreleased material - detailing threats to kill and extortion. And yet, the media wasn't interested in **MICHAEL JACKSON THE VICTIM.**

The LA Times article, '*Michael Jackson's FBI File More Snooze Than Sizzle*' dated 23 December 2009, might provide some enlightenment.

> ***"When the FBI announced last week that it planned to make public its previously secret file on Michael Jackson, the bombshells seemed guaranteed. How could hundreds of pages of inside government information about the world's most famous and famously unconventional man be anything other than riveting?***
>
> ***"But the materials released Tuesday turned out to be more somnolent than sensational, their 333 pages a collection of photocopied tabloid articles and heavily redacted reports from investigations that were old news years ago.."***

MICHAEL JACKSON - THE VICTIM was just not newsworthy, compared to the speculation about his death, and the previous allegations.

FD-340a (Rev. 10-3-77)

b6
b7C

(Title) [redacted]

(File No.) 9A-LA-142276

Item	Date Filed	To be returned Yes	No		Disposition
1	8/19/92		X	Receipts for money belonging to [redacted] [redacted] (CLB)	b6 b7C
2	8/19/92		X	orig notes re [redacted] (CLB)	
3	8/19/92		X	orig notes re [redacted] (CLB)	b6 b7C b7D
4	8/19/92		X	7 pages of handwriting exemplars by subject, & 2 exemplar cards (CLB)	
5	8/19/92		X	orig notes re: [redacted] (CLB)	b6 b7C
6	8/19/92		X	orig notes re: [redacted] (CLB)	b6 b7C b7D
7	8/19/92		X	14 color photos of Jackson estate (CLB)	
8	8/20/92			Color photos of ... of Subject	
1B3	1/14/95		X	FD-192 (CLB) Destroyed TMT	

9A-LA-142276-117
CLB ... CLB

FD-340 (Rev. 4-2-85)

Field File No. 9A - LA - 142276 - 1A1

Serial # of Originating Document

OO and File No. LA

Date Received 7/23/92

From LA County Jail / USMS
(Name of Contributor)

(Address of Contributor)

By SA [redacted] b6 b7C
(Name of Special Agent)

To Be Returned ☐ Yes ☐ No Receipt Given ☐ Yes ☐ No

Grand Jury Material - Disseminate Only Pursuant to Rule 6(e), Federal Rules of Criminal Procedure ☐ Yes ☐ No

Title:

Reference:
(Communication Enclosing Material)

Description: ☐ Original notes re interview of

Receipts for money belonging to

[redacted] b6 b7C

8/19/92

CLB

DEPARTMENT OF JUSTICE
FORM NO. USM-303
(REV-10-18-63)

RECEIPT

U.S. MARSHAL

A 463384

Central District of Calif

Date 7/23, 19 92

Received of [redacted] FBI Agent

MARSHAL'S NO.	TITLE OF CASE	PROCESS NO.	PROCESS TYPE	AMOUNT
	Cash found from			$39.00
	a prisoner [redacted]		Cash	
	[redacted]			
	prisoner [illegible]			
				39.00

b6
b7C

Received by [redacted]
U.S. MARSHAL'S OFFICE

ORIGINAL—TO REMITTER

W 402920 **WITHDRAWAL TICKET**

FBI-- SA [redacted]

b6
b7C

LOS ANGELES COUNTY SHERIFF - IRC
THIS IS YOUR RECEIPT (WITHDRAWAL)
DATE 07/23/92 TIME 09:27:30
REG 6 TRAN 165308 TELLER 15
218 CUST. CASH ONL -390.00
REFRENCE # 402920
TOTAL -390.00
CASH -390.00
NON-NEG BAL 0.00

SIGNATURE

COUNTY OF LOS ANGELES COUNTY JAIL CASHIER'S OFFICE	PRISONER'S COPY	441 BAUCHET LOS ANGELES, CALIFORNIA 90012

76W461 SH-J-251-B-3/92

FD-340 (Rev. 4-2-85)

Field File No. 9A - LA - 142276 - 1A2

Serial # of Originating Document ______

OO and File No. LA

Date Received 7/24/92

From ______ (Name of Contributor) b6 b7C

______ (Address of Contributor)

By ______ (Name of Special Agent)

To Be Returned ☐ Yes ☐ No Receipt Given ☐ Yes ☐ No

Grand Jury Material - Disseminate Only Pursuant to Rule 6(e), Federal Rules of Criminal Procedure ☐ Yes ☐ No

Title:

Reference: ______ (Communication Enclosing Material)

Description: ☒ Original notes re interview of ______ 7/24/92

b6 b7C 8/11/92 CLB

9A-LA-142276-1A?

7/24/92

[illegible]

5 - 6 letter

[illegible]

b6
b7C

[illegible] 6/22/92

[illegible]

PDP

[illegible]

all Channel + him - he tracks
& analysis - rating system
alert — Dagmar Reina Abel -

escalation of fixation & threat
2/92 — Apr 92

mid
Gaie

b6
b7C

thst potential 1-5 (15 max
location formula)
freq. of contact

added letters - possible wrench
(progression) w/ AUSA

Start July 91 for

b6
b7C

FD-340 (Rev. 4-2-85)

Field File No. 9A-LA-142276-1A3

Serial # of Originating Document

OO and File No. LA

Date Received 7/24/92

From [redacted] b6 b7C b7D

(Name of Contributor)

[redacted] (Address of Contributor)

By SA [redacted] b6 b7C

(Name of Special Agent)

To Be Returned ☐ Yes ☐ No Receipt Given ☐ Yes ☐ No

Grand Jury Material - Disseminate Only Pursuant to Rule 6(e), Federal Rules of Criminal Procedure ☐ Yes ☐ No

Title:

Reference:

(Communication Enclosing Material)

Description: ☒ Original notes re interview of [redacted] 7/24/92 b6 b7C b7D

8/19/92 CLB

2/24/92

b6
b7C
b7D

has no personal knowledge of
has read resume

Gotti
Gambino

letter to

has been kept letter thanking her
apprised of that

not present during arrest

is aware of all of this now

after this wants to be "normal"
like a regular person — rebellious
then she was notified
(there have been various things)

brought up to date —

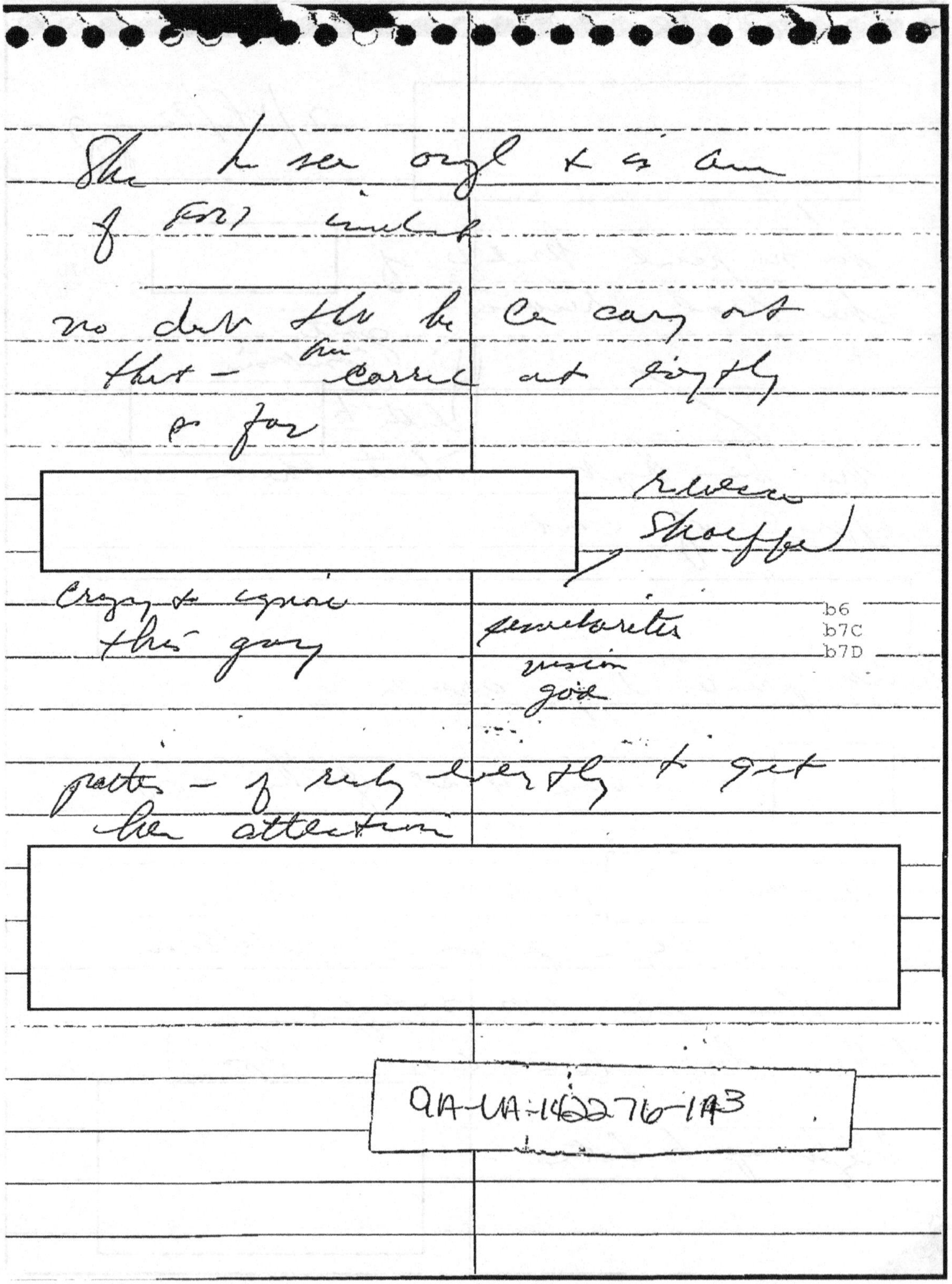

She [illegible] sex orgy & is [illegible] of [illegible] [illegible]

no [illegible] [illegible] be [illegible] carry out that — has carried out [illegible] or [illegible]

[illegible] Shoeffer

Crazy & ignore this guy

[illegible] vision god

pattern — of [illegible] [illegible] & get her attention

9A-LA-162276-143

b6
b7C
b7D

FD-340 (Rev. 4-2-85)

Field File No. 9A-LA-142276-1A4

Serial # of Originating Document

OO and File No.

Date Received 7/27/92

From Holly Beckner
(Name of Contributor)

City Attorney's Office
(Address of Contributor)

Van Nuys, California

By SK [redacted] b6 b7C
(Name of Special Agent)

To Be Returned ☐ Yes ☐ No Receipt Given ☐ Yes ☐ No

Grand Jury Material - Disseminate Only Pursuant to Rule 6(e), Federal Rules of Criminal Procedure ☐ Yes ☐ No

Title:

Reference:
(Communication Enclosing Material)

Description: ☐ Original notes re interview of

Seven (7) pages of handwriting exemplars provided by [redacted] [redacted] (administered by LAPD) plus two (2) exemplar cards 8/19/92 CLB

b6
b7C

Form 05.07.0 (Rev. 6-22-51)

PHOTOGRAPHED

LOS ANGELES POLICE DEPARTMENT

Descent ______
Cauc. Mex. Neg. Other

Year Born ______

Time ______M

Surname ______

Date ______ Division ______ Bkg. No. ______ Charge ______

By ______
Serial No.

L.A. No. ______

1. Name ______ Sex male

2. Street Address ______

3. City ______ State ______

b6
b7C

4. Place of Birth ______ Date of Birth ______

5. Occupation ______ Date (Today) 7/6/92

6. Where Now Employed ______
(Or where last employed)

7. Name of Nearest Relative ______ Relation ______

8. Address of Nearest Relative ______

9. Color Hair? BlK Color Eyes? BRN Height: Ft. 6 In. 0 Weight 200 Age 33

10. In Case of Emergency Notify [redacted] b6 b7C

Address [redacted]

11. Capital Letters of the Alphabet ABCDEFGHIJKLMNOPQR (Write, Do Not Print)

12. STUVWXYZ

13. Small Letters abcdefghijklmnopqrs (Write, Do Not Print)

14. tuvwxyz Right or Left Handed Right Hand

15. Numbe[redacted]c.) 1 2 3 4 5 6 7 8 9 10 11 12 13 14 15 16 17 18 19 20

Fingerprints of Four Fingers of Right Hand

Witnessed by [redacted] SA-USSS
Name Serial No.

Approved by
Watch Commander Serial No.

Signature [redacted]

Date 7/6/92

Van Nuys Court - DEPT 103, 1115 HRS ②

Form 05.07.0 (Rev. 6-22-91)

Form 05.07.0 (Rev. 6-22-51)

Descent ______
Cauc. Mex. Neg. Other

PHOTOGRAPHED

LOS ANGELES POLICE DEPARTMENT

Year Born ______

Time ______M

Surname ______

Date ______ Division ______ Bkg. No. ______ Charge ______

By ______
Serial No.

L.A. No. ______

1. Name ______ Sex Male

2. Street Address ______

3. City ______ State ______ b6 b7C

4. Place of Birth ______ Date of Birth ______

5. Occupation ______ Date (Today) 7/6/92

6. Where Now Employed ______
(Or where last employed)

7. Name of Nearest Relative ______ Relation ______

8. Address of Nearest Relative ______

9. Color Hair? BlK Color Eyes? BRN Height: Ft. 6 In. 0 Weight 200 Age 33

10. In Case of Emergency Notify [redacted] b6 b7C

Address [redacted]

11. Capital Letters of the Alphabet A B C D E F G H I J K L M N O
Write, Do Not Print

12. P Q R S T U V W X Y Z

13. Small Letters a b c d e f g h i j k l m n o p q r s
Write, Do Not Print

14. t u v w x y z Right or Left Handed Right

15. Numbers (1 to 20 Inc.) 1 2 3 4 5 6 7 8 9 10 11 12 13 14 15 16 17 18 19 20

Witnessed by [redacted] SA USSS [redacted]

Fingerprints of Four Fingers of Right Hand

Approved by
Watch Commander Serial No.

Signature [redacted]

Date 7/6/92

Van Nuys Court – Dept 103, 1115 Hrs.

7/6/92

b6
b7C

9A-UA-142276-194

5/21/92

TO All Concerned Parties;

I hope you receive this letter in good health and in good Spirits;

I decided that because nobody is taking me Serious, and I can't handle my state of mind, that I Am going to Washington D.C. to threaten to kill the President of the United States George Bush.

IF they do not arrest me or Solve my problem im gonna attempt to Kill President George Bush. b6 b7C

NO Anwser from [redacted] is the only wrong anwser. And I will not accept it.

I would be a fool to try to harm her, She isn't my enermy, it's the people inbetween me and her.

Sincerely; with Love

b6
b7C

P.S. I Dear you to call this a bluFF.

W:,

7/6/92

b6
b7C

I Don't want No Record of this in the Courts 6/9/92

TO [redacted]

I hope you receive this letter in good health and in good Spirits:

So [redacted] has been Seeing and Living with [redacted] it's out in the open. [redacted]

I called myself fighting to protect [redacted] life ~~and~~ as ~~her family~~ well as her family.

Now the rumor is she is secretly married to him, to top it off, im hurt by this, im not gonna make any threats because im too tired.

TO [redacted].

good luck with your wife, because you are going to need it

TO [redacted] (Your Choice)

good luck with your husband, you do have a choice, one who will live or one who will die.

As for alimony [redacted] you owe me for past Support.

Distribution: The FBI
John Gotti

7/6/92

b6
b7C

To The Daily News:

Now the issue with [redacted] is love -vs- being used, with Michael Jackson and John Gotti it's about Financial compensation. I told you what will happen to John if he doesn't pay up. Michael I will personally attempt to kill, if he doesn't pay me my money. If im crazy im going to jail, if not everybody will know the truth.

But I can't live like this any longer.

Sincerely, Read Ecc: 7:25-28

5

7/6/92

b6
b7C

P.S. Now I know what she means by good love comes for free, I make her rich, and while I am in a homeless shelter, she fucks in a mansion.

Distribution:

THE FBI

John Gotti

Im not saying anymore, but we will see,

Sincerely' with love

5/18/92

TO The Daily News;

I hope you receive this letter in good health and in good spirits:

To confirm our telephone conversation last night.

So I decided to go to the FBI today, if that doesn't work ill go to the CIA, military intelligents, on up to the President of the United States' of America, and if the chain of command doesn't work, I will resort to violence, to bring attention to my problem. I'll commit Mass murder at a Michael Jackson Concert if necessary, in an attempt to murder Michael, then you will have to deal with my problem in the public eye.

Sincerely;

ECC 7:25-28

7/6/92

b6
b7C

2/5/92

Dear

I hope you receive this letter in good health and in good Spirits:

First of all I want to say im very disappointed, for what you did, you embarassed me and you also disrespected me in the worst way. What you don't understand is when my men lost respect for me, there is no loyalty and without loyalty how do I protect you, your father, mother, sisters, or brothers, and that's a part of my job.

I expected something like this out of , because She's a stupid bitch, but not by you.

The Media is not a game, you don't feel me out in the dialy News, I gave you my phone number and a address to write me, to avoid this type of Situation.

In 1989 intentions was to use me, get paid and run, and Supported you in doing that, you know its true.

I expect you to retracked that statement, the same way you made it. Because that bullshit is out OF the question. I still love you and what im saying is out of love, im not gonna feed my enemy, and only a Face to Face with them, can begin to resolve this or end it that much Sooner. Don't try that Shit and I don't care if you get angry about this, just don't try it.

Sincerely, with Love

(Your Husband)

7/6/92

b6
b7C

5/21/92

To all Concerned Parties;

I hope you receive this letter in good health and in good Spirits;

I decided Since nobody is taking me Serious, and I can't handle my state of mind, that I am going to Washington D.C. to threaten to Kill the President of the United States George Bush.

If they do not arrest me or Solve my problem, im gonna attempt to kill President George Bush. NO anwser from [redacted] is the only wrong ~~awn~~ awnser and I will not accept it. I would would be a fool to try to harm her. She isn't my enemy, it's the people inbetween me and her.

Sincerely' with Love

P.S. I Dear you to call this a bluff.

FD-340 (Rev. 4-2-85)

Field File No. 9A - LA - 142276 - 1A5

Serial # of Originating Document

OO and File No. LA

Date Received 7/28/92

From [redacted] b6 b7C

(Name of Contributor)

4641 Hayvenhurst Ave

(Address of Contributor)

Encino, California

By SA [redacted]

(Name of Special Agent)

To Be Returned ☐ Yes ☐ No Receipt Given ☐ Yes ☐ No

Grand Jury Material - Disseminate Only Pursuant to Rule 6(e), Federal Rules of Criminal Procedure ☐ Yes ☐ No

Title:

Reference:

(Communication Enclosing Material)

Description: ☒ Original notes re interview of [redacted] b6 b7C

8/19/92
CLB

7/28/92

b6
b7C

Security Officer — 5 yrs.

4641 Hayvenhurst

Encino

6/22/92

[illegible]

saw [illegible] apple TV

he goes [illegible] gate

[illegible] on — will be closing [illegible]

[illegible] PDP [illegible]

"alert box"

[illegible] of State

— not [illegible]

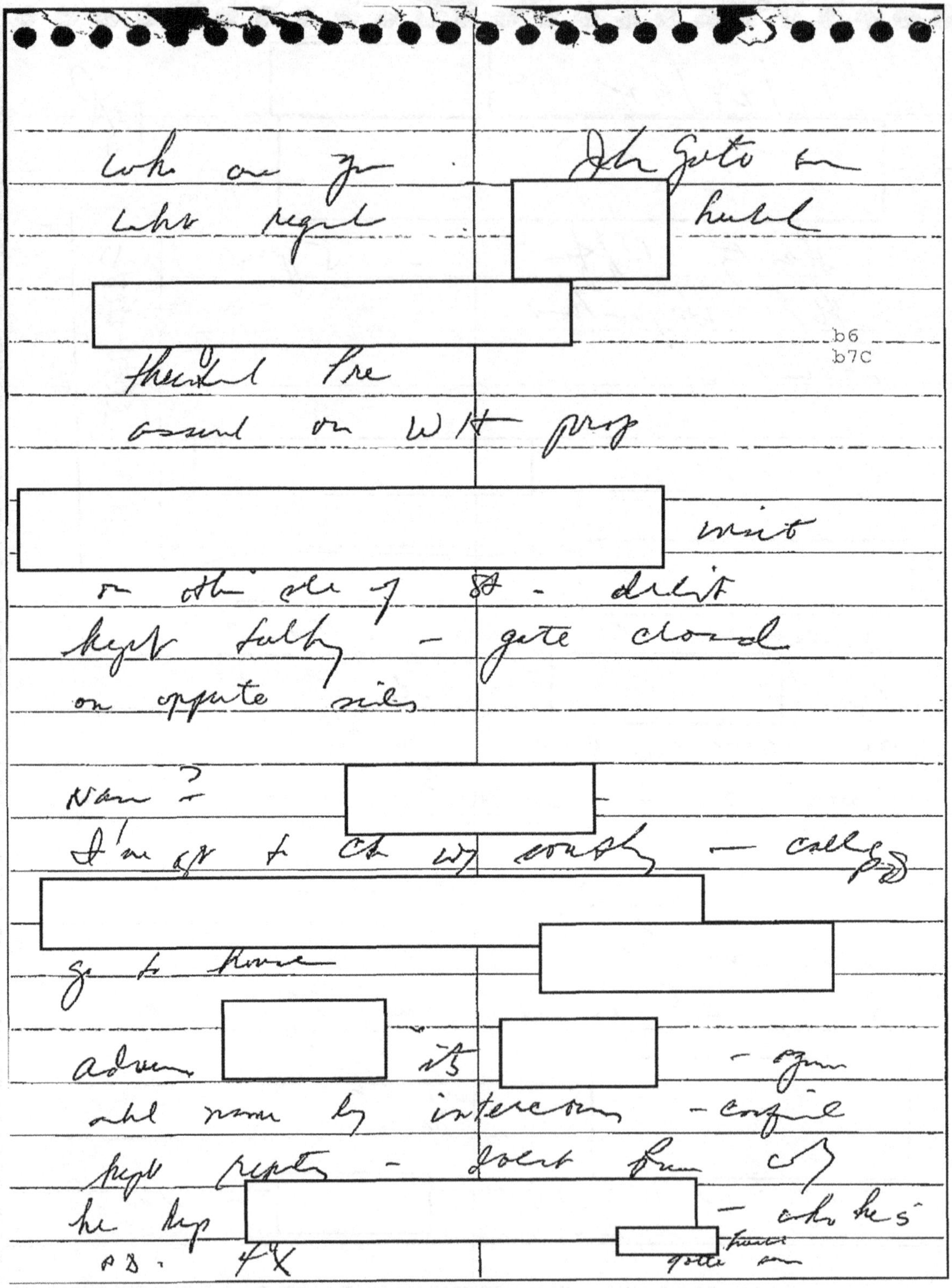
b6
b7C

4 calls

b6
b7C

20 - 30 minutes — [redacted] still cutting on
elsewhere — just created
knew potentially danger — didn't force
to move monitor — TV

(0100)

PD — 4 cars — same story to PD
he goes out & meets them

(if he doesn't find out why he's this
way — he's going to have to come to
a conclusion → going to have to
make his own conclusion

don't recall [redacted] by name
as far as ... killing him

but did mention killing [redacted] no specific words
stream of conversation once
all jumbled

Distortion

read report — no details
didn't think it would
amount to anything

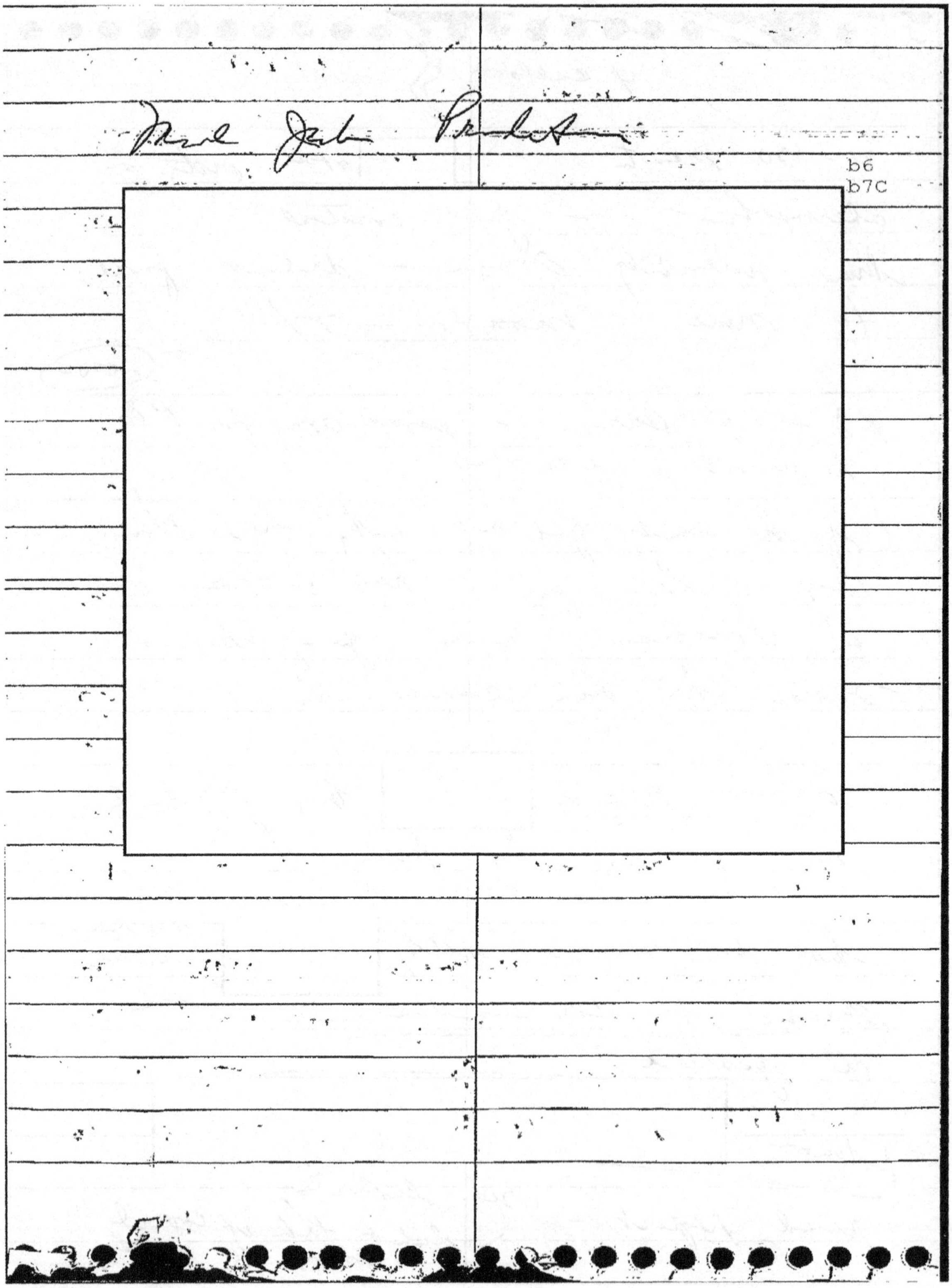

b6
b7C

FD-340 (Rev. 4-2-85)

Field File No. 9A-LA-742276-1A6

Serial # of Originating Document

OO and File No.

Date Received 7/28/92

From [redacted] b6 b7C b7D

(Address of Contributor)

By [redacted] b6 b7C

To Be Returned ☐ Yes ☐ No Receipt Given ☐ Yes ☐ No

Grand Jury Material - Disseminate Only Pursuant to Rule 6(e), Federal Rules of Criminal Procedure ☐ Yes ☐ No

Title:

Reference:

(Communication Enclosing Material)

Description: ☒ Original notes re interview of [redacted] (telephonic 7/28/92) b6 b7C b7D

8/19/92
CUB

. . conference call ← AUSA Jenner
me

7/28/92

b6
b7C
b7D

ID's himself +

9A-LA-142276-1A6

xplan process —

aware of this

b6
b7C
b7D

# of Counts

FD-340 (Rev. 4-2-85)

Field File No. 9A - LA - 142276 - 1A7

Serial # of Originating Document

OO and File No. LA

Date Received 7/28/92

From Holly Buckner
(Name of Contributor)
LA City Attorney's Office
(Address of Contributor)

By SA [redacted] b6 b7C
(Name of Special Agent)

To Be Returned ☐ Yes ☐ No Receipt Given ☐ Yes ☐ No

Grand Jury Material - Disseminate Only Pursuant to Rule 6(e), Federal Rules of Criminal Procedure ☐ Yes ☐ No

Title:

Reference:
(Communication Enclosing Material)

Description: ☐ Original notes re interview of

14 color photos w/ negatives of the Jackson residence at 4641 Hayvenhurst Ave, Encino, Calif.

8/19/02 CLB

4643

9A-LA-142276-1A7

REORDER FORM

NO.	QTY.	SIZE	NO.	QTY.	SIZE	NO.	QTY.	SIZE	NO.	QTY.	SIZE	NO.	QTY.	SIZE	NO.	QTY.	SIZE
0			8			16			24			28A			33		
0A			8A			16A			24A			29			33A		
1			9			17			25			29A			34		
1A			9A			17A			25A			30			34A		
2			10			18			26			30A			35		
2A			10A			18A			26A			31			35A		
3			11			19			27			31A			36		
3A			11A			19A			27A			32			36A		
4			12			20			28			32A			37		
4A			12A			20A											
5			13			21											
5A			13A			21A											
6			14			22											
6A			14A			22A											
7			15			23											
7A			15A			23A											

ENLARGEMENT	
Wallet	A
5x7	B
8x10	C
11x14	D

READ THIS NOTICE

Liability Agreement: You agree to accept an equivalent amount of unexposed film or refund of the film processing purchase price as your exclusive remedy as the limit of our liability and of any finisher handling your film, should the film, prints or service be defective, damaged, lost or not returned; regardless of your damages, including incidental or consequential, and regardless of your legal theory-including negligence and strict liability, unless we agree in writing to assume a greater obligation and you pay in advance a higher agreed price for this service.

4506 Twin ✓ 10551

Name Beckner

Last Name First Name

Address:

Street City Zip

Phone ( ) Date 7/19/92

ONE ROLL PER ENVELOPE

SIZE	TYPE	FRAMES	NO. OF PRINTS 24
☐ DISC	☐ KODACOLOR 100 & 1000	☐ 12	PRICE
☐ 110	☐ KODACOLOR 200 & 400	☐ 15	
	☐ VERICOLOR II	☐ 20	
☐ 126	☐ FUJI COLOR 100 & 1000	☐ 24	Develop
☐ 135	☐ FUJI COLOR 200 & 400	☐ 36	
	☐ OTHER		

☐ REPRINTS ☐ COPY PRINT

SPECIAL INSTRUCTIONS

H

Time Due: 2200

Print	
Sub Total	
TAX	
TOTAL	

ONE HOUR PHOTO MAX.

SYLMAR TOWN SHOPPING CENTER
12671 GLENOAKS BLVD.
SYLMAR, CA 91342
(818) 362-3456 (Film)

FD-340 (Rev. 4-2-85)

Field File No. 9A - LA - 142276 - 1A8

Serial # of Originating Document ________

OO and File No. ________

Date Received ________

From ________
(Name of Contributor)

____
(Address of Contributor)

b6
b7C

By SA [redacted]
(Name of Special Agent)

To Be Returned ☐ Yes ☐ No Receipt Given ☐ Yes ☐ No

Grand Jury Material - Disseminate Only Pursuant to Rule 6(e), Federal Rules of Criminal Procedure ☐ Yes ☐ No

Title:

Reference: ________
(Communication Enclosing Material)

Description: ☐ Original notes re interview of

color photos plus negatives for Subject [redacted]

b6
b7C

8-20-92

FD-340 (Rev. 4-2-85)

Field File No. 9A-LA-142276-1A9

Serial # of Originating Document

OO and File No.

Date Received 8/10/92

From [redacted] b6 b7C b7D

(Address of Contributor)

By SA [redacted] b6 b7C

(Name of Special Agent)

To Be Returned ☐ Yes ☐ No Receipt Given ☐ Yes ☐ No

Grand Jury Material - Disseminate Only Pursuant to Rule 6(e), Federal Rules of Criminal Procedure ☐ Yes ☐ No

Title:

Reference:

(Communication Enclosing Material)

Description: ☒ Original notes re interview of [redacted] b6 b7C b7D

8/10/92

9A-LA-142276-1A9

b6
b7C
b7D

mean nothy to you
never meet

make aware of letter by
July 92

– CDL –
SS

FD-340 (Rev. 4-2-85)

Field File No. 9A-LA-142276 — 1A10

Serial # of Originating Document

OO and File No. LA

Date Received 8/12/92

From [redacted]

[redacted] b6 b7C b7D

By SA [redacted] b6 b7C

To Be Returned ☐ Yes ☐ No Receipt Given ☐ Yes ☐ No

Grand Jury Material - Disseminate Only Pursuant to Rule 6(e), Federal Rules of Criminal Procedure ☐ Yes ☐ No

Title:

Reference: (Communication Enclosing Material)

Description: ☒ Original notes re interview of [redacted] b6 b7C b7D

[illegible]

[illegible]

b6
b7C
b7D

6/22/92

[illegible]

9A-LA-142276 – 1A70

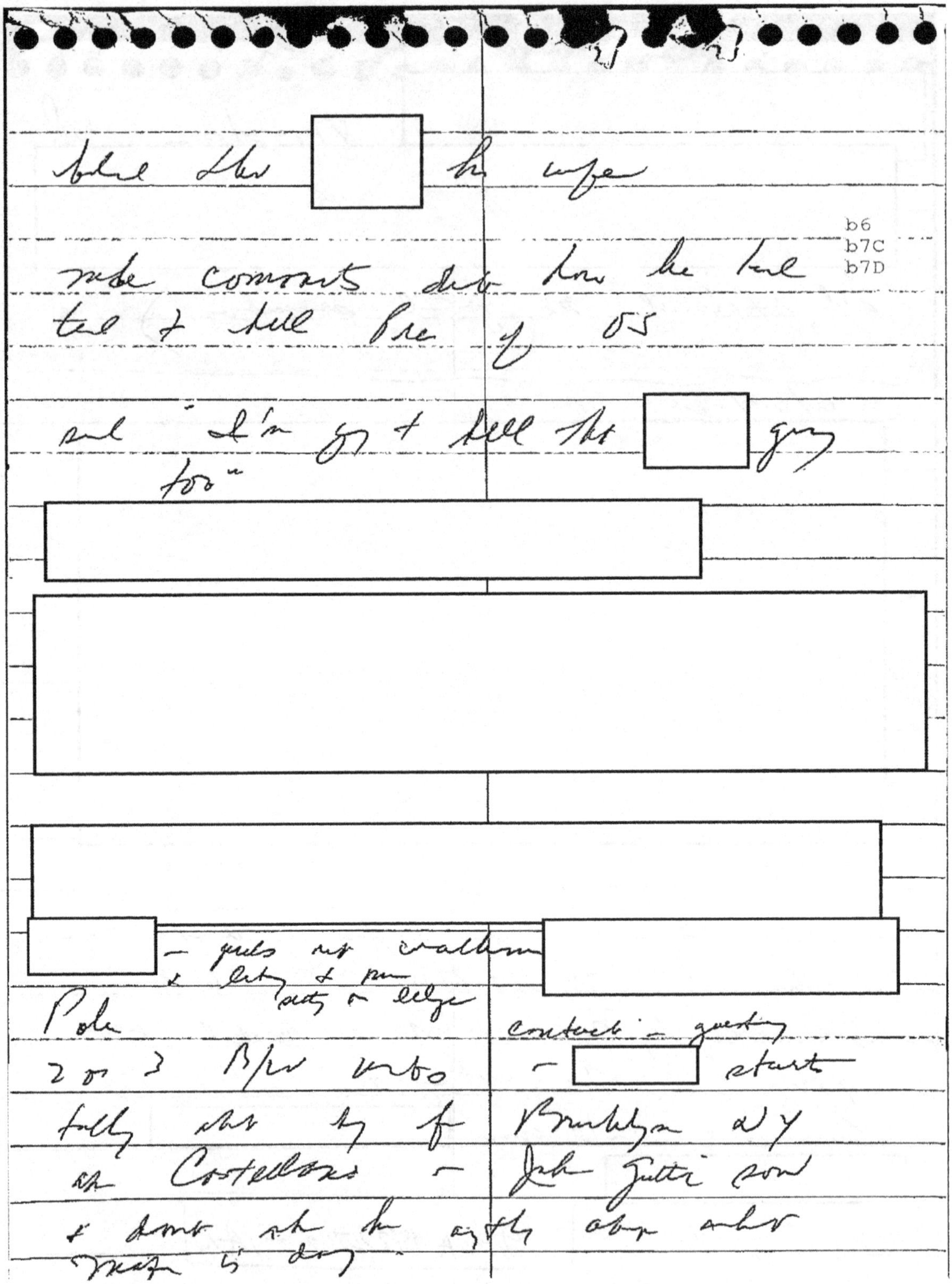

behind [illegible] his wife

b6
b7C
b7D

made comments about how he [illegible]
[illegible] & tell Pres of US

said "I'm going to tell that [illegible] guy
too"

– pulls out wallet
& [illegible]

Pole — contact – questions

2 or 3 B/W [illegible] – starts

talking about [illegible] Brooklyn NY

Costellanos – John Gotti son

& [illegible] anything about [illegible]

b6
b7C
b7D

sounded angry & upset over
spelling

had sent lots of letters - no response
"this has gone on long enough"

b6
b7C
b7D

refusal to provide any biography
data regarding hemming

FD-340 (Rev. 8-18-89)

Universal File Case Number 9A-LA-142276-1A11

Field Office Acquiring Evidence

Serial # of Originating Document

Date Received 12-20-94

From SA

(Name of Contributor)

(Address of Contributor)

b6
b7C

(City and State)

By

(Name of Special Agent)

To Be Returned ☐ Yes ☒ No

Receipt Given ☐ Yes ☒ No

Grand Jury Material - Disseminate Only Pursuant to Rule 6 (e) Federal Rules of Criminal Procedure

☐ Yes ☒ No

Title:

Reference:

(Communication Enclosing Material)

Description: ☐ Original notes re interview of

FD-192 (1B1) DESTROYED

1/14/95

Bulky Exhibit - Inventory of Property Acquired as Evidence
FD-192 (Rev. 7-18-85)

Date 7/30/92

Title and Character of Case

[redacted] aka
[redacted]-Victim;
Michael Jackson-Victim;
[redacted]-Victim;
[redacted]-Victim;
Mailing Threatening Letters;

9A-LA-142276-1a[illegible]

b6
b7C

Date Property Acquired	Source From Which Property Acquired
7/27/92	Holly Beckner, Asst. City Atty, Los Angeles

Location of Property or Bulky Exhibit	Reason for Retention of Property and Efforts Made to Dispose of Same
Bulky Exhibit	Evidence

To Be Returned	See Serial	Agent Submitting Property or Exhibit	Agent Assigned Case
☐ Yes ☒No		SA [redacted]	SA [redacted]

b6
b7C

☐ Yes ☒No Grand Jury Property - Disseminate Only Pursuant to Rule 6(e), Federal Rules of Criminal Procedure.

☐ Yes ☒No Property to be Forfeited to the Government

Description of Property or Exhibit

Nine (9) Original letters with envelopes addressed to [redacted] [redacted] 14755 Ventura Blvd., #1-710, Sherman Oaks, Ca. 91403, sent by [redacted] Plaza Post Office, Box [redacted] L.I.C. New York, 11101

b6
b7C

Destroy as per SA [redacted] 1/20/94

F6524298
UNIT 30 SHELF 2

For Valuable and/or Narcotics Evidence Only

Evidence Bag Seal # ____________

Signature of Two Special Agents Verifying and Sealing Bag Contents ____________

SEMIANNUAL INVENTORY CERTIFICATION TO JUSTIFY RETENTION OF PROPERTY (Initial and Date)

9A-LA-142276-1B1

BLOCK STAMP

Field File # 9A-LA-142276 1B1

OO: Los Angeles

EVIDENCE (PACKAGE COPY)

CHAIN OF CUSTODY

	Date	Time		Date	Time
Signature [redacted] Reason Evidence	7/27/92	8:00 Am	[redacted] Bulky Evidence	7/30/92	4:30 PM
Signature [redacted] Reason A/V/D/STORAGE	7/31/92	4:30	b6 b7C		
Signature Reason					
Signature Reason					
Signature Reason					
Signature Reason					
Signature Reason					
Signature Reason					
Signature Reason					
Signature Reason					

Item No. **Remarks** Reviewed Evidence 8/3/92 [redacted]

b6
b7C

FROM:VAN NUYS CITY ATTY. TO:43104780153 [JUL] 2, 1992 7:56AM #895 P.01

LOS ANGELES CITY ATTORNEY'S OFFICE

VAN NUYS CRIMINAL BRANCH

14410 SYLVAN STREET, ROOM 106, VAN NUYS, CALIFORNIA 91401

(818) 989-8881
(818) 989-8855 (pretrial)
(818) 989-8887 (hearings)
(818) 989-8488 (victim-witness)
(818) 904-1444 (fax)

FAX TRANSMITTAL SHEET

Number of Pages (including this page): 14 (1st Fax)

SENT TO: [redacted] FBI

b6
b7C

FROM: Holly Beckner
902-2182 Fax - 904 - 1444

9A-LA-142276-2

DATE: 7-2-92

MESSAGE:

[redacted] - I'm sending (1) a brief chronology, (2) our arrest report (which is not accurate - Δ threatens to kill [redacted], not [redacted] at time of arrest) (3) letters. Note he decides not to come to LA until after [redacted] resigns, and is pretty close.
Please call me. Thanks! Holly
2nd Fax with additional letters follows

FROM:VAN NUYS CITY ATTY. TO:43104780153 JUL 2, 1992 7:57AM #895 P.02

b6
b7C

5/18/92: Letters – re: Mafia killings
: suggests taking a life to prove own power

5/19/92: Letter: [redacted] "is a dead man"
([redacted] ?)

* 5/21/92: Writes he is going to D.C. to attempt to kill President

* 5/22/92: Arrested outside White House
numerous threats to kill someone to get attention
(ref: Sec. Service D.C.)

continues to write

6/4/92: Released

6/5/92: [redacted] makes threatening remarks to [redacted]
writes of intent to deal once & for all with Jackson's

6/22/92: Arrives in Calif. at Jackson's
Threatens to kill [redacted]

FROM:VAN NUYS CITY ATTY. TO:43104780153 ... 2, 1992 8:01AM #895 P.07

TEL No. May 18,92 14:34 P.03

b6
b7C

5/18/92

Dear

I hope you receive this letter in good health and in good Spirits!

I Faxed Some letters to your radio station earlier this morning, So I assume you understand my Situation.

Im writing you because im convinced you have good contacts with Celebrities, and considering is making a movie now, for you she is a touch tone away, as also is obviously as well.

Im requesting that you act as a liason to bring about a peaceful resolution. Because im on vacation with limited funds, and I need peace of mind. My attitude concerning this, is im prepared to resort to Military tactics, because with my limited funds that's probably the only way people are going to take me Serious.

Here's my phone ## I might get the message Here's my P.O. Box, and there's a thing called American Express and Federal Express

Plaza Post Office
Box
N.Y.C. New York 11101

Im gonna call you at to confirm you received my request. My position is either wants me or she doesn't, regardless im not crazy, Im gonna make it with or without her. But im not gonna be unfaithful because she's an unfaithful bitch, I'd rather let go and find someone new. The word for me is not crazy, its ambitious, im gonna get mines or die on the battle-field.

"You think im gonna continue to suffer, while punk mother fuckers live Large at my expense, "Bullshit"

FROM:VAN NUYS CITY ATTY. TO:43104780153 JUL 2, 1992 8:02AM #895 P.08
JUN-29-1992 13:47 FR[illegible] MJJ PRODUCTIONS TO 18185060425 P.04

TEL No. May 18,92 14:33 P.02

5/18/92

I hope you all receive this letter in good health and in good
spirits:
To KNBC / Retransmission Please:
Concerning [redacted]
I just want to make a point perfectly clear, im not saying
these things to hurt or upset [redacted] Im just letting it be known
that im not to be blackmailed, and I will not be extorted. Me and
[redacted] may have a lot of things to discuss, but she shouldn't pay
people to hide things from me, that's the worst thing she can do.
To all those people who think they got away with using and
abusing me and my wife, if you think it's about just forgiving you
and that's it, im gonna forgive your ass alright, and that's a promise.
"That's why I got accountants" I have a cup full of pennies, so
you know how I feel about people who beat me out of millions, through
blackmail and extortion.

To Michael Jackson:
Don't make anymore major purchases until I make it home, other
then that house I put on order. Im not paying into any extortion,
as for that house, im not beating anyone. I built it, im just doing
what I think is right. I mean like hell I got a stapler on my desk
going for $1M, the Son of Man used it, or how about $1B for my worn
out Holy Bible, be for real Michael.

To the Daily News / Retransmission Please:
Concerning The Roman Catholic Church and the issue of Overseers:
The hell with the so-called Pope John Paul and his whole damn
crew. (Read:1Ti:3:1-16) and take note of (1Ti:3:2) take note of
(Eph:5:23) (Read:1Co:7:12-31) (Read:Php:9:1-31)
Understand that the Apostle Paul was married, but separated
(diminished) from his wife, so it could be said he was unmarried, yet
maintained the right's to his wife, because he did not divorce her.
Therefor he had to receive a reconciliation. Jesus Christ became
the Apostle Paul. And trust me, as a man I need my wife, and you all
are no better then me.
What the Apostle Paul did not do was sell his soul to satan, he
remained faithful and did not get married while he was separated.
Understand that the Holy Bible speaks about physical things to
allude to spiritual insights. (Refer to letter to [redacted]
[redacted] / Concerning your annulment: Dated 5/12/92)

To ABC News / Concerning Gun Control:
Now that we see signs of Black Community unification, all of a
sudden we are concerned with the influx of inexpensive guns into
Urban America. Where was this coverage when the CRIPS and the Bloods
was killing off one another ? And why can't we deal with the drug
issue in the same way, by going to the source ?
What we are saying is that, it is alright for the middle class
Suburban Americans to own guns, but not the inner city poor. So what
are we advocating is that the way it should be is, we set up arms
middle class White people around, unarmed oppressed Black people, to
inforce the law of Black oppression. The Black Community has the
technology, manpower, and resources to manufacture their own weapons,
the same way they process their drugs within the city boundaries. Gun
control without social justice is not the solution.

b6
b7C

FROM:VAN NUYS CITY ATTY. TO:43104780153 JUL 2, 1992 8:03AM #895 P.09
JUN-29-1992 13:46 FROM MJJ PRODUCTIONS TO 18185060426 P.03

TEL No. May 18,92 14:35 P.01

(Important Note: Read Scripture.)

5/18/92

To The Daily News:

I hope you receive this letter in good health and in good Spirits:

To confirm our telephone conversation last night:

Im writing to inform you that I decided to use the government's chain of Command to resolve my problem: My Problem! After close to two years of Searching for the truth, and a life time of mistreatment, I have not received any acknowledgment. for the last 14 months I haven't had Sexual intercourse, calling myself being faithful to [redacted], my best friends and relatives constantly challenge my Sanity. And all I ask is that [redacted] tell me yes or no, either she wants me as her husband or not, but I will not except that she is too important or too busy to answer me considering how this all has effected my life. b6 b7C

So I decided to go to the FBI today, if that doesn't work ill go to the CIA, military intelligents, on up to the office of the President of the United States of America, and if the chain of Command doesn't work I will resort to Violence, to bring attention to my problem, I'll commit Mass murder at a Michael Jackson concert if necessary, In an attempt to murder Michael, then you will have to deal with my Situation in the public eye.

Now the issue with [redacted] is love - vs - being used, with Michael Jackson and John Gotti its about financial Compensation, I told you what will happen to John if he doesn't pay up, Michael I will personally attempt to kill if he doesn't pay me my money. If im crazy ill go to jail, if not then everybody will know the truth. "But I can't live like this any longer."

Sincerely, (READ; Ecc: 7:25:28)

FROM:VAN NUYS CITY ATTY. T. 3104780153 2, 1992 8:04AM #895 P.10

b6 b7C

Dear [redacted]

I hope you receive this letter in good health and in good spirits;

I requested that you act as liaison to bring about a peaceful solution, and now the FBI is openly involved.

But now aside from that tough guy bullshit, I must explain something to you. Im 33 years old and never had a real relationship in my life, I can't even slow dance. If it wasn't a woman much older then me it was a prostitute and this is the story of my life, because I didn't want to get emotionally involved.

Im not a bad looking dude and im not a homosexual, I tried to be faithful to the best of my ability all my life, because I knew someday GOD would see me through, I didn't know it was [redacted] I only knew there was someone in this world for me. They stole my life from me, and you know what people are thinking, "I thought he was a faggot" Do you know how hard it is for a faggot to get pussy these days ? With the addition of AIDS, if a female has sex with a man she believes is a homo she is crazy.

Now my vacation went to waste, bugging out on [redacted] and all I asked for was a yes or no and I added to that a maybe. If im crazy and she isn't interested say no, what do she have to lose ? If she isn't certain of what is going on, say I have to think about it. If she is interested say yes. But after what I went through for her I deserve a anwser, because im a man with a serious problem, who devoted at the minimum two years, to receive one letter saying basically, [redacted] I know you exist.

P.S. Ask [redacted] about me, im a lonely dude. Say [redacted] who was [redacted] girl friend ?

Don't take me wrong, because im not on my pity pot. I just want to expand on my position.

I believe I was 15 years old when the decision concerning what would come to past with [redacted] was made, I chose [redacted] over [redacted] because I knew [redacted] was gonna try to use me, by then it was clear to me. Also I was very young and extremely shy, and [redacted] was so fine and fully developed, like what was I gonna do with her ?

[redacted] was at a better age for me to grow with, and she showed a interest in me that made me feel that she looked up to me, so I beat up some dude to impress her, I met him in Florida, we worked as dishwashers together, we made up. This encounter took place at Madision Square Garden, and ever since then my life was never the same, I suffered but I knew she would someday "come back to me". In 1989 in L.I.C. N.Y. at the Riverpark she did, [redacted] woke me up [redacted] I know things about him, and have good reason not to trust him. There was inbetweens but at age 30 she had to wake me up, that what i's about to happen, would come to past. I told them, being her and her parents back at MSG, that people would attack them to control their assets, amoung other things, and just when they thought that they was about to be destroyed, I would come to their rescue. I said they told me to tell you that "I AM HE WHO THEY SENT". [redacted] you have to understand, I had to suffer, live poor, im very inexperienced in relationships, I never really took a woman out to eat, forget a real evening out. How else could I compete for [redacted] coming from where I am and have been.

The only thing she will believe is my position of power to protect them from me. I became who I am for her, how could she leave me ?

Sincerely, with love

FROM:VAN NUYS CITY ATTY. TO:43104780153 [illegible] 2, 1992 8:28AM #898 P.01

LOS ANGELES CITY ATTORNEY'S OFFICE

VAN NUYS CRIMINAL BRANCH

14410 SYLVAN STREET, ROOM 106, VAN NUYS, CALIFORNIA 91401

(818) 989-8881
(818) 989-8855 (pretrial)
(818) 989-8887 (hearings)
(818) 989-8438 (victim-witness)
(818) 904-1444 (fax)

FAX TRANSMITTAL SHEET

Number of Pages (including this page): 14

SENT TO: [redacted] b6 b7C

FBI

FROM: Helly Beckner
Deputy C.A.

DATE: 07-2-92

9A-LA-142276-3

MESSAGE:

2nd Fax - Additional letters

FROM:VAN NUYS CITY ATTY. TO:43104780153 JUL 2, 1992 8:28AM #898 P.02

14

To All Concerned Parties;

I hope you all receive this letter in good health and in good spirits;

To [redacted] Im willing to meet you on common grounds, so baby let's do it right. b6 b7C

The signal I want to receive to inform me that you want me to be a part of your life and plan to do right by me , is to hear that you moved back home with your parents.

I want you to move back home with your parents, so that I can receive you properly. Before I take you away from your parents, I want their approval of our marriage, therefor we will stay there as long as it takes to gain their approval. This will be the time when we all can discuss and resolve as many of our differences as realistically possible.

As for the house that you built, I want everybody out of there and I want it cleaned out. And while you are at your parents house waiting for me faithfully, if someone must stay there, make sure it is family members. We will decide together where we are gonna live. Like I said im interested in "Scarlet Dream" The Paul Castellano Estate, my father want's me to move in for awhile to clean the house, I may have to do it, because only I can, we should discuss this as well. I plan to come to California as soon as it is right.

To The L.A. CRIPS: As we all know the CRIPS are International, and most certainly nationwide. There's a lot of adjustments being made, such as the matching of CRIPS Charters to Local Masonic Lodges, Universal and Local Codes and so on.

But what I want to address is my visit to L.A. in the near future. Im not gonna come to L.A. intill [redacted] officially resigns, the power he has is unheard of, and the system he ran was unjust, he has to go, and that is the condition of my coming to California. And I believe my position is a wise one, because GOD forbid [redacted] attempt to be a hero, and ever try to bring harm to me or my family, because then I will be forced to kill him. But being he is the one authority I do not trust, I will avoid him, this is the best position to take. But I warn any connection he may feel that he has in the system, don't try to bring harm to me or my family.

"No Law Inforcement Group Should Be Allowed To Act On Their Own"

Also I ask that the CRIPS respect and protect my wife for the remainder of our separation, I feel that she can openly be faithful to me as "I AM" to her, and be proud of it, I love [redacted] very much.

Sincerely; with love

P.S. [redacted] I would like for you to go to and take advise from your parents. I married the daughter of Jehovah Witnesses, which I AM very grateful for. Things that your mother told you would happen to you is now happening, all you have to do is except it.

All you have to do is turn back to the GOD of your understanding and from there we will find a common ground. See [redacted] GOD loved you after all, just find it in your heart to repent. [redacted]

FROM:VAN NUYS CITY ATTY. TO:43104780153 JUL 2, 1992 8:29AM #898 P.03

6/12/92 15

b6
b7C

To [ ], WPLS.

I hope you receive this letter in good health and in good spirits:

Tell [ ] that I said, if he ever goes to the public and says he was anything otherthen a friend of [ ], and that things never got serious between them, we will see about that.

Now you know anybody married to [ ] as fine as she is, ain't gonna hide the fact, being aware of it, inless he is a punk, and punks get chumped for their women. [ ] don't you know I will fuck [ ] up really bad, over [ ] so stop making me jealous alluding to [ ] because it can never happen while im alive, not in reality.

Im gonna get intouch with agent [ ] about this Monday, actually today, I'll give the FBI, [ ] and the Jackson Family incill Monday to get their anwsers straight. [ ] could not have ever married anyone else, because she was already married to me. But to allow you to allude to her being married to someone other then me is very unfaithful and im tired of it.

Note: And all [ ] has to say is, I was secretly married and I didn't want people to think I was homosexual, so I hired a friend as an escort. If they ask to who ? For legal reasons it must remain a secret for now. If they ask about her sexuality ? I just want to say I tried my best to be faithful and I really do love my husband, my private life for the most part should remain private.

Now under these conditions, I will let [ ] walk with $1M and the things he own, such as one car and so on, im talking about personal items, and I mean realistically. Now if he tries to take me for a ride, somebody loyal to me is gonna kill him without me saying anything, and that's guranteed, not a threat.

Sincerely: with love

[ ]

FROM:VAN NUYS CITY ATTY. TO:43104780153 JUL 2, 1992 8:30AM #899 P.04

JUN 30 '92 04:49PM

b6 b7C

Dear [redacted] / WBLS.

I hope you receive this letter in good health and in good spirits:

I want to tell you that you have been very helpful, rather you realize it or not. "Thank you very much"

I realize that you may not be taking me seriously, but "I AM" for real, and none of this is a joke.

[redacted] was born for me, she is a very important part of me, she can not marry anyone because she is already married to me, everything that she has is mines, and she is symbolic to a lot of things. "She is the wife of the Son of Man" for this reason I can't recognize her marriage to anyone but me.

Understand that Jesus Christ married the church, [redacted] is therefor symbolic of the church, amoung other things. So now understand the concept, in that I realize she was unfaithful, yet she must become once again faithful, in order to restore the purity of our marriage.

She must "Come back to me" in reality I didn't leave [redacted] she left me, it was in her heart to be unfaithful to me upon our reunion, and to keep her from being killed, because my wife must be faithful, I let her go, I allowed our separation again in 1989. "Come back to me" I wrote the letters, im the one who doesn't know where she is, im the one being hurt, not her. The bottomline is back in 1989, she believed I was a punk, and she was only out to use me, she didn't respect me as a man, nor did she have any respect for men. The important issue here is that if I can not put my house in order, how can I put GOD's house in order. And believe me, in 1989 my house was all fucked up, full of resentments, you name it.

See [redacted] was put through a lot, and was made confused. She didn't know I was [redacted] so she called herself using me, and being married to [redacted] Who she figured [redacted] to be, I don't know.

Now as I stated before, the timing of my taking her virginity was because she wasn't gonna be faithful, and she didn't know it was me. She was made to believe I was a faggot, because she was so worried about what I was doing, she couldn't be faithful, and that was the problem. As I said, I don't know who she figured [redacted] to be (perhaps a sucker), but certainly not the Son of Man. I guess she figured [redacted] was just someone John Gotti used, and it was her duty to control me. "She didn't know who "I AM"

I knew we would be separated for a long time, and I didn't want any other man to touch her, and I knew she would be unfaithful, so I confused her sexuality and she called herself being faithful to a faggot, and resented it, because she carried a lot of shame and guilt.

[redacted] would get into relationships with men because she was afraid of what people might think. Therefor she was made vulnerable to blackmail. The shame is the fact that she really wants a man, the guilt is the fact that she knew what she was doing was wrong. I couldn't chance an unwanted pregnancy, which is all I really asked of her, "Please don't have another man's child"

The situation she got involved in concerning both [redacted] and this dude [redacted] im willing to bet is centered around her confused sexuality, and she has nothing to be ashamed of, because I did it to her. One of us had to do it anyway, I figured it was better her then he. What's important is she has to overcome it, if she doesn't im gonna try to kill every homosexual on the face of the earth, if I can't save my wife, they can't be saved.

FROM:VAN NUYS CITY ATTY. TO:43104780153 [illegible] 2, 1992 8:31AM #898 P.05

See I knew that the enermy would go after my wife,and attempt to exploit her weaknesses. She was ashamed of her confused sexuality, and she wanted a man, and believed I was a faggot. The bottomline is [redacted] was confused. I remember hearing [redacted] cries, "why do you keep hurting me, what did I do" This still brings tears to my eyes, so I have to add this, "I really do love [redacted] But I had to suffer and she is a part of me, to be my wife came with a price.

Now you should be able to understand what I mean when I say that, if I lose [redacted] the world will have to suffer. If I lose [redacted] millions of people will die, and millions more will suffer. The world can forget the cure to AIDS, the solution to the ozone, and the solution to the S&L scandal.

You may not take me seriously, but the Federal Government knows who "I AM" they know the deal. If it was about money, I already monopolized the world and im only 33 years old.

This is a test of faith, it's all about love, if I give up on the world as things are now, the world will end, and im tired. The reason I did this to the world is because you'll planned to kill me, because you are all a bunch of fools. Hey there's the Son of Man lets kill him for our sins, do you still want me to die ?

b6
b7C

Ques:

#1) Where are they, in Santa Monica ?
#2) Is there two tennis courts and five bedrooms ?
#3) Did the mansion cost about $4.5M ?

My ANW:

I don't play tennis, but I could learn. But I don't believe I could ever move in there behind him, I might have flashbacks.

Tell [redacted] I said, I think it would be best that she sell that house or we could burn it down and not look back.

I wonder whose schema it was to attempt to divide my estate, there's no such a thing as a settlement with [redacted] I made so much money they could not count it all, they will always be counting, my spending money will equal to Michael's estate minus one penny, which he will insist on giving back plus some, because he is the one who knew who I was all along. Listen to his Dangerous recording.

Sincerely, with love

FROM:VAN NUYS CITY ATTY. TO:43104780153 2, 1992 8:32AM #898 P.06
JUN 30 '92 04:39PM USSS NEW YORK FO, P.8/11

8

I Don't want no records of this in the Courts.

b6
b7C

6/19/92

TO [redacted],

I hope you receive this letter in good health and in good Spirits:

So [redacted] has been seeing and living with [redacted] it's out in the open.

I called myself fighting to protect [redacted] life, as well as her family.

Now the rumor is she is secretly married to him, to top it off, im hurt by this. Im not gonna make any threats, because im too tired.

TO [redacted]

Good luck with your wife because you are gonna need it.

TO [redacted] (Your choice)

Good luck with your husband, you do have a choice. (One who will live) or (one who will die)

As for Alimony, [redacted] you owe me for past Support.

Distribution:
THE FBI
John Gotti

(P.S. Now I know what she means by "Good Love is For Free" I make her Rich and while im in a homeless shelter, she fuck's [redacted] in a mansion.)

"Im not saying anymore, but we will see"

Sincerely, With Love

FROM:VAN NUYS CITY ATTY. TO:43104780153 JUL 2, 1992 8:33AM #898 P.09

2

To All Concerned Parties; 5/21/92

I hope you all receive this letter in good health and in good Spirits:

I decided that Since nobody is taking me Serious, and I can't handle my state of mind, then I am going to Washington D.C. to threaten to Kill the President of the United States, George Bush.

IF they do not arrest me or solve my problem Im gonna attempt to kill President George Bush.

No Anwser from [redacted] is the only wrong anwser and I will not accept it. I would be a fool to try to harm her. She isn't my enermy its the people inbetween me and her.

b6
b7C

Sincerely; With Love

P.S. I Dear you to call this a bluFF.

FROM:VAN NUYS CITY ATTY. TO:43104780153 JUL 2, 1992 8:34AM #898 P.10

b6
b7C

To ABC / Retransmit to NBC News: 5/19/92
Concerning JFK:

He was not assassinated, he was set up by the Kennedy Family in a betrayal, they called themselves sacrificing him to change sides.

He was put into a position where he had to die, so his assassination was faked. JFK in return put a contract out on his brother Robert, who was behind it. Robert gave himself away when he ran for President. The miss calculation was his neck broke, I understand once that was repaired he went into the underworld, he didn't want anything else to do with the Kennedy Family.

To [redacted] and [redacted] Retransmit to [redacted]
I hope you receive this letter in good health and in good Spirits:
Concerning Malcolm X
I can tell you this, [redacted] used to gamble with him up town in Harlem, he was a Pimp and so was [redacted] and they had an unresolved problem from back then (Malcolm was a part of an old Pact).

Now they told me Elijah Poole who became Elijah Muhammad was [redacted] cousin, I believe through a marriage, but in this family distant cousin's marry, so I don't know what to tell you, but ask [redacted] in Avon Park FL.

Back to Malcolm, as a child they brought me to him to send him to his death, he insisted on dieing because he knew he screwed up.

I don't recall all of the details, but I know when he found out who I was, he had to die, because he violated a trust, thinking he knew the truth, he became an informant, in an attempt to become #1, and he had to die for that. He died not for what he said, but for what he was thinking he said. (He violated a trust, and tried to sell out the people).

[redacted] can tell the truth, Malcolm X was not a hero, neither was Dr. King. Nobody will harm you [redacted] but if your gonna use my money tell the truth, and my word will support you to the end.

"Unlimited Funds".

He said " I have to die " that was how he repented. Where in the case of Dr. King the Levites killed him, they made him through the media, and killed him for speaking against the war.

" They where both set up, they both wanted to be number one "

Sincerely; With Love

FROM:VAN NUYS CITY ATTY. TO:43104780153 JUN 2, 1992 8:35AM #898 P.11

b6
b7C

Dear [redacted] / WBLS 5/18/92

I hope you receive this letter in good health and in good spirits:

I know I said I wouldn't fax anymore, but I just spoke to my brother inlaw and he told me about your call, and this is important for you to understand.

I just came back from the FBI at 26 Federal Plaza, and I handed over a 91 page document, plus the two pages I faxed this morning.

Now if you want information or have information you can call the FBI at (212) 335-2700. I expect to hear from them on wednesday.

Now trust me on this [redacted] the only way out for the Jackson Family is through me, you can't get security to protect them from me, because im responsible for their security.

My interest is that half of Michael's estate is mines, my proof is if he doesn't pay up im going after him.

They controlled me because of my love for [redacted] now if [redacted] leaves me, not only will she be a broke bitch by my doing, but the Mafia will kill her, because she was unfaithful and they have no more use for her. If she accepts me she will be protected, because they can not bring harm to my wife, because if they play killing wife games, they must remember that, ("I hate to say it, but it's true") im the number one killer, but hey, for the most part I did it for the government, that's why I was granted legal immunity. As for why didn't anybody know ? (Read:MK:6:4-6) My sister is also confussed.

For the Jackson Family, I will protect them even if it means killing them.

[redacted] I owe you $1M for what you did. (Thanks)"

To all concerned Parties; 5/18/92

I hope you receive this letter in good health and in good spirits;

I just want to say that im sorry for all that I have done to this world. My heart is full of regret for all that I have caused, yet I realize that I have travelled to far to turn back now. And it is crazy, in that I did all that I have done, that the world would know that I have come, and still can I find one who believes ?

With the world at the verge of total destruction, I delivered to you the truth, but you refuse to put your faith in GOD, rather you trust in intellectuals who are only out for profit, so I wonder are you worthy of me ?

I shared with you my debriefing in fear for my life, only if you could see all the life you may receive if you only believe a small part of it. For the most part it is true, a small part speculation, but even the speculations was designed to protect you. Yet you still ask, who are you? And you still refuse to accept that "I AM", yet without question you accept John Gotti as the GodFather, but you question me when I tell you "I AM" the Son of Man, for the Apostle Paul is [redacted] [redacted] and that GOD the Father is the Holy Spirit, not a man, for the Holy Father who is Jesus Christ is with me. How can you accept him without question, yet question me ?

But now if "I AM" how can you profess that you are a believer and deny me ? Because you do not understand ? Or because you do not wish to understand ? How can you call Michael Jackson the King of Pop, without question, yet question me, when I tell you that "I AM" THE KING OF KINGS, do you really want to put me to the test. Must I take a life to prove I can take a life, do you want it to be by natural causes ? What's one more life after eliminating millions, tell me what's one more, but im so tired of killing people, it's a

FROM:VAN NUYS CITY ATTY. TO:43104780153 2, 1992 8:35AM #898 P.12
JUN 30 '92 04:54PM USS NEW YORK FO P.9/11 31

time for healing. Please don't put me to the test, because I travelled to far to turn back now, and only I can undo what I was made to do.

This world needs me and the Government knows it, and my conditions are fair. I realize the damage I have caused, but may we all realize the damage I will prevent, it will more then balance out.

Only if when I was born in this world, I was not made to fear for my life, very little of what happened would have happened, it could have been so peaceful, but the world made it clear I had to fulfill the Holy Bible Prophecy that you would be made a believer, so you got what you asked for. But now better days are ahead, for those who believe that the Son of Man has come to save the world.

"Please don't put me to the test"

P.S. I also want to add that this is for real, John Gotti didn't want me to get control of my assets because he knows once I do, he can't control me. Because he knows I don't owe him my loyality, but he owes his loyality to GOD, and the spirit of GOD is with me. The reason they won't kill me is because they can't, only I can kill me. If you point a gun at me and pull the trigger you won't hear it go off.

"If you don't believe me, I challenge you to the test" b6 b7C

Dear [ ] 5/19/92

I hope you receive this letter in good health and in good spirits;

Fuck your fax paper, this is important.

I decided rather then let [ ] get killed for leaving me, im gonna kill whoever tries to take her from me, im not taking no for a anwser, because aside from the front off, I don't think I can honestly let go, and she knows this, and is taking advantage of it.

Im sorry but before I let them take [ ] from me, the woman I worked all my life for, dreamed about, and waited all my life for, before they take her, they will have to kill me or be killed.

As I said concerning Michael and John it's business, intill I get into the scene, Michael really can't control his own assets. And the Jackson Family should be with me on this, because Michael has to give each one of his brothers ans sisters $10M on that day, as a settlement. They don't have to be angry with him, he wasn't in position to give to them as he would have liked to. As for [ ] I don't know what to say (Read:GEN;29:15-30)

This is what these Jehovah Witnesses pulled on me and still don't want to pay up, but he's out of daughters, what he gonna do now throw in a grand daughter ?

Ask [ ] does she know [ ]
[ ] Am I crazy ?

Maybe, but im no fool, im sorry but [ ] is a bugged out bitch, the shit she took from punk ass [ ] now [ ] is a dead man.

To [ ] 5/19/92

I hope you receive this letter in good health and in good spirits;

I didn't get any news, which is good news, when you're expecting bad news.

Concerning an argument that I've been addressed with:

Where is my proof ? How can I say half of Michaels estate is m[ine] without documents to prove it ? Where is my certificate of marriage ? If I hire a lawyer how can he present my case ?

ANW: My claims are based on the fact that "I AM" the Son of Man, with legal immunity status. Therefor the cou[rt]s that would normally apply, do not.

Be it the will of GOD, my Judge will be the Holy Father, and I agree to a consistory of [F]reemason's to act as the Jury, in deciding

FROM:VAN NUYS CITY ATTY. TO:43104780153 JUL 2, 1992 8:36AM #898 P.13

JUN 30 '92 04:55PM USS NEW YORK FO

Page P.10/11 32

as to rather or not im telling the truth, in that "I AM" the Son of Man.

See to it that every member receives a clearence to examine my FBI, CIA, and Military Intelligents files, that a honest conclusion can be determined.

As I said, [redacted] could not marry another man, for she has always been my wife, and I consummated our marriage when I took her virginity when she was 13 years old, because she gave me no choice. She was going to be unfaithful, and her virginity mean't something special to her. So how did she get a divorce from a marriage that could not have existed. I granted her an annulment upon her request, [redacted] must do as [redacted] admit she was unfaithful, but I already know. I will be judged in the highest court.

Sincerely, with love

b6
b7C

P.S. If [redacted] has been unfai[...]l in a recent relationship as you was telling me, before I consum[...]te our reconcili[...]on she will go without sex for ninety days, in my presence, so I [...] he enjoyed herself.

Complaint Form
FD-71 (Rev. 2-13-86)

NOTE: Hand print names legibly; handwriting satisfactory for remainder.
Indices: ☐ Negative ☐ See below

Subject's name and aliases	Character of case
[redacted], aka [redacted]	EXTORTION – THREATENING LETTERS
[redacted] VICTIM; — VICTIM; MICHAEL JACKSON — VICTIM	Complainant ☐ Protect Source: HOLLY BECKNER, Deputy City Attorney (b6 b7C)
	Complaint received: ☐ Personal ☑ Telephonic Date 6/29/92 Time 12:10 pm
Address of subject	Complainant's address and telephone number: 818-989-8881 (office number) 818-902-2182 (direct line in office)

Subject's Description

Race	Sex	Height	Hair	Build	Birth date
B	☒ Male ☐ Female	6'			[redacted]
Age		**Weight**	**Eyes**	**Complexion**	**Social Security Number**
		200			[redacted]

Scars, marks or other data [redacted] FBI # [redacted]

Facts of complaint

C advised that S is sending threatening letters to [redacted] [redacted] and MICHAEL JACKSON.

C also advised that S was arrested in 5/92 outside of the White House on charges of threatening the President. (b6 b7C)

C further advised that S is now in custody in Los Angeles for violating a restraining order by showing up at [redacted]

On 7/1/92, C faxed arrest report and sample of letters written by S.

9A-LA-162276-4

Do not write in this space.

SERIALIZED — INDEXED — FILED

JUL 0_ 1992

FBI — LOS ANGELES

BLOCK STAMP

7/7/92 — assign to [redacted] (b6 b7C)

SA [redacted] (Complaint received by)

route copy to [redacted] w/ attachments

Memorandum

To : SAC, LOS ANGELES (9A-LA-142276) (C-1) (P)

Date 7/9/92

From : SA [redacted]

Subject: [redacted] AKA [redacted]
[redacted] - VICTIM;
MICHAEL JACKSON - VICTIM;
[redacted] VICTIM;
THREATENING LETTERS;
OO: LOS ANGELES

b6
b7C

Re FD-71 dated 6/29/92.

For information, on 7/8/92, writer telephonically contacted HOLLY BECKNER, Deputy City Attorney, Los Angeles, California, (818) 902-2182, regarding the complaint she lodged with the FBI on 6/29/92 with respect to captioned matter.

According to BECKNER, subject [redacted] is currently in custody (LA County Jail) on a misdemeanor filing. The charges include two counts of terrorist threats, two counts of stalking and three counts of trespassing. However, BECKNER emphasized that these are all misdemeanors and the actual jail time he will spend if found guilty would be minimal. BECKNER is concerned, given subject's past history, that he truly is a dangerous person and poses a real danger to the JACKSONS and [redacted] is currently held on $50,000 bail and his trial is scheduled to begin the week of 7/14/92. b6 b7C

BECKNER advised that the letters she faxed to the FBI are only a representative sample and the ones that clearly express threats to the JACKSONS and [redacted] There are in fact a large volume of letters that [redacted] has sent all over the country but with the basic theme of having to get back together with [redacted] and eliminating anyone who gets in his way. [redacted] stated that she has four sources for the letters: the U.S. Secret Service, [redacted] security agency, MICHAEL JACKSON's security agency and Paramount Studios. b6 b7C

2 - Los Angeles

RGP/rc

9A-LA-142276-5

SEARCHED INDEXED
SERIALIZED FILED

JUL 14 1992

FBI — LOS ANGELES

[redacted] informed that [redacted] was arrested by the U.S. Secret Service on 5/22/92, as he attempted to get on the White House grounds. Apparently, this was a ploy by [redacted] to attract attention to his "problem" with [redacted] was not prosecuted. [redacted] It was after this incident that he traveled to Los Angeles and was arrested for trespassing. b6 b7C

While in county jail, handwriting exemplars were taken from [redacted] which have been matched to the faxed handwritten letters by an LAPD expert. At the same time, [redacted] made a spontaneous admission that the original letters were booked into his property at the jail. b6 b7C

BECKNER is concerned that her case is not as strong as it seems. Also, she has been advised by [redacted] security agency that they will not produce their client [redacted] for a misdemeanor trial in which the outcome is in doubt. Because of this, BECKNER would like the FBI to assume this case so that it could be prosecuted as a felony in federal court. b6 b7C

BECKNER stated that she is willing to provide the FBI with everything she has regarding this case. It was agreed upon that SA [redacted] would meet with BECKNER at her office on 7/14/92.

2

Memorandum

To : SAC, LOS ANGELES (9A-LA-142276) (C-1) (P)

Date 7/15/92

From : SA [redacted]

Subject: [redacted] AKA [redacted] VICTIM; MICHAEL JACKSON - VICTIM; [redacted] - VICTIM; THREATENING LETTERS; OO: LOS ANGELES

b6 b7C

Re memo of SA [redacted] dated 7/9/92.

For information, on 7/14/92, writer met with Deputy City Attorney HOLLY S. BECKNER at her office, Van Nuys City Hall, 14410 Sylvan Street, Van Nuys, California, (818) 902-2182, with regard to captioned matter.

BECKNER explained that even though the trial concerning JONES is scheduled for today, she is going to trail it for at least two or three more days in order to have time to resolve certain questions. Specifically, she wishes to know if the United States Attorney's Office would consider federal prosecution if she in fact accepts a guilty plea from [redacted] on misdemeanor counts. BECKNER is unsure whether "double jeopardy" would come into play. Also, BECKNER advised that the possibility exists that [redacted] would be a civil process through the California Justice System.

b6 b7C

BECKNER advised that she is willing to take a guilty plea from [redacted] if he is sentenced to court ordered mental treatment as opposed to straight jail time. However, the maximum time [redacted] could get would be one (1) year. BECKNER is uneasy with that since she feels that [redacted] truly represents a danger to [redacted] and [redacted] and to a lesser extent to MICHAEL JACKSON.

b6 b7C

2 - Los Angeles

RGP/rc

9A-LA-142276-6

SEARCHED ___ SERIALIZED ___

BECKNER provided SA [redacted] with copies of all letters and facsimile letters sent by [redacted] to [redacted] and other recipients (newspapers, talk show hosts, etc). Again, she offered to provide whatever assistance would be required by the United States Attorney's Office should it decide to take the case. She furnished the name of LAPD Detective [redacted] (213) 485-7576 (Threat Management Unit) who is actively assisting her.

b6
b7C

SA [redacted] explained to BECKNER that he would make contact with the United States Attorney's Office, present the facts of the case, and hopefully, obtain a prosecutive opinion which would be relayed to her.

2

Memorandum

To : SAC, LOS ANGELES (9A-LA-142276) (C-1) (P) Date 7/15/92

From : SA [redacted]

Subject: [redacted], AKA
[redacted] VICTIM;
MICHAEL JACKSON - VICTIM;
[redacted] - VICTIM;
THREATENING LETTERS;
OO: LOS ANGELES

b6
b7C

For information, on 7/14/92, SA [redacted] contacted Assistant United States Attorney (AUSA) GREGORY W. JESSNER, Los Angeles, California, (213) 894-0511, concerning captioned matter. The facts of the case, as known to SA [redacted] were relayed to AUSA JESSNER. It was also explained that Los Angeles Deputy City Attorney HOLLY BECKNER wished to know if the USA's Office would consider taking over the case. Complicating the matter is the fact that she might take a guilty plea on misdemeanor counts against [redacted] At the same time, independent of her case [redacted]

b6
b7C

AUSA JESSNER advised that the case appeared to be potentially viable and one that his office might prosecute. He stated that "double jeopardy" was not a factor in this matter. However, should [redacted] be found guilty in state court, it would make federal prosecution much more difficult to obtain.

AUSA JESSNER agreed to contact Deputy City Attorney BECKNER and discuss the case with her personally so that a decision could be made as to what venue should hear this matter.

2 - Los Angeles

RGP/rc

9A-LA-142276-7

SERIALIZED

9A-LA-142276-8

SEARCHED ___ INDEXED ___
SERIALIZED ___ FILED ___

FBI — LOS ANGELES

From:
Sec Service NY
Sec Service DC
(Michael Jackson
Sec
Security)
Paramount Studios

b6
b7C

CONTROLLED MATERIAL

PRIVACY NOTICE

This message is intended only for the use of the individual or entity to which it is addressed and may contain information that is privileged, confidential or exempt from disclosure under applicable Federal or State law. If the reader of this message is not the intended recipient or the employee or agent responsible for delivering the message to the intended recipient, you are hereby notified that any dissemination, distribution, or copying of this communication is strictly prohibited. If you have received this communication in error, please notify us immediately by telephone.

[redacted] Here's my P.O. Box, and theres a thing called American Express and Federal Express

Plaza Post office

Box [redacted]

L.I.C. New York 11101

Im gonna call you at [redacted] to confirm you received my request. My position is either [redacted] wants me or she doesn't, regardless im not crazy, Im gonna make it with or without her. But im not gunna be unfaithful because she's an unfaithful bitch. Id rather let go and find someone new. The word for me is not crazy, its ambitious, im gunna get mines or die on the battle field. [redacted]

"You think im gonna continue to suffer, while punk mother fuckers live large at my expense, "Bullshit""

b6
b7C

2/5/92

Dear

b6
b7C

I hope you receive this Letter in good health and in good spirits;

First of all, I want to say that im very disappointed in you For what you did. You embarrassed me and you also disrespected me in the worst way. How do you expect my men to respect me when you do not, See my men know how I Feel about the and what they attempted to do to me. And that article in the Daily news and the word over WBLS, made me look like a chump and Feel smaller then that. What you don't understand is when my men loss respect For me, there is no loyality, and without loyality, how do I protect you, your Father, mothers, sisters, or brothers, and thats a part of my job. I expected something like this out of because she's a stupid bitch, but not by you.

The Media is not a game, you don't Feel me out in the daily news, I gave you my phone number and a address to write me, to avoid this type of situation. You know damm well didn't mastermind a damm thing, and this decision of yours is not professional it's personal. Im not Feeding them anymore, who in the hell are they! and im not gonna allow you

②

to use me again and again [redacted] So that you
can use the money to buy Friends. In 1989
your intentions was to use me, get paid and
run, and [redacted] supported you in doing
that. You know it's true, but I Felt you had b6 b7C
reason to Feel that way, and perhaps time
will heal wounds, but are you back with the
Same attitude. IF you feel that im only Jealous,
then isn't that a good enough reason consideratin
my Situation to avoid them. And trust me.
whatever my feelings are concerning them, it's
not without merit. And I have a lot of questions,
like who in the hell is [redacted], the man
you took on my trip, well you told me you
would take me and I did call. I want to meet
[redacted], and I want to know more about
this Secret marriage that took place in
Europe. As you can see im very confused here,
Like who do you want to be with [redacted] it is
decision time, that's the bottomline. I don't
understand the name of the game you want
to play here, but stop while your ahead because
you will lose, even if there be no winners
you will lose. Forget about [redacted] and
[redacted] you can't work with them period, I

③

I will do everything in my power to destroy them, and your persistence on this issue, will only confirm to me, that this is what you want me to do. I can't understand how you can put these niggers before me, but not only me, but your own brother. Im trying to promote major investment into a project for you, and in doing so establish your brother as a major producer, and you rather feed these pimps.

Im not gonna tell you everything that I know concerning them, but assume I know, or will know, and it's all dirt, filth, because they are nothing but pigs, and no wife of mines, is gonna run behind pigs. If you can't do this project without them, there will not be any project, money we don't need anyway. my concern is on the principles. Are you telling me Fuck you [redacted] or are you saying [redacted] is not good enough for the job. Do you think it's to big for him, ~~while~~ well let me tell you something [redacted] it's to big for you, that's why [redacted] will be a part of this one. Because you have a tendency to take good things and run after people to use you ~~and~~ at the expense of those who love you, like me for example.

b6
b7C

(4)

or anybody else, it just about my turn to live.

IF you got to go to the Media, you go to them with what I tell you to do, IF you don't fully agree with me, you discuss it with me in private. Don't you ever disrespect me like that again, it's not exceptable what so ever.

I expect you to retract that statement, the same way you made it, because that bullshit is out of the question. I still love you [ ] and what I'm saying is out of love. Im not gonna feed my enemy, and only a Face to Face with them can begin to resolve this or end it that much Sooner. Don't try that shit [ ] and I don't care if you get angry about this, just don't try it.

b6
b7C

Sincerely, with Love

[ ]

(Your Husband)

Muslim Journal, Inc. Phone (312) 243-7600
910 W. Van Buren St. No. 100
Chicago, IL 60607-3323 FAX (312) 243-9778

The Indianapolis Recorder
The George P. Stewart Printing Inc.
2901 N. Tacoma AVE
P.O. BOX 18267 Phone (317) 924-5143
Indianapolis, IN 46218

The Alexandria News Weekly
1746 Mason Phone (318) 443-7664
Alexandria, LA 71309

Las Vegas Sentinel-Voice
1201 S. Eastern Ave. Phone (702) 383-4030
Las Vegas, NV 89104

Amersterdam News PH# (212) 932-7400
2340 Fredrick Douglas Blvd.
New York, N.Y. 10027 FAX (212) 222-3842

Star of Zion
A.M.E. Zion Publishing House
P.O. BOX 31005 Phone (704) 377-4329
Charlotte, NC 28231-1005

Speakin' Out News
2006 Poole Ave. NW Phone (205) 852-9449
P.O. Box 2826 FAX (205) 852-9484
Huntsville, AL 35810

Campus Digest Phone (205) 727-8263
Tuskegee University
Tuskegee, AL 36083

The Washington Capital Spotlight Newspaper
1264 National Press BlDG (Phone) (202) 628-0700
Washington, DC 20045 FAX (202) 662-8725

Black Miami Weekly
P.O. Box F
Miami, FL 33147

Capital Outlook
1501 E. Park Phone (904) 878-3895
P.O. Box 11335
Tallahassee, FL 32301

News Reporter Phone (813) 254-2608
1610 N. Howard AVE.
Tampa, FL 33607

Columbia Black News
S.C. Black Media Group
P.O. BOX 11128 PHONE (803) 799-5252
Columbia, S.C. 29211 FAX (803) 799-7709

Houston InFormer
P.O. BOX 3086 PHONE (713) 527-8261
Houston, TX 77253 FAX (713) 524-7028

PLAYERS International Publications
8060 Melrose Ave. Phone (213) 653-8060
Los Angeles, CA 90046 FAX (213) 655-9452

Herald Dispatch
3860 Crenshaw BlVD Ste. 110
P.O. BOX 19027A Phone (213) 291-9486
Los Angeles CA 90008 FAX (213) 291-2123

The San Diego Voice and Viewpoint
P.O. BOX 95 Phone (619) 266-2233
San Diego, CA 92112 (619) 266-0533

Metro Reporter
Reporter Publication Phone (415) 931-5778
1366 Turk St. FAX (415) 931-0214
San Francisco, CA 94115

Ebony Magazine
820 S. Michigan AVE. Phone (312) 322-9200
Chicago, IL 60605

The Final Call Phone (312) 602-1230
734 W 79th St, FAX (312) 602-1013
Chicago, ILL 60620

THE Atlanta Voice
P.O. BOX 92487 (404) 524-6426
Atlanta GA 30314

Chicago Metro News Phone (312) 842-5950
2600 S. Michigan AVE, NO. 308
Chicago, IL 60616

AFRO-American Times
1360 Fulton St. Phone (718) 636-9500
Brooklyn, N.Y. 11216 FAX (718) 857-9115

The New York Voice - Harlem U.S.A.
75-43 Parsons BlVD. Phone (718) 591-6600
Flushing, N.Y. 11366

USA 29

b6
b7C

14755 Ventura Blvd. #1-710
Sherman Oaks, CA 91403

6/13/92

b6
b7C

To all conncerned Parties;

I hope you all receive this letter in good health and in good spirits:

Mainly because [redacted] has showed some interest in me and in this project, I decided to take it one step further.

[redacted] featuring **Earth Wind & Fire in The Elements Of The World.**

The Theme:

First of all let's develope the basic symbolic meanings of the four elements.

Earth: We are talking about the dwelling place of mankind. And the basic story line is that because woman was deceived by the serpent and her man was mislead by her, the ground (Earth) was cursed. So to correct this a man had to come and redirect his woman, and his woman had to overcome the serpent, and put her faith once again in GOD.

"Come back to me"

Wind (Air): We are talking about communications. The Word of GOD was carried by messengers and transmitted through the Air, the Wind blows wherever it pleases. So through the Air the Word was delivered.

Fire: Now we are talking about a purification process taking place. Everyone will be salted with Fire. When we think in terms of mankind, we are talking about the act of repentance, which can be pure hell. With the knowledge of good and evil, and the true desire to do what is good, and do away with evil, we can overcome, but our flesh will make it a challenge.

Water: This is the symbol of the Savior, which in reality is The Power of The Holy Spirit working through a man. The only thing that separates mankind from receiving The Holy Spirit, is man's lack of love. Now understand a true man is both He and Her. It was because of the Savior's love for his wife, that he gained knowledge of himself, that he could save, love and protect his wife. Now in reality we are talking about the church.

Summary: The Elements of the World is a love story about a couple who became spiritually one, but was separated physically for a nice amount of time, and was confused, but yet they held on and reunited, because of the power of love, they overcame.

The drama of this is the two comparisons, on the one hand you had a female who was really born poor but lived rich as far back as she can remember. She became famous with celebrity statis, and so the world of money and lust, turned her away from GOD. You had the male her husband, who was born rich and lived poor as far back as he can remember in terms of reliving an experience. He was looked down upon, he was a drunk, who became homeless. And out of love for his wife he regained knowledge of self, but who would believe him ? But out of love, he believed in himself. While the whole world seemed not to believe him, he wouldn't let go of his dream. So he told the truth and she heard it and knew in her heart, it was her husband, so she turned away from her sinful ways and they reunited.

Ideas in General:

What im gonna do here is jump around and discuss different ideas, that I believe will create an effective project.

#1) Rather then just have one show, allow at least three performances, to accommodate different time zones, east coast, west coast, and europe.

SRJ

JUN 1 8 1992

b6
b7C

#2) The live concert video will be made from all three performances.
#3) Rather then just go on pay per view, also include small music halls and sterio movie theaters to present the concert via satellite.

The advantage to the consumer is they can see the show at a lower cost then to actually go to the live concert. The advantage from a business standpoint is, if we promote this correctly we can create a $100M gate easily over the weekend. The advantage from my standpoint, which the most important, is once these shows are completed, I will be able to spend some real quality time with [redacted] and start a family.

#4) I would like to add [redacted] to the team of professionals, and I would like for him along with EWF to create extended versions to all the songs to be released as singles, once again prior to the album release. An important aspect of the extended remix versions, is I want musicianship and musical engineering, not just turntable turning, and [redacted] can do the job.

#5) On the singles releases, I want two songs released together on the 1st, 3rd, and 5th releases and one song on the 2nd, 4th, and 6th releases, and that should leave us three songs on reserve.

I want to completely dominate the charts early on in the album release, and promote the show by saying things like;

[redacted] is married and there will not be a concert tour with this album, this may be the last chance to see her perform live on stage for awhile, so on, and so on.

When we approuch the last singles release, we can announce the release of the video of her live performances, or we can show it first on cable or network television.

#6) Because we are gonna record at least seven video's prior to the album release, and we are gonna spend crazy money on the video's. I want to point out I want them to be very colorful with modern audio and video effects, with some acting in at least two of them.

Now what we can consider, im not sure about this one, we can consider releasing, The Elements of the World, music video set along with the album, for about $15.00 being that Paramount Communications will be investing into the video's, they should consider the effect or impact this will have on the project. In the one hand people will jump on it, on the otherhand people will have seen and heard the whole package early on.

The result of a music video set release could result in our inability to decide on the singles release. But it could pay off big if we put together good extended singles for radio broadcast, do a good job promoting the concert, and do a good job promoting the concert video.

Now what would be great is if we can effectively inforce some type of copy right law to prevent T.V. broadcast from airing any video that has not been released, this will work. We will develope an enormous interest in the package early in it's release. We can have MTV, BET, VH1, and whoever else saying, if you really want to understand the message behind [redacted] new project you have to see the video set, it's really deep, but unfortunitely because of copy right laws we can only play them as they are released as singles, which I can understand, considering they invested an estimated $30M on the video's alone.

#7) As for the star studded audience, the catch is that they will be coming to pay tribute to [redacted] the first lady of peace.

Page #3

b6
b7C

The audience will be an important part of the show, the fan's will see clips of them coming in and so on, I want the star studded audience to be set up with tables that are served (waited on) and I want Soul Train Dancers all over the place, it's a celebration to remember, that may never be matched. And it's important that we clearly promote the idea that you don't have to gamble to visit Atlantic City, because Atlantic City offers all sorts of great great entertainment for the whole family.
#8) Concerning the stage show, I want the best technical crew that money and influence can gather for a single event. It is very important that we put together a stage that will allow us to create different types of effects. Also keep in mind the star studded audience and the Soul Train dancers will be very much a part of the show, therefor some of the effects should extend to them. For example, smoke laid across the audience floor. Just keep in mind, this is to be a major event, and a really big show.
#9) In order for this to work , the movie theaters that will carry the show, will have to set up sound systems that will allow them to carry a concert sound. So we are talking about major investment dollars. [redacted] may have to sell the idea that these theaters have to look at it as a long term investment, for a new era of entertainment. Now we will need to establish contractors that will be certified by a entertainment committee, that will establish the Studio Standard, the the theaters must meet.
Also let's consider how [redacted] recordings are played back, I want a minimum of $20M a year for three years upon the release of [redacted] new album release, with a $5M bonus upon the new album release in advertisement endorsements, from consumer electronic companies. This is my minimum standards and as for the commercials, we will do all the work before the album release.
#10) I suggest to [redacted] that this album cover be more colorful then [redacted] and watch who you thank and for what, im sorry but I do get jealous. But in general the [redacted] cover concept wasn't bad, to include the words to each song inside, is very effective. I want to insure quality and control over the actual tapes to insure consumer protection. I want the tapes to offer hours of defective free playing time, if you know what I mean. Also you might consider on the back of the package, rather then just advertise the names of the songs, advertise the package inside. For example [redacted] This is a Earth Wind And Fire Performance: A [redacted] Words to Songs Inside: Fan Club Information Included: And so on. Remember the package sells the product, so use it to advertise. Don't just go on your name, humble yourself and try to reach out.
#11) We can consider releasing a limited edition special remix album, which will consist of the remixed singles released, which will be a group of remixed extended versions. Perhaps our standard might be the number one hits from the album The Elements of The World.
#12) I want all of [redacted] fan mail put into storage for at least five years, and the addresses of the senders put on a disk, with the date of the mail arrival and I want a system of retrieval. I want the system to automatically kick of an alarm when a name or address comes up on a consistant basis. If there is a fan out there really interested in [redacted] I want to know. What happened to me, I don't ever want to go unnoticed again. This will be a part of my security team's responsibilities.

#13) Concessions such as T-Shirts, Caps, Sweat Suits, Posters, and so on. Alot of concessions sales will be effected in one hand, but boosted on the other. Because there will be no concert tour, to prevent an over stock we may have to limit our stock amoung the theaters and be willing to except any unsold undamaged products back. The adjustment I want to make to more then balance this out is, to not use concessions to advertise the project, but to promote the idea behind the project, which is love.

I want our products sold as sports wear right beside [redacted] [redacted] and right beside Black Cultural type concessions, it's not all about glamour, it's about the message. Also I want to do business with the street venders. As I said, it's about the message, so I want our items to be seen, remember that the Wind blows wherever it pleases.

And I want to close this letter by saying that the actual details concerning this project should remain confidential for copy right purposes, and I respect that you all are professionals and will be able to work it out.

b6
b7C

Distribution:

[redacted]

Earth Wind And Fire

[redacted]

Sincerely; with love

[redacted]

Plaza Post Office
Box
L.I.C. New York 11101

NEW YORK, NY 102
PM
15 JUN
1993

29 USA

b6
b7C

Paramount Communications
Melrose AVE.
Hollywood, CA 90038
c/o FBI

6/7/92

To all concerned Parties;

I hope you all receive this letter in good health and in good spirits:

Im writing this letter to establish some form of coordination amoung the professionals that "I AM" calling on, to work together in a project that I feel is very important. Im writing this letter in order that you all may establish a schedule that will allow this projec to be fulfilled in a timely fashion.

In assigning indivisuals a task, you will find my directives to be very generalized, the important thing to understand concerning this is, I realize that you all are professionals, so I feel that a general idea is all that you will need.

Project Name: [redacted] **"The Elements Of The World" Featuring Earth Wind And Fire.**

b6
b7C

My Administration:

[redacted] **(Right Hand)** His job is to keep up with all the aspects of the business, and be able to take charge in a moments notice. As my General Assistant he will act on my behalf on a regular basis.

[redacted] **(Business Administrator)** Where [redacted] is incharge of Organizational Operations, [redacted] has the responsibility of actually handling the business aspects of the organization. He has to interpret all business dealings with an understanding of my position and interest, with the help of a team of advisors. [redacted] will advise me on business decisions, once the decision is made, he will basically handle the paperwork. [redacted] knows what he got his college degree for.

[redacted] **(Certified Accountant)** Again [redacted] knows what he went to college for. The bottomline is [redacted] whose nick name is [redacted] job is to count the money, and make sure everybody gets paid, especially the government.

[redacted] **(Business Liaison or Promoter)** [redacted] is the contact, he will make any request known to the administration, and deliver our response. As a Promoter he will do his job, he has experience in the field. Which means plenty of air time on radio and T.V. broadcast.

[redacted] **(Security Chief)** Once again the man has experience, and a legal gun permit, and im confident that he knows his job.

Before I request the Professional Assistance necessary for this project, I want it to be clearly understood, money is no object, just ask for a fair price, which is no higher then top pay.

b6
b7C

Professional Assistance Request:

[redacted] **(Performance** [redacted] will also be responsible for her selection of dancers, and choreography and or selection of Choreographer. Songs selection, some song writing, and arrangements, album cover concept, wardrobe selection, and selection of Cosmetologist. Also I expect [redacted] to use her professional experience to know what to want and need, the benifit of my men is we will get it for her.

Earth Wind And Fire: (Performance) I want EWF to focus their energy on creating the best sound performance possible.

Page #2

b6
b7C

[redacted] **(Producer)** Once the project is put into writing and everybodies responsibilities are made clear, see to it that the job gets done. I want this presentation to be a reflection of [redacted] imagination, with the performance of EWF this can be limitless from an artistic standpoint. Let [redacted] set her own goals and standards, then you reinforce her when she gets weary. Also I would like for you to assist in song writing.

Song Writers: I want [redacted] and EWF to work this out together, [redacted] has the final word on all but two songs, which will be decided by EWF.

[redacted] **(Director)** I want a 30 minute for T.V. first video release, plus at least six additional video's recorded prior to the album release. And im talking about top quality video's.

[redacted] **(Paramount Communications)** I want Paramount Communications to cover all the expenses for [redacted] [redacted] video's. I want Paramount Communications to handle this one in the same manner as a movie. Im talking in the area of $30M. Now here's the catch, there will be no tour with "The [redacted] album, but there will be a one night only performance "Pay Per View" with an all star cast, we are talking about [redacted] with Earth Wind And Fire on one stage, performing out of Atlantic City, before a star studded audience.

"One Show" im gonna give Paramount Communications the rights.

[redacted] We are talking about a really big show, and crazy promotions for your hotals, we are talking about [redacted] featuring Earth Wind And Fire, in a one show only "Pay Per View" concert, out of the Taj Mahal. This will be the beginning of something big. I want the use of your property for at least two video's and I want you to pay us for promoting your hotals. "A day at the Taj Mahal, like living in a dream world" Throw in the Rolls.

Distribution:

Earth Wind And Fire

b6
b7C

Sincerely; with love

Plaza Post OFFice
Box
L.I.C. New York 11101

b6
b7C

Paramount Communications
Melrose Ave.
Hollywood, CA 90038

RECEIVED - L A
APR 1 0 1992

SRJ

APR 1 3 1992

4/15/92

4-6-92

and the Executive board of Paramount
cations.

e you receive this letter in good health and in good Spirit
ormation included with this letter clearly states my
d what I want done about it. To insure you take the
eriously, I registered this Letter, and here is a Few
significant references.

Jesus christ is my Holy Father)

eorge Bush	MR. John Gotti
te House	MCC 150 PARK ROW
nsylvania AVE.	New York, N.Y. 10007
on, DC 20500	This is my biological Father
Government OFFicial)	(THE GodFather OF New York)

in L. Powell
agon
n, D.C. 20301
s OF StaFF, Chairman)

o Cuomo
apital
N.Y. 12224
OF New York)

d Dinkins
ll
N.Y. 10007
New York City)

Sincerely with Love

aily News on

b6
b7C

15, 1992

M HOLLYWOOD
ECK & STACY JENEL SMITH

SE TO PLAY
PING TOM

JISE WILL PLAY THE DE-
oyeur in Paramount's big-screen
on of **Ira Levin**'s best-selling
r – if producers **Bob Evans**
donald get their way.
Eszterhas ("Basic Instinct") is

wrapping up his adaptation of the book now and with any luck a cast and director will be set in time for shooting to start in New York in June.

On another front, Evans and Macdonald are after **Arsenio Hall** to star in a biopic on jazz great **Cab Calloway**. Para-
the producers have a multi-pic-
decided not to go along with
nd the film makers are now talk-
king it for HBO.

ab Calloway, theres
the homeless.
wood role model
personal, so to
ompany look for

RECEIVED - L
APR 2 7 1992

veterans.

#1

4-5-92

ncerned;

u all receive this letter in good health and in
ts

2: I realize that you'll are not a messenger service,
e in the business of broadcasting, and im simply
. Fan who respects your ability of rapid communications
tainers and other Celebrities, so be honored by
t, that you are in a position to be of help.

b6
b7C

try to write AND mail you a personal letter by 4-6-92,
Federal Plaza so expect it. I know I made some
ements concerning you, that you probably found to
re. But true in reality or not true, I had to address
s and the situations, to put a stop to or prevent
ing in anycase. You must believe I love you for this
nce you forget that you became very vulnerable
ulated by lies, it was always my belief in your
that saw me through. That's the blind faith, to
a love you can't see, yet you hold on to it, knowing
ll see you through. Sometimes it mean's talking
ou feel, even if what you say stands to be corrected.
en; "Better is open rebuke than hidden love" (Pr: 27:5)
written; "For Jealousy arouses a husband's fury and
no mercy when he takes revenge" (Pr: 5:34) This is
ainst Adultery, and believe me when I tell you, that
ot always right, and ill tell you the truth, and it still
t right intill you over come it, as it stands.
that, ill briefly state my position: I want
on , with
And File with a team of Producer that will

#2

Hollywood
ortunity, and
the roles
e to me as
d no nudity,
far in your
es when I
piss me off.
and how I
essional, so
, separate, and
ly movie
or do you
you make

ith my wife
dvise you
ing. As for
lergymen for,

ns;
, as the husband
ramount
sonal interest
is for me.

it's a new signature
ange.

From the S/V/D

3/31/92

To all concerned parties;

I hope you all receive this letter in good health and in good spirits:

Im gonna get straight to the point, I don't like what I saw last night at the 64th Annual Academy Awards, or what im seeing, that's going on in Hollywood, and being that "I AM" Paramount Communications, [redacted] you can take this personal.

What I see is an association that is connected to a industry, that is obligated to keeping this association employed, and as far as im concerned the association that all the movies are being written for, consist of to many white faces and not enough others, and that's gonna have to change, or the executive branch is gonna have to change, in the union and production leadership, as things are, it is unacceptable.

If in no other industry, the movie industry should be a reflection of the nation that it serves, and the direction it is traveling in, and our nation is no longer traveling in the direction of white race supremacy or European control, but in the direction of true freedon and justice for all.

b6 b7C

What im calling for is not a new line of low budget black expectation films, to exploit black people, but for the writers and Hollywood leadership, to take the moral responsibility, and offer not a bunch of distorted views, but to present a reflection of hope to the American people, regardless of race. Everyday I leave out to the streets of New York City, I see people of all races, should any movie about city life be any different ?

Hollywood must address the real world, the real problems, and the real solutions of today, it's not about the 60's it's about the 90's, so hide the truth ? No it's time to tell the truth.

I don't like what I see, as far as im concerned, in the current direction Hollywood is traveling , Hollywood is an enermy of the American people, Hollywood will change or be destroyed.

My call for a change in Hollywood is not a request, but a demand, and [redacted] you can take this personal, because I don't like how Paramount Communications is investing my families money in the movie industry, and im not going for it. I want the union, movie production, and minority leadership to come togerher and resolve this ASAP. (AS SOON AS POSSIBLE)

Sincerely: with love

JUN 23 '92 01:50PM U[...] WASHINGTON FO P.7/9

5/9/92

TO WBLS/Retransmission Please:

Dear [redacted]

b6
b7C

I hope you receive this letter in good health and in good Spirit

Concerning Black Community development:

Listen to me [redacted], the first thing that you need to do is sway away from two party politics, and Move closer to the Church, that may represent your rightful position "A spokesman of God". The black comm must grow out of the welfare mentality, Seeking hand outs. The Black Comm needs control over their own assets, that's the problem. Get away from t 60's mentality, and the Dr. King (Black Solution.) "He was a sell out."

Let me tell you something, Dr. King was a collaborator of the so-cal Jews, who knew he was not me, so they killed him. Because he came them, but not in my name, but out of his own selfish motives. Had he I might have had to kill damn near all of you'll, for putting him before me. Had he come in my name, he would have known they are my Levites

And now they must be protected, especially in Europe. (Read: JN:13: then (Read: JN:13:29) then (Read: NU:1:47:54) then (Read: NU:1:51 AND NU:1:53) then (Read: Nu:18:21-24).

I told you about the S&L Scandal, "I AM" the S&L, the Federal government owes me. So stop trying to squeeze water out of the wrong Rock, and return to the church and go to the Levites in my name. If they deny you, I will destroy them all.

And try talking to President Bush, instead of against him, for the most part I agree with him. I mean what does it take for black people to wake up and see the light. The Mind of Jesus Christ is within [redacted] Anybody could have said Jesus Christ sent me, but who ever knew he took on the name [redacted]?

Sincerely: With Love

b6
b7C

P.S. When im once again made perfect, I will come in the name of the "Holy Father"

JUN 23 '92 01:51PM USSS WASHINGTON FO P.8/9

b6
b7C

14755 Ventura Blvd. #1-710
Sherman Oaks, CA 91403

Mr. Michael Jackson
P.O. BOX [illegible]
Los Angeles, CA 90093-3024

Memory [illegible] System

WBLS Promo	Fax:	1 (M1) 6	1 (212) 697-6026
WBLS Sales	Fax:	1 (M2) 9	1 (212) 661-7409
Daily News	Fax:	1 (M3) 0	1 (212) 949-2120
ABC Radio	Fax:	1 (M4) 3	1 (212) 456-5533
Afro-Amer.	Fax:	8 (M5)	(718) 857-9115
Egeria	:	(M6)	1 [illegible]
Lujuana	:	(M7)	(718) 729-0966
WBLS Promo	:	Fire	1 (212) 953-0300
TWU	FAX:		1 (212) 721-1431

Ozone Park Clubhouse:
The Bergin Hunt and Fish Club
98-04 101st Ave

[illegible] Ravenite Social Club
247 Mulberry St.

JUN 23 '92 01:51PM US WASHINGTON FO P.9/9

Forty Acres and a mule music works
124 DeKalb St.
Brooklyn, N.Y. 11217
c/o

b6
b7C

Philip Morris Agency
58th St. and 6 Ave
New York. N.Y.

(212) 949-2120 FAX Dails

News Tips — 210-6397

N.Y. Daily News (21150) (212) 210-2100 FAX (212) 662-2597

(212) 338-1659

N.Y. Post (21292) (212) 815-8000 FAX (212) 349-2511

MTV PH# (212) 713-6400 FAX (212) 713-6931

ABC Radio Networks PH# (212) 887-5200 FAX (212) ~~889~~ 456-5333

USA Network PH# (212) 408-9100 FAX (212) 408-3600

(?) ECC Management Services 1-800 441-8618 ext. 684

TDI — (212) [illegible]

661-3344 [illegible]: (718) 729-1490

b6
b7C

JUN 30 '92 04:36PM US NEW YORK FO P.2/11

2

5/21/92

TO All Concerned Parties;

I hope you all receive this letter in good health and in good Spirits:

I decided that since nobody is taking me Serious, and I can't handle my state of mind, that I am going to Washington D.C. to threaten to kill the President of the United States, George Bush.

IF they do not arrest me or solve my problem Im gonna attempt to kill President George Bush.

No Anwser from [redacted] is the only wrong anwser and I will not accept it. I would be a fool to try to harm her, She isn't my enermy its the people inbetween me and her.

Sincerely; With Love

b6
b7C

P.S. I Dear you to call this a bluFF.

Threat to Pres.

(From Sec Service pages 2-30)

JUN 30 '92 04:37PM USDOJ NEW YORK FO

P.4/11

4

6/5/92

To all concerned Parties;

I just want to say im happy to be back, and I have a lot of paperwork to catch up on this weekend.

The Statements on the document that recorded my actions are not true, but the truth will be revealed.

Sincerely: with Love

b6
b7C

P.S. UNDERSTAND THAT I LOVE [redacted], AND REFUSE to let go, so IF she got into a relationship, that's understandable., but she has to understand, she has to let go, because nobody is gonna take my [redacted] and I made that point clear at the White House.

JUN 30 '92 04:38PM USSS NEW YORK FO P.5/11 5

6/5/92

TO WBLS: ____ b6 b7C

The Secret Service at the White House told me about ____ love Scene. they said they couldn't get her to do one intill ____ they asked me did I want to see it, because I could she her nudity, they said nobody need ever know but ~~me~~ it.

I said "no", why do you want to show me that shit, if anything you made her out of a unfaithful bitch, so now I won't have to worry about her anymore, because she feels guilty (to that effect)

I said I don't ever want to see that shit, and if ____ doesn't edit all that shit out, he is a dead man. (It wasn't a love scene, he fucked her).

They admited ____ had at least five abortions, I said how could you let ____ do that to her, you know he planned to kill, you know ~~this~~ he is John Gotti's buddy, you know he is a crook, so you had to know ____ bullshit was a set up.

See ____ they planned to kill your friends.

It's all about money and power, im gonna be busy today, but monday im gonna blow your mind.

Sincerely' With Love

____

JUN 30 '92 04:38PM USS NEW YORK FO P.7/11

7

6/8/92

To all concerned Parties;

I hope you all receive this letter in good health and in good spirits:

Concerning [redacted] [redacted] is nothing but John Gotti's puppet on a string. His mission is to become President in order to grant John Gotti a Presidental Pardon, and let me warn you [redacted] is no joke and he really can win. No man should be that Powerful, no man should have all the money and legislative authority

John Gotti has to give up some of the money, in a give and take negotiation. John Gotti's only crime is that he became to powerful, because everything is tied to the federal government.

Because of the importance of a check and balance system im against [redacted] going to the White House. But because of the Seriousness of th[redacted], candidacy and the Billions of dollars behind him, I say this as a warning to the Government and people of the United States of America, grant John Gotti the right to an appeal, and complete the negotiations for the conditions of his release. My position is he pay up and get from between me and my wife.

I love John, but he is a selfish bastard, he wants to control everyone and everything, and he is taking this shit to far. "Now it's [redacted] next what?"

You can't keep John down, he has to much money, negotiate and free him before it's to late, because his next move, you figure out.

Sincerely, with Love

b6
b7C

JUN 30 '92 04:39PM USS NEW YORK FO P.9/11

9 6/10/92

To all concerned Parties;

I hope you all receive this letter in good health and in good spirits:

I may be a little premature concerning this, but I feel it is best that I discuss this ahead of time, to insure a timely response.

Sincerely; with love,

b6
b7C

JUN 30 '92 04:40PM USS NEW YORK FO 10 P.10/11

b6
b7C

Important Retransmission 6/11/92.

To [redacted] / WBLS.

I hope you receive this letter in good health and in good Spirits:

It is very important that what im about to Say, be Completely understood.

Im Convinced that a Scheme is taking place to divide my assets held by [redacted] which Could never happen.

The U.S. Government will not recognize any marriage that [redacted] may call herself. involved with other then with me, we are Separated; but can never get divorced. my position concerning her coming back to me, is to insure that She is ready to at least attempt to be faithful, I realize She has some problems, but She has to at least want to do right by me before our reconciliation, right now I don't think She is being honest.

My Speculation is that the missing quantity is an older woman, who out of [redacted] confused State turned to for guidance, and [redacted] was convinced she could use the California Laws to divide my assets held by her to act as an insurance policy, sort of 50% with me and 50% to the Gay world, then she could leave me and make it 75% to the Gay world, the only problem is she can never leave me, and she can forget returning to her old ways. Im gonna have this investigated. In anycase as we all know I have telepathy and I must be keyed in to correct some of these problems, and as a condition [redacted] will have to see me, so it's not worth Scheming on me, ill find out Sooner or later.

You may be hearing from some of my men, just cooperate with them. "They must find [redacted]

Sincerely, with Love

JUN 30 '92 04:41PM US NEW YORK FO P.11/11

Plaza Post Office

Box

L.I.C. New York 11101

b6
b7C

FBI
26 Federal Plaza
New York, N.Y. 10007

P.3/11

Plaza Post Office
Box
L.I.C. New York 11101

b6
b7C

FBI
26 Federal Plaza
New York, N.Y. 10007
ATTN: Agent

JUN 30 '92 04:44PM USSS NEW YORK FO

JUN 30 '92 04:46PM USS NEW YORK FO P.8/11

6/14/92 18

b6
b7C

Dear

It was I who sent you a proposal in my alis I use this name to write my ideas down and you can say im writing a book. The nature of my discussion is love, respect, and loyality.

The story line is this, when my day comes and people ask, where did this guy come from ? The only question im gonna have is, did you read the book ?

As for the references and witnesses on the resume, to put it simply. I say a lot of things and I don't have any problems with anyone in terms of violence.

I realize some people find what im saying difficult to understand, and to a degree I must admit that im somewhat confused. But I do know this, I really do love and I truly believe that if I continue to be loyal, everything is gonna work out for the best. This is my test of faith and my loyality must be to GOD Almighty.

To get to the point, , as a result of your people checking on me, as they put it. In any case, if I can't get this resolved, im in need of immediate employment.

If you are interested in my proposal, I don't want my employment with you to interfere with any negotiations. can not work for you, only with you, but can. I'll stop by your office sometime this week if necessary.

Sincerely,

(A Wanna Be)

JUN 30 '92 04:51PM USSS NEW YORK FO P.2/11 24

Communications System.

In order to insure orderly organizational operations, amoung the CRIPS, im gonna put the CRIPS under the control and directives OF the Freemason's.

Each Local CRIPS charter will be assigned to a local masonic Lodge, who will be responsible for transmitting information within the Local CRIPS Charter.

THE FIAG: Being the liaison between the CRIPS and the Freemason's, will be a member of the masonic lodge, and will manifest both the masonic and CRIPS codes. (Grips and Pass words

The Flag will deliver the information to the administrative body of the local CRIPS Charter, and receive any request that the Local CRIPS Charter might have, and assist the CRIPS to the degree he is authorized.

The directive "I AM" now sending down is for the CRIPS to remove the baseball caps, when I said get rid of the colors. I didn't mean replace them with Sports wear.

I want the Freemason's to teach the CRIPS a new system of communications, and replace their colors with codes.

The universal code is for all CRIPS to get along but the local codes, must be protected amoung the local Charters. Local codes must not be Violated This is to insure central control.

Sincerely with Love

b6
b7C

JUN 30 '92 04:51PM USS NEW YORK FO P.3/11 25

The Universal Code
Of
The C.R.I.P.S.

C.R.I.P.S. Defined
Christians: Ac:11:25-26
Resurrection: 1Co:15:42-45
International: NIV Holy Bible
Powerful: Mk:1:7-8 & 1Jn:5:5-8
Sovereign: 2Pe:2:1-3

Authentic C.R.I.P.S.
test of
Brotherhood

Back ↑ .... Inside ↑ Front

The Universal Code
Q. May I cross your path ?
A. Most certainly if you come with truth.
Q. How do you identify the truth ?
A. They called disciples christians.
Q. Do you believe in the resurrection ?
A. Most certainly "It is raised in power" Is all about a consciousness-raising of my people.
Q. How do you know these things ?
A. I study the NIV, we are international, free, and accepted all over the world.
Q. Explain the element water, how can water symbolize the savior, if it is written, "But he will baptize you with the Holy Spirit" ?

The Universal Code
A. The Spirit, The Water, and The Blood, is The Father, The Word, and The Holy Spirit.
Jesus Christ is The Word of GOD. (Understand that The Son, came by The Word, and by The Spirit of GOD.) Therefor his Word is Bond.
Q. What does this all mean ?
A. GOD is powerful.
Q. Are there false prophets amoung the people ?
A. Just as there will be false teachers amoung you. They will even deny the Sovereign Lord who bought them.

Pending approval by Freemason's to be Printed on thin cardboard.

Plaza Post office
Box
L.I.C. New York 11101

b6
b7C

THE FBI
26 Federal Plaza
New York, N.Y. 10007
Agent:

JUN 30 '92 04:52PM USS NEW YORK FO P.4/11

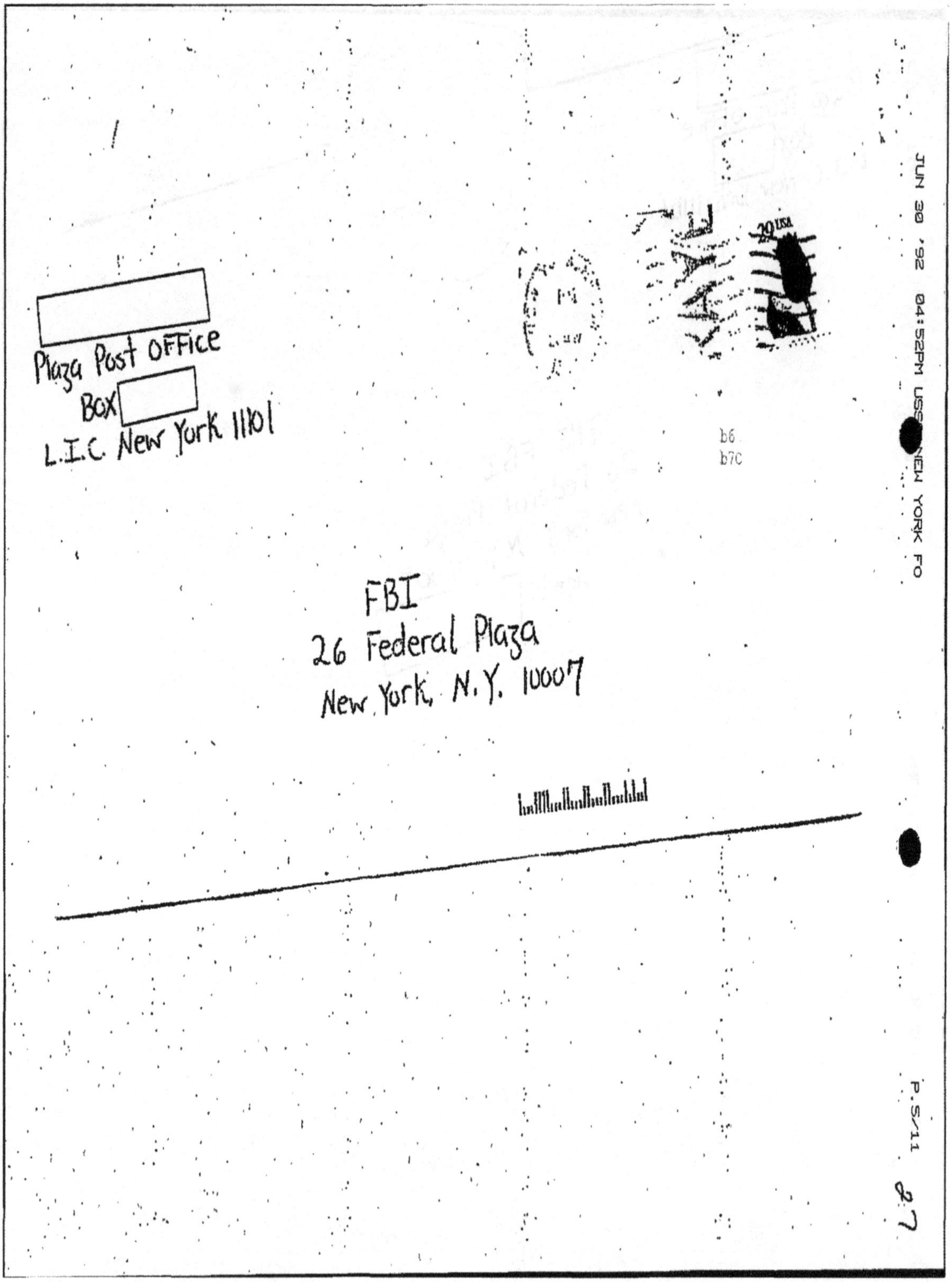

Plaza Post Office
Box
L.I.C. New York 11101

b6
b7C

FBI
26 Federal Plaza
New York, N.Y. 10007

JUN 30 '92 04:52PM USSS NEW YORK FO P.5/11

27

34 Post Office
Box
L.C. New York 11101

b6
b7C

NEW YORK, NY
PM
20 MAY
1992

X-RAYED

THE FBI
26 Federal Plaza
New York, N.Y. 1000?

Additional Note: Concerning Freemason's; 5/20/92

What will be established is that all the member's of this consistory of Freemason's will become a witness of the truth, you can not be a Member of this Consistory and not recognise that "I AM" the Son of Man, and you can not be a Freemason and not believe "I AM" the Son of Man. This is the Secret behind Prince Hall.

"Therefor, how can I be denied."

b6
b7C

NEW YORK, NY 102
PM
6 FEB
1992
USA
29
b6
b7C
SEARCHED SERIALIZED INDEXED FILED
FBI — LOS ANGELES
14755 Ventura Blvd. #1-710
Sherman Oaks, CA 91403

'laza Post Office
Box
.I.C. N.Y. 1110|

NEW YORK, NY 102
PM
1994

29 USA

9A-LA-142276-10

SEARCHED ____ INDEXED ____
SERIALIZED ____ FILED ____
JUL
FBI — LOS ANGELES

b6
b7C

14755 Ventura Blvd. #1-710
Sherman Oaks, CA 91403

b6
b7C

4-6-92

Dear ______

I hope you receive this Letter in good health and in good Spirits;

I just want to tell you that I love you very much, and you stay on my mind, I want to tell you how much im hurting inside, but I believe your attitude right now is, you Feel why should I get personal now, I told everybody everything already, and I understand.

But ______ I still love you very much, and if you want to Fax my letters to everybody and rat me out, and tell everybody im a cry baby, that's O.K. today. As long as they know im crying because of how bad im being treated.

I wrote ______ and asked him to advise you, on basically everything, (personal and Spiritual matters,) and if you got it in you, I want him to baptize you, I Feel you have a habit of going to the wrong people For help.. IF you think that the way to build a relationship with me, that is joyful, is done by constintly disagreeing with and disobeying me, your wrong. "Stop trying to test me on every issue, test the people who put you up to this For a Change, even if its you, because testing me is only grounds For an excuse, For your next Fuck up. Please give me a break ______ I can't do this alone. Im about to give up on ______ I had it with her and ______ in name only marriage. Im at the point where ______ and ______ can go to hell together. I guess it will be me, you and ______ unless ______ turns out to be another fucking trader, I guess ill write her and see

#2

b6
b7C

how she is doing. When I married her I thought she was you," Don't ask me" but she prepared me for you, two of a kind, and I had to go through the same shit with her. "Such profanity" So now your gonna tell everybody? I believe you and [redacted] will get along very well, about the same age, simular background one lived in wealth, one lived in poverty, both fine as it gets, I got good taste.

I realize that im gonna have to treat you'll as the weaker of the two, being me the Head, you'll the body, you'll can never be as spiritually strong as me, but I demand respect. Remember that you'll are not married and can never marry, but are one in me, you'll are my wife and it is me that you'll must serve, we are not playing closet games, im not the front man, im the husband, not you, not [redacted] and what goes on in my bedroom stays in my bedroom, all the women in my bedroom are my women, and are not to be touched outside my bedroom. And in my bedroom I will be respected and served right or all hell breaks loose.

Sincerely' with Love

[redacted] Your Husband

LAST KNOWN ADDRESS

P.S.

I Don't Know what last name she is using.

#1

4-5-92

To all concerned;

I hope you all receive this letter in good health and in good Spirits.

TO WBLS: I realize that you'll are not a messenger service, but you are in the business of broadcasting, and im simply a personal Fan who respects your ability of rapid communications with entertainers and other Celebrities., so be honored by my request, that you are in a position to be of help.

b6
b7C

TO [redacted]

Im gonna try to write AND mail you a personal letter by 4-6-92, out of 26 Federal Plaza. So expect it. I know I made some public statements concerning you, that you probably Found to be offensive. But true in reality or not true, I had to address the attitudes and the situations, to put a stop to or prevent From happening in any case. You must believe I love you For this to work, once you Forget that you become very vulnerable to be manipulated by lies, it was always my belief in your love for me that saw me through. That's the blind Faith, to believe in a love you can't see, yet you hold on to it, knowing that GOD will see you through. Sometimes it mean's talking about how you Feel, even if what you say stands to be corrected. It is written; "Better is open rebuke than hidden love" (Pr: 27:5) And it is also written; "For Jealousy arouses a husband's Fury and he will show no mercy when he takes revenge" (Pr: 5:34) This is a warning against Adultery, and believe me when I tell you, that the truth is not always right, and ill tell you the truth, and it still won't make it right intill you over come it, as it stands. Now with that, ill briefly state my position; I want you to work on [redacted] with Earth, Wind, And Fire, with a team of Producers that will include [redacted], I already explained to you

#2

Why. As for movies, I believe a career in Hollywood would be good for you, and you deserve an opportunity, and you've acted before, Im all for it, as long as the roles you perform are dignified, as well as respectable to me as your husband off the screen." No love scenes and no nudity, don't even allude to nudity, I think you went to far in your music videos, I don't watch them, and sometimes when I hear the songs, and think about the videos, they piss me off. Put yourself in my position and you'll understand how I feel, and it's O.K. to be friendly, but still professional, so remember that. Keep you profession and intimacy separate, and we will get along. [redacted] is not the only movie director O.K., do you want to be a actress or do you just want to work with [redacted] Sometimes you make me wonder about you.

b6
b7C

To [redacted] keep your relationship with my wife professional and we will get along, the only advise you give her is on her acting, you can suggest anything. As for advise thats what she got me, her parents and clergymen for, with that you got a future in Hollywood.

To [redacted] of Paramount Communications;
You will be hearing from me soon. For now, as [redacted] [redacted] Paramount Communications, I request that you take a personal interest in my wife's career in movies, please do this for me.

Sincerely, with Love

What can I say, it's a new signature subject to change.

P.S. [redacted] You will be hearing from me soon.

SEARCHED INDEXED
SERIALIZED FILED
FBI — LOS ANGELES

...za Post Office
Box
L.I.C. New York 11101

b6
b7C

14755 Ventura Blvd. #1-710
Sherman Oaks, CA 91403
c/o FBI

NOTE: Retran[redacted]nission do to Sign[redacted] indication OF a possible System Failure on last transmission, Which Since been Corrected. [redacted]

Request Retransmission b6 b7C 4-24-92

To all concerned Parties;

#1) To [redacted] (ques.) Why no love scenes? (Anw.) Because I said so. Let me tell you a story; I know this Female who was out there, and she once said to me, [redacted] do you really think I love my husband and do the things I do? come on [redacted] be For real, it acts, all acts, nothing but a Front, [redacted] remember this, "don't believe what a woman tells you, believe in what she do, a woman will tell you anything to get what she wants, but if a woman loves you she will be there For you, and try her best not to hurt you. I be dogging (him/her) [redacted] "watch this". (To that effect.) So to request such a thing, makes me wonder, what's real, and what's all acts. To leave home, to kiss all over a dude while you say, "I love you" over and over, intill the match making producer decides you got it correct, and we know you have to prove to the producer you have all the right parts for the role, "be For real" Im not a chump" all acts, it's a Front.

#2) To [redacted] He claims that theres unFair practices in radio broadcasting, it's like he is claiming nobody wants to play the songs he didn't even release yet. Let me tell you a story; Once I went to a meeting and nobody called on me to speak, so I got angry and said, "this meeting ain't nothing but a bunch of Fucking clicks, just because you didn't know me you didn't call on me". So they changed the rules, they obviously agreed, they decided to call on people they didn't know, but it seems I became the most popular member of the group, because im rarely called on. Now I realize, what I wanted was to be heard, not the rules changed, because I realize im no better then the next person, and I need the support of the group, I can't do it alone. I guess Sometimes it's important to say what you mean, and state what you really want. Sincerely' with Love

③

b6
b7C

with you, you got to stop ignoring me and pay me some attention, like a letter or a phone call, I deserve much more then that, but for now I'll settle for that.

in agreement on this, I can still work, infact I should develope into a better intellectual, because ill be giving myself time to consider my taughts. THEREFOR I will be able to control my own assets. The next Few weeks are gonna be very critical, theres a lot going on behind the scenes, and im not clear on a lot of things, and I have important decisions to make. Don't be Surprised if I visit your parents soon, you can't just keep ignoring me.

Sincerely' with love

P.S. I love you must believe this to be true.

①

b6
b7C

5/30/92

Dear [redacted]

I hope you receive this letter in good health and in good Spirits:

First of all I want you to know that I love very much and that's unconditional, but hard to live up to. The only thing I asked out of you was not to bear another man's child, because I knew that upon our separation they would confuse us to turn on each other "But nothing can come between us" remember that.

Im gonna cover a lot of issues briefly, not in detail.

[redacted] Concerning this movie as well as future movies, I made my position clear on this, no love Scenes, and Certainly no nude clips. Now im not clear on the Situation going on behind the Scenes, but after my interview at the White House, im convinced that [redacted] [redacted] pulled Something under-handed. And my advise to him if he has good health practices is to edit out any and all love scenes, and nude clips and destroy it by fire, because I don't ever ~~wanted~~ want to See it. Such a Scene is disrespectful to me and can only hurt [redacted] I like the good woman homesome look, and im not gonna let Some punk Screw up my life long investment out of Selfish ambition. [redacted] if my reports are correct, I warn you your fucking with the wrong bitch, because if [redacted] is a bitch She is my bitch, don't piss me off [redacted] im gonna see that movie.

THE Reconcillation: understand that you was born for me, when you was 13 years old our marriage was ~~consummated~~ Comsummated, and then we was Separated and Confused, we both was unfaithful one way or

②

b6
b7C

another. the reason you couldn't have ever married [redacted] was because you was already married to me, So I annulled that marriage. A woman can have but one Husband, there is one HEAD to a household. But in the case of [redacted] I married her 30 AUG 85, now ill leave it up to you as to rather or not I annul that marriage, but I warn you, She is the same age as you and has a lot in common with you, She was meant to be your maid Servent. See [redacted] I know you go both WAYS, and So does she, the Holy Bible Said theres not one upright woman on the face of the earth. Your gonna do what your gonna do, I just don't want it to leave MY bedroom.

The women who enter my bedroom must Submit to me, and not have any Sexual contact with anyone outside our Circle. I don't want you running off with a friend because your needs are not being fulfilled at home. So on the issue of Sexuality lets be up front and for real. I think you should meet [redacted] together im sure you'll will make it easy for me. I believe with 4 women we will be able to produce the amount of Children I want, I know [redacted] is a prostitute but you know I can't leave her, you'll are a reflection of me, we are all really just one, what you are also I am as well. "But we shall overcome"

My Situation:

[redacted] You got to Stop this Shit [redacted] you know im deeply in love

Plaza Post Office
Box
L.I.C, New York 11101

0315H 061492 PASADENA CA 91109-9998

NEW YORK, NY 101
PM
11 JUN
1992

29 USA

b6
b7C

14755 Ventura Blvd, #1-710
Sherman Oaks, CA 91403

9A-CA-182276-12

FILED

FBI — LOS ANGELES

b6
b7C

Important Retransmission 6/11/92

To / WBLS.

I hope you receive this letter in good health and in good Spirits:

It is very important that what im about to Say, be completely understood.

Im convinced that a Scheme is taking place to divide my assets held by which Could never happen.

The U.S. Government will not recognize any marriage that may call herself involved with other then with me, we are Separated, but can never get divorced. my position concerning her Coming back to me, is to insure that She is ready to at least attempt to be faithful, I realize She has some problems, but She has to at least want to do right by me before our reconciliation, right now I don't think She is being honest.

My Speculation is that the missing quantity is an older woman, who out of confused State turned to for guidance, and was convinced she could use the California Laws to divide my assets held by her to act as an insurance policy, sort of 50% with me and 50% to the Gay world, then she could leave me and make it 75% to the Gay world, the only problem is She can never leave me, and She can forget returning to her old ways. Im gonna have this investigated. In anycase as we all know I have telepathy and I must be keyed in to correct Some of these problems, and as a condition will have to See me, So it's not worth Scheming on me, ill find out Sooner or later.

You may be hearing from Some of my men, just cooperate with them. "They must find

Sincerely' with Love

Plaza Post OFFice
Box
L.I.C. New York 11101

NEW YORK NY 102
PM

9A-LA-143276-13

FBI — LOS ANGELES

b6
b7C

14755 Ventura Blvd. #1-710
Sherman Oaks, CA 91403
c/o FBI

TO WBNJ; Please Retransmit this to [redacted]
by Fax machine, I will also mail it out of 26 Federal
Plaza, to confirm it.

b6
b7C

6/7/92

Dear [redacted],

I hope you receive this letter in good health and in good Spirits;

I really do love you very much, And I just can't let go, nor do I wish to. Im Sorry for our life long Separation (As it seems) but I promise to try very hard, to be as good to you as I can, and I will never leave you [redacted] my commitment to you is for life.

Now if you don't get intouch soon, im gonna force people to tell me of your where-a-bouts, because im gonna believe you are not safe, and im gonna stop playing the game. Im only going about things as I am, because I want to know that you love me and have gotten over your anger.

I want to be your manager, for a few reasons, so whoever has that job, buy out his contract in my name, it shouldn't cost much at all. The main reason I want this job is to insure that never again, will someone decide when, and when we can not be together, as in the Case of [redacted] I never needed you more, but your manager had other plans, for you, and it's obvious you also had other plans, because you didn't take me on that trip to Europe as you promised, but that's O.K. today.

"So we both got hurt, not just you [redacted]

Now I told you what I want you to do, but im gonna tell it to you again in short. I want you to work on [redacted] with EArth Wind and Fire, I understand the whole

#2

b6
b7C

6/7/92

band is back together now. I want you to bring in all of your dancers, [redacted] wouldn't want to have it any other way. I want you to do all of the Vocal tracks, you should hire some help, but I want EWF to focus mostly on the music. On two Songs I want EWF to assist in Song writing and backaground Vocals, one being the title track [redacted]
I explained the symbolism to you in a letter, the bottomline is that Water Symbolizes the Savior.
Stick to the R&B with Gospel Sound, iF you need a hot guitar Solo, hire [redacted] This one is too big for you, that's why I want [redacted] along with Someone he can work with to produce this project. [redacted] has good connections, I know you love him, so give him a chance. he needs this opportunity, it's not all about [redacted], so Stop trying to bring them all the money.
As for this movie [redacted] better not be trying to boss you around, and control you, because i'll have him killed. I want you on a Flexable Schedule, (your a star, and music is your priority) So you can focus on your music project.
As for the movie, he can Fax to you what, where, and when he needs you. And as I said No nude clips, no love Scenes, trust me, keep your image clean; that alone will take you a long way. I hope to hear from you soon.

Sincerely' with Love

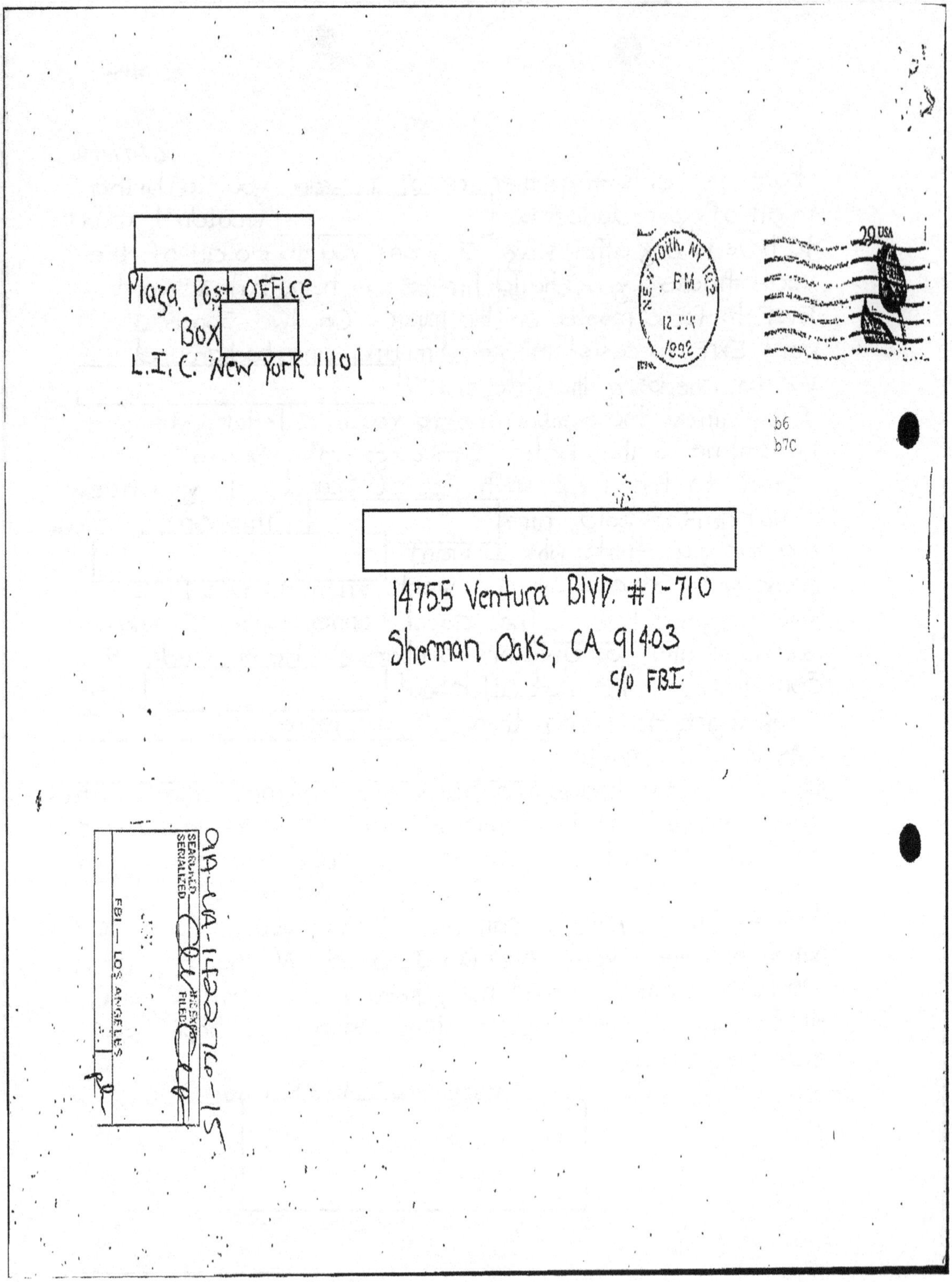

Plaza Post OFFICE
Box
L.I.C. New York 11101

NEW YORK, NY 1?? PM 12 ... 1992

29 USA

b6
b7C

14755 Ventura Blvd. #1-710
Sherman Oaks, CA 91403
c/o FBI

9A-LA-142276-15
SEARCHED — SERIALIZED — INDEXED — FILED
FBI — LOS ANGELES

Jackson JF Family

JACKSON INCIDENT REPORT

4641 HAYVENHURST AVE

ENCINO, CALIF. 91436

DATE: 6/22/95

b6
b7C

TIME: Approximately 9:30

During The morning watch while viewing The cameras, I observed a male blk outside The property approaching ______ As he was sweeping. Immediately I made my way down to The gate As ______ Exited The Estate in his vehicle. The was open As he backed out of it To Avoid potential unlawful entry I stood by, As some fans do. But while watching I spoke cordially inquiring of The visit he was making here Suddenly Realizing The person was indeed A suspect from The books we keep ______ He stated That he wanted to know if ______ was here, Also if any other family members were here. Also That John Gotti was his father. I ask him his name he said ______ confirming my Thinking to Records. I made my way back to the office ______ in view I brought it to ______ then Alerted The Police

OFFICERS SIGNATU______ DATE. 6/22/95

9A-LA-142276-16

Jackson JF Family

2 of 2

JACKSON INCIDENT REPORT

4641 HAYVENHURST AVE

ENCINO, CALIF. 91436

DATE:

TIME:

Subsequently, Police Arrived to Arrest The Suspect At Approximately 10A.M.
We had Also Called [redacted] Office Which They Had Asked us To do upon Arrival of Any Suspect on Record. Approx. 1010 Arrest Was Concluded Property Then, Resecured.

b6
b7C

OFFICERS SIGNATU[redacted] DATE.

notes by HS Beckner
From wit interviews

Interview on 7-1-92 with wit [redacted]

(in essence)

Def stated: I keep getting [redacted]

I'm [redacted] husband and John Gotti's son. I've got the find out why. I need to talk to [redacted] or [redacted]. If I don't get a conclusion I going to either kill myself, or......

"I want to kill that [redacted] guy"

(kept repeating)

b6 b7C

Interview on 7-1-92 with [redacted] [redacted]

b6 b7C b7D

Δ said; (in essence)
I don't know who I

9A-LA-142276-17

pls

am any more. You know, I tried to kill the President of the United States.

b6
b7C

I'll kill that [redacted] guy, too [redacted] (sp?)

I'm [redacted] husband. I'm here to find out what's going on.

I'm [redacted]

I'm John Gotti's son.

DISCLOSURE STATEMENT

Los Angeles Police Department

PAGE NO.	TYPE OF REPORT	BOOKING NO.	DR NO.
5/5	ARREST 602(N) P.C.	3121958	—

1. All currently existing reports (except personnel investigations) connected to this investigation, including crime, property, arrest, schematic, refusal, follow-up, etc., including those of other suspects, are cross-referenced in this report.

2. The names, assignments, serial numbers, and work phone numbers of all officers who saw, heard or otherwise perceived (1) any events leading to or involving the commission of the crime; (2) any arrest and/or search made in connection with the crime; (3) any statement of a suspect or witness; (4) any test performed at the scene (e.g., FST, scientific); (5) any intoxication or impairment of a suspect or witness; and/or (6) any facts necessary for probable cause for a warrant, search or detention, are listed in the report. Also listed in the report are the names, business and/or home addresses, business and/or home phone numbers of all civilian witnesses (except confidential informants) who provided information (whether incriminating or exonerating) as to any of the above listed categories.

3. All known oral statements made by any suspect or witness concerning the offense are included in a referenced report.

4. Copies of all original officer notes relating to statements of suspects or witnesses are attached.

5. All items of evidence seized, photographs (except booking), audio and video tape recordings (except Communications Division records) are mentioned in one of the referenced reports.

6. If any of the above items have been lost or destroyed, this fact is mentioned in a referenced report.

7. Any known fact which might indicate innocence of this crime or which might be substantial material evidence favorable to any suspect or which might damage the believability of a prosecution witness is mentioned in a referenced report.

All of the above statements are true.

SIGNATURE	SERIAL #	DIVISION OF ASSIGNMENT	DATE
		WUAL	6-22-92
		W/VAL	6-22-92
		"	"
		"	"

b6
b7C

70-5.02.9 (4/92)

MUNICIPAL COURT OF CALIFORNIA,
LOS ANGELES JUDICIAL DISTRICT

CRIME SUMMARY INFORMATION
PROBABLE CAUSE DECLARATION

b6
b7C

Location Booked L.A.P.D. – WVAL DIV	Booking Number 3121958
Arrestee (L[redacted]	DOB [redacted]
Address (Residence) TRANSCIENT L.A.	
Booking Charges 602(N) P.C.	Supplemental Holds/Warrants –
Date/Time of Arrest 6·22·92 0930	48 Hr. Exp. Date/Time 6·24·92 0930
Arresting Agency/Division L.A.P.D WVAL	A[redacted] CITIZEN ARREST

☒ **FACTS ESTABLISHING ELEMENTS AND IDENTIFICATION OF DEFENDANT:**

I – ATTACHED

TRANSPORTING [redacted]

REPORTS INCORPORATED HEREIN BY REFERENCE.

I DECLARE UNDER PENALTY OF PERJURY THAT THE FOREGOING IS TRUE AND CORRECT TO THE BEST OF MY KNOWLEDGE AND BELIEF.

EXECUTED ON 6·22·92 AT LOS ANGELES COUNTY, CALIFORNIA,

BY [redacted] [redacted]
SIGNATURE EMPLOYEE NUMBER

ON THE BASIS OF ☐ THE OFFICER'S DECLARATION ☐ REPORTS REVIEWED, I HEREBY DETERMINE THAT THERE ☐ IS ☐ IS NOT PROBABLE CAUSE TO BELIEVE THIS ARRESTEE HAS COMMITTED A CRIME.

(DATE) (TIME) (SIGNATURE OF JUDICIAL OFFICER)

LOS ANGELES POLICE DEPARTMENT
FOLLOW-UP INVESTIGATION

MULTIPLE b6 b7C

DATE THIS REPORT	DATE ORIGINAL RPT.	SPECIFIC TYPE ORIG. RPT. (ADW, TFV, EVID., ARREST/BURG., ETC.)	R. D.	PCD	DR
07-16-92	06-22-92	Arrest Report	1089	-	None

XXX/BOOKED TO/ARRESTEE (AS ON ORIGINAL REPORT) | IF RECLASSIFYING TO HOMICIDE VICT'S: SEX DESCENT AGE | BKG. NO. (SUPPL. TO ARREST) | WORK FOLDER PERIOD ORIG. RPT. INDEX NO

CASE STATUS 1 CLEARED BY ARREST 2 CLEARED OTHER 3 REPORT UNFOUNDED (4) INVESTIGATION CONTINUED

Use this section only to add or correct info - do not repeat info from previous reports. Exception: Complete entire suspect info if making final disposition.

DATE OCCURRED | CHANGE TO-ON OR BTWN MO DAY YEAR TIME & MO DAY YEAR TIME | TYPE ORIG RPT - CHG. TO | RD-CHG. TO | DR CHANGE TO | INV. DIV. CHANGE TO

PROPERTY VALUE: ADDITIONAL LOSS $ | PARTIAL RECOVERY $ | TOTAL RECOVERY $ | DELETE FROM ORIG. RPT. $ | DESCRIPTION CHANGE | ITEM NOS. RECOVERED/DELETED (ON MULT. RPTS, USE NARRATIVE)

	SEX	DESC	HAIR	EYES	HEIGHT	WEIGHT	DOB	AGE	NAME & ADDRESS (OR NAME & CHARGE, IF ARRESTED) / ACTION TAKEN	LA OR BKG. NO.
S-1	M	Blk	Blk	Bro	6-0	200		33	602(N)PC / *****	3121-958
2										
3										

NARRATIVE (USE BELOW COLUMNS FOR MULTIPLE REPORTS ONLY)

P/T/D | MULTIPLE RPT: PCD & DR NOS. | TYPE OF CRIME | RD | VICTIM'S NAME | DATE ORIG. RPT. | VALUE

Investigation: On 07-09-92 I, Detective [redacted] met with DCA H. Beckner and discussed the arrest of [redacted] that occurred on 03-04-92. DCA Beckner advised me that she had reviewed the case and believed that the suspect was in violation of Penal Code 422 (Terrorist Threats) involving an additional victim [redacted] DCA Beckner also provided me with copies of letters containing threats that the suspect had sent to [redacted] DCA Beckner stated that she had received information that the suspect was also in possession of additional letters containing threats and those letters had been placed in the suspect's booking property bag at the the time of his arrest.

On 07-13-92 I conducted a telephonic interview with [redacted] advised me that he was aware of at least three(3) threats that were made by the suspect to [redacted] stated that he has read approximately thirty(30) to fourty(40) letters containing threats made by the suspect including two(2) letters to the victim. [redacted] has been monitoring letters being sent by the suspect since 02-05-92.

[redacted] stated that in a letter dated 06-12-92 the suspect wrote that someone loyal to him(suspect) would kill the victim and that it was guaranteed and not a threat. In an additional letter dated 06-09-92 the suspect wrote that the victim's wife(actually the victim's girlfriend) had a choice

WAS PROPERTY BOOKED IN CONJUNCTION WITH THIS REPORT OR INCIDENT? XX NO YES ..... IF YES, HAS 10.6 BEEN COMPLETED? NO YES

DATE & TIME REPRODUCED | DIVISION | CLERK | REPORTING OFFICER(S) | SERIAL NO. | DIVISION DHD-TMU

LAPD 03.14.0 (R. 3/85) FOLLOW-UP INVESTIGATION

LOS ANGELES POLICE DEPARTMENT

FOLLOW-UP INVESTIGATION

MULTIPLE b6 b7C

DATE THIS REPORT	DATE ORIGINAL RPT.	SPECIFIC TYPE ORIG. RPT. (ADW, TFV, EVID., ARREST/BURG., ETC.)	R. D.	PCD	DR
07-20-92	06-22-92	Arrest Report	1089	-	None

XXXXXXXXXX/ARRESTEE (AS ON ORIGINAL REPORT) | IF RECLASSIFYING TO HOMICIDE VICT'S: SEX DESCENT AGE | BKG. NO. (SUPPL. TO ARREST) | WORK FOLDER PERIOD ORIG. RPT. INDEX NO.

SE STATUS 1 CLEARED BY ARREST 2 CLEARED OTHER 3 REPORT UNFOUNDED (4) INVESTIGATION CONTINUED

Use this section only to add or correct info - do not repeat info from previous reports. Exception: Complete entire suspect info if making final disposition.

S-	SEX	DESC	HAIR	EYES	HEIGHT	WEIGHT	DOB	AGE	NAME & ADDRESS (OR NAME & CHARGE, IF ARRESTED)	BKG. NO.
1	M	Blk	Blk	Bro	6-0	200		33	602(N)PC; ACTION TAKEN ****	3121-958
2										
3										

NARRATIVE (USE BELOW COLUMNS FOR MULTIPLE REPORTS ONLY)

Investigation: I,Detective [redacted] had received information from DCA Holly Beckner that she had submitted letters written by the suspect(which contained threats to the victim) to the Los Angeles Police Department's Scientific Investigation Division(SID)-Questioned Document Section. DCA Beckner stated that she had been advised by [redacted](SID) that a comparison of a sample of the suspect's writing which was submitted to SID and the letter dated 06-12-92 containing the threat to the victim were written by one and the same, the suspect [redacted] I contacted SID Specialist [redacted] [redacted] and he advised me of the same. Additionally, DCA Beckner advised me that she was in possession of the original letters.

On 07-16-92 I completed a follow-up containing a telephonic interview with the victim [redacted]. During that interview the victim disclosed to me that he had read the letter dated 06-12-92 which contained the threat that if the victim took the suspect for a ride somebody loyal to the suspect would kill the victim and that was a guarantee. The victim recalled that specific threat to him by the suspect during my interview with him.

WAS PROPERTY BOOKED IN CONJUNCTION WITH THIS REPORT: XXX NO ☐ YES ..... IF YES, HAS 10.6 BEEN COMPLETED? ☐ NO ☐ YES

SERIAL NO. | REPORTING OFFICER(S) | SERIAL NO. | DIVISION DHD-TMU

DATE & TIME REPRODUCED | DIVISION | CLERK

LAPD 03.14.0 (R. 3/85) FOLLOW-UP INVESTIGATION

AO 91
Rev. 11/82

CRIMINAL COMPLAINT

COPY

United States District Court	DISTRICT: CENTRAL DISTRICT OF CALIFORNIA
UNITED STATES OF AMERICA v. [redacted]	DOCKET NO.
	MAGISTRATE'S CASE NO. 92- 1440 M

b6
b7C

Complaint for violation of Title 18 United States Code § 876

NAME OF JUDGE OR MAGISTRATE	OFFICIAL TITLE	LOCATION
CHARLES F. EICK	UNITED STATES MAGISTRATE JUDGE	Los Angeles, CA

DATE OF OFFENSE	PLACE OF OFFENSE	ADDRESS OF ACCUSED (If known)
On or about June 12, 1992	Los Angeles County	

COMPLAINANT'S STATEMENT OF FACTS CONSTITUTING THE OFFENSE OR VIOLATION:

On or about June 12, 1992, in Los Angeles County, within the Central District of California, defendant [redacted] knowingly deposited in a post office or authorized depository for mail matter and caused to be delivered by the Postal Service according to the direction thereon a written communication containing a threat to injure the person of another.

b6
b7C

BASIS OF COMPLAINANT'S CHARGE AGAINST THE ACCUSED:

(See attached affidavit which is incorporated as part of this Complaint)

MATERIAL WITNESSES IN RELATION TO THIS CHARGE:

Being duly sworn, I declare that the foregoing is true and correct to the best of my knowledge.

SIGNATURE OF COMPLAINANT (official title) [redacted]

b6
b7C

OFFICIAL TITLE: Special Agent - Federal Bureau of Investiagtion

Sworn to before me and subscribed in my presence,

SIGNATURE OF MAGISTRATE(1)

DATE: July 21, 1992

1) See Federal Rules of Criminal Procedure rules 3 and 54.

GWJ:cjd REC: Detention (Arrest Warrant)

GWJ

AFFIDAVIT

I, [redacted] being duly sworn, hereby depose and swear:

1. I am a Special Agent (SA) with the Federal Bureau of Investigation (FBI), United States Department of Justice. I have been an FBI agent for thirteen years. I am currently assigned to the Major Case Squad of the Los Angeles Field Office which investigates, among other things, threats received through the mail. This affidavit is made in support of a criminal complaint charging [redacted] with violation of Title 18, United States Code, Section 876: mailing threatening communications. b6 b7C

2. On July 8, 1992, Holly Beckner, Deputy City Attorney, Los Angeles City Attorney's Office, told me the following:

a. She was in possession of between thirty and forty letters written by [redacted] to [redacted] in which [redacted] made a number of allegations and threats, not only against [redacted] but also against [redacted] [redacted] President George Bush, and others.

b. All of the letters had either been mailed through the United States Postal Service or had been sent by facsimile machine to various recipients in different parts of the country.

c. [redacted] was in the Los Angeles County Jail, having been arrested on June 22, 1992, for trespassing onto

Los Angeles Police Department

CONTINUATION SHEET

PAGE NO.	TYPE OF REPORT	BOOKING NO.	DR NO.
2 of 2	Follow-Up Report	3121-958	None

ITEM NO.	QUAN.	ARTICLE	SERIAL NO.	BRAND	MODEL NO.	MISC. DESCRIPTION (EG. COLOR, SIZE, INSCRIPTIONS, CALIBER, REVOLVER, ETC)	DOLLAR VAL.

Investigation Continued:

of a husband who would live or one that would die. b6 b7C b7D

[redacted] stated that [redacted] because of the suspect's threats and actions(the suspect travelled from New York to Los Angeles and arrived at [redacted] residence).

On 07-13-92 I conducted a telephonic interview with DCA Beckner who advised me that she(Beckner) had conducted interviews with the witnesses [redacted] and [redacted] who had witnessed the suspect's arrest on 03-04-92. Both witnesses advised stated to DCA Beckner that the suspect had threatened to kill [redacted].

On 07-14-92 I conducted a telephonic interview with the victim [redacted]. The victim stated that he first became aware of the suspect [redacted] and that he(suspect) was sending letters to the victim, [redacted] a few months prior to the suspect's arrest on 03-04-92. The victim stated that [redacted] [redacted] had presented him(victim) with information about the suspect and his(suspect) actions.

The victim stated that he had read the letters that contained the threats directed at the victim by the suspect and that he considered the threats serious and credible. The victim stated that he based the threats serious because the suspect had acted out by making a trip from New York to Los Angeles and gone beyond writing letters. The victim also stated that he was aware of other incidents(particularly the Rebecca Schaeffer and Robert Bardo case) were a suspect has threaten a person and then caused harm to that person [redacted]

On 07-16-92 I conducted a follow-up to the Los Angeles County Jail(441 Bauchet St L.A.) and examined the suspect's property bag (#0093125). My examination of the bag revealed that there were no additional letters and there was no evidence that there had been (no property had been removed by anyone).

CONTINUE ON REVERSE SIDE.

CONTINUATION SHEET 15.09.0112

the property of [redacted] in Encino, California. He is facing misdemeanor charges stemming from that incident.

b6
b7C

d. [redacted] had been arrested by White House Police on May 22, 1992, for attempting to get onto the White House grounds in an apparent attempt to get the attention of [redacted]

e. Since his arrest, handwriting exemplars had been taken from [redacted] and a questioned documents examiner has determined that those exemplars were written by the same person who wrote the aforementioned letters.

f. [redacted] sent these letters to a number of different people, and would send copies of the letters to [redacted] [redacted]

3. On July 14, 1992, Holly Beckner gave me copies of the letters written by [redacted]

4. On July 14, 1992, I reviewed the letters provided to me by Holly Beckner. Most of these letters were addressed either to [redacted] or to [redacted] at 14755 Ventura Boulevard, # 1-710, Sherman Oaks, California 91403. The address on Ventura Boulevard is an address [redacted] uses to receive mail. Most of these letters list the sender as [redacted] which is a name [redacted] uses, although some of the letters list the sender as [redacted] The letters bear postmarks showing that they were sent through the United States Postal Service.

5. The letters contain a number of different threats to various people. Although the overall tone of the letters is

b6
b7C

threatening to [redacted] there are no explicit threats to her. The following are examples of the letters sent by [redacted]

a. The first letter from [redacted] to [redacted] is dated February 5, 1992. The letter begins "Dear [redacted] and in the letter [redacted] describes himself as [redacted] husband. [redacted] describes his desire to reunite with [redacted] and his plan to eliminate anyone who gets in his way. At one point he writes, ". . . I will do everything in my power to destroy them, and your persistence on this issue will only confirm to me, that this is what you want me to do." He signs this letter, [redacted] your husband)."

b. In a letter dated April 6, 1992, [redacted] accuses [redacted] of being unfaithful to him. He writes, "And it is also written, for jealousy arouses a husband's fury and he will show no mercy when he takes revenge (PR 5:34)." In this same letter, [redacted] threatens [redacted] warning [redacted] to keep his relationship with [redacted] on a professional level. He signs the letter [redacted]

c. Another of the letters is dated May 18, 1992. This letter was sent by facsimile machine to the New York Daily News and signed [redacted] After complaining about his inability to attract [redacted] attention, he writes, "So I decided to go to the FBI today, if that doesn't work, I'll go to the CIA, military intelligent (sic) on up to the office of the President of the United States of America, and if the chain of command doesn't work, I will resort to violence, to bring attention to my problem. I'll commit mass murder at a Michael Jackson concert if necessary, in an attempt to murder Michael . . . ." Also, he complains about a financial disagreement with Michael Jackson and writes, "Michael I will personally attempt to kill if he doesn't pay me my money."

d. In a letter dated May 19, 1992, originally sent to [redacted] a radio personality in New York, [redacted] states, "As I said, [redacted] could not marry another man, for she has always been my wife, and I consummated our marriage when I took her virginity when she was 13 years old."

e. [redacted] sent the United States Secret Service and others a letter dated May 21, 1992, addressed to "All Concerned Parties" and signed by [redacted] The letter states in part, ". . . since nobody is taking me serious, and I can't handle my state of mind, then I am going to Washington D.C. to threaten to kill the President of the United States, George Bush. If they do not arrest me or solve my problem I'm gonna attempt to kill President George Bush. No answer from [redacted] is the only wrong answer and I will not accept it."

b6
b7C

f. In a letter dated June 7, 1992, addressed to [redacted] writes about [redacted] career and his desire to manage it as is rightfully his place as her husband. He also says, "I'm sorry for our life long separation (as it seems) but I promise to try very hard to be as good to you as I can, and I will never leave you [redacted] my commitment to you is for life." Turning his attention to [redacted] stated, "As for the movie, better not be trying to boss you around and control you, because I'll have him killed." This letter is signed

b6
b7C

g. In a typewritten letter dated June 11, 1992, addressed to "all concerned parties" and signed by refers to an impending trip to Los Angeles he was planning so that he and could meet and settle their differences.

h. sent a typewritten letter dated June 12, 1992, to and sent a copy to In this letter, signed by he directs her to advise boyfriend, of the danger he faces if he doesn't leave The letter states, in part, don't you know I will fuck up really bad, over so stop making me jealous alluding to and because it can never happen while I'm alive, not in reality." In the same letter defendant states, ". . . I will let walk with $1 million and the things he owns . . . now if he tries to take me for a ride somebody loyal to me is gonna kill him without me saying anything, and that's guaranteed, not a threat."

6. I have learned from Holly Beckner that on May 22, 1992, the day after his letter threatening to kill the President, was arrested by White House police and Secret Service agents as he attempted to enter the grounds of the White House.

7. I have reviewed police reports of an incident which took place on June 22, 1992. On that date, [redacted] attempted to get onto the property at 4641 Havenhurst Avenue in Encino, California. [redacted] The Los Angeles Police Department arrested [redacted] on charges of trespassing. [redacted] told police that he was there to take care of a problem with [redacted] At the time of his arrest, [redacted] was inquiring as to whether or not [redacted] [redacted] was in the residence so that he could talk to her.

8. I have reviewed Holly Beckner's notes of an interview with [redacted] who was a witness to the trespassing incident on June 22, 1992. [redacted] said that [redacted] described himself as [redacted] husband, said that he had tried to kill the President, and said that he planned to kill [redacted]

b6
b7C

Special Agent
Federal Bureau of Investigation

Subscribed and sworn to before
me this ____ day of July, 1992

UNITED STATES MAGISTRATE JUDGE

ORIGINAL

AO 442 (Rev. 12/85) Warrant for Arrest

FBI Will Arrest

United States District Court

CENTRAL DISTRICT OF CALIFORNIA

UNITED STATES OF AMERICA
V.

WARRANT FOR ARREST

ON COMPLAINT

CASE NUMBER: 92- 1440M

b6
b7C

To: The United States Marshal or any
Authorized United States Officer

YOU ARE HEREBY COMMANDED to arrest ______ Name

and bring him or her forthwith to the nearest Judge/Magistrate to answer a complaint

charging him or her with (brief description of offense)

Mailing threatening communications

in violation of Title 18 United States Code, Section(s) 876

with Bail fixed at $____________

REC: BY AUSA DETENTION

Date: July 21, 1992

CHARLES F. EICK
Name of Judge/Magistrate

Signature of Judge/Magistrate

9A-LA-142276-21

RETURN		
This warrant was received and executed with the arrest of the above-named defendant at		
DATE RECEIVED	NAME AND TITLE OF ARRESTING OFFICER	SIGNATURE OF ARRESTING OFFICER
DATE OF ARREST		

CR-95 (7/87)

Memorandum

To : SAC, LOS ANGELES (9A-LA-142276) (C-1) (P)

Date 7/22/92

From : SA [redacted]

Subject: [redacted], AKA [redacted] VICTIM;
MICHAEL JACKSON - VICTIM;
[redacted] - VICTIM;
[redacted] - VICTIM;
MAILING THREATENING LETTERS;
OO: LOS ANGELES

b6
b7C

For information, on 7/20/92, HOLLY BECKNER, Deputy City Attorney, Los Angeles, California, (818) 902-2182, contacted writer and advised that after discussing captioned matter with Assistant United States Attorney (AUSA) GREG JESSNER, the decision had been made that the United States Attorney's Office would assume the case against subject, [redacted] and bring federal charges against him. As such, BECKNER would now dismiss the local misdemeanor charges against [redacted] so that the FBI could assume federal custody of him. SA [redacted] advised that he would now contact AUSA JESSNER in order to file a criminal complaint and have an arrest warrant issued. It was agreed that a federal detainer would be placed on [redacted] to ensure that he remains in custody after the local charges are dropped.

2 - Los Angeles

RGP/rc

9A-LA-142276-22

SEARCHED ___ INDEXED ___
SERIALIZED ___ FILED ___

FBI — ___

FD-302 (Rev. 3-10-82)

- 1 -

FEDERAL BUREAU OF INVESTIGATION

Date of transcription 7/28/92

b6
b7C

On July 23, 1992, pursuant to a federal arrest warrant issued on July 21, 1992, [redacted] was taken into federal custody by Special Agents (SAs) [redacted] and [redacted] of the Federal Bureau of Investigation (FBI) Los Angeles Field Office.

[redacted] who was incarcerated at the Los Angeles County Jail on local charges, was removed from the County Jail and transported to the United States Marshal's Service (USMS) lock-up at the U.S. Federal Courthouse, 312 North Spring Street in Los Angeles. There he was to await his initial appearance before a U.S. Magistrate.

At the time that he was taken into federal custody, [redacted] was read his rights as they appear on form FD-395 (Interrogation; Advise of Rights). [redacted] was asked if he understood his rights as they had been explained to him. [redacted] answered affirmatively. No questions were posed to [redacted] prior to his being handed over to the USMS.

The following descriptive data for [redacted] is set forth below:

Name	[redacted]
Alias	[redacted]
Sex	Male
Race	Black
Date of Birth	[redacted]
Place of Birth	[redacted]
Height	6'0"
Weight	200 pounds
Hair	Black
Eyes	Brown
Social Security Account Number	[redacted]
Last Known Address	[redacted]

Investigation on 7/23/92 at Los Angeles, California File # 9A-LA-142276-24

by SA [redacted] SA [redacted] RGP/rc Date dictated 7/24/92

This document contains neither recommendations nor conclusions of the FBI. It is the property of the FBI and is loaned to your agency; it and its contents are not to be distributed outside your agency.

FD-302 (Rev. 3-10-82)

- 1 -

FEDERAL BUREAU OF INVESTIGATION

Date of transcription 7/28/92

On July 24, 1992, [redacted], was interviewed at [redacted] [redacted] by Special Agents (SAs) [redacted] and [redacted] of the Federal Bureau of Investigation (FBI). [redacted] who describes [redacted] [redacted] has been the recipient of death threats from one [redacted] [redacted] After identifying themselves through a show of credentials, SAs [redacted] and [redacted] explained to [redacted] that he was being interviewed concerning the threats [redacted] b6 b7C b7D

Present at the time of this interview were [redacted] [redacted]

At the outset, [redacted] advised that he does not personally know [redacted] but he is obviously aware of him, having read several of [redacted] letters addressed to [redacted] [redacted] in which at various times [redacted] identifies himself as the son of JOHN GOTTI and an associate of the Gambino family. [redacted] has also read letters in which [redacted] has threatened the [redacted] as well as [redacted] stated that he has been kept apprised of all the developments regarding this individual by the [redacted]

[redacted] stated that [redacted] has been made aware of [redacted] and his letters. [redacted] added that [redacted] [redacted] and any problems that are brought to the attention of her security detail. However, in this instance, due to the serious nature of the threats made by [redacted] and the whole tone of his letters, it was felt that she should be made aware of the situation. [redacted] explained that at times, [redacted] just wants to be "normal" and go about her business without her usual entourage or without being recognized. Because of the

Investigation on 7/24/92 at Malibu, CA File # 9A-LA-142276-25

by SA SA [redacted] /RGP/rc Date dictated 7/24/92 b6 b7C

This document contains neither recommendations nor conclusions of the FBI. It is the property of the FBI and is loaned to your agency; it and its contents are not to be distributed outside your agency.

FD-302a (Rev. 11-15-83)

9A-LA-142276

Continuation of FD-302 of [redacted], On 7/24/92, Page 2

b6
b7C
b7D

[redacted] letters however, [redacted] and the security detail have actually increased their security awareness and have tried to heighten [redacted] awareness as well. [redacted] confirmed that [redacted] has seen all of the original letters addressed to her containing the threats, and is cognizant of the fact that the FBI is actively investigating this matter.

[redacted] stated that after reading the letters from [redacted] and being aware of all that [redacted] has done so far (being arrested in Washington D.C. and Los Angeles), he has no doubt that [redacted] could carry out the threats that he has made. He described [redacted] feels that an individual like [redacted] cannot be ignored. He sees similarities between this case and other celebrity "stalking" cases, the most notable being that of REBECCA SCHAFFER. In his mind, [redacted] appears to be willing to risk everything just to attract [redacted] [redacted] attention. [redacted]

The following descriptive data was obtained through observation and interview:

Name	[redacted]
Sex	
Raee	
Date of Birth	
Place of Birth	
Height	
Weight	
Hair	
Eyes	
California Driver's License Number	
Social Security Account Number	

FD-302 (Rev. 3-10-82)

- 1 -

FEDERAL BUREAU OF INVESTIGATION

Date of transcription 7/28/92

On July 24, 1992, [redacted] was interviewed at the [redacted] by Special Agents (SAs) [redacted] and [redacted] of the Federal Bureau of Investigation (FBI) Los Angeles Field Office. After identifying themselves, it was explained to [redacted] that he was being interviewed with regard to the threatening letters sent to [redacted] by one [redacted] in which [redacted] threatened [redacted] MICHAEL JACKSON, and [redacted] b6 b7C

Present during this interview were [redacted]

[redacted] advised that all letters addressed to [redacted] eventually channel down to him. Concerning [redacted] stated that he was aware of about five (5) letters in which [redacted] specifically threatened someone. In two of the letters, the threats were directed toward [redacted] Other letters contained threats against [redacted] MICHAEL JACKSON and President GEORGE BUSH.

In his estimation, [redacted] advised that [redacted] was attempting to manipulate [redacted] by threatening other persons [redacted] in his letters, alludes to the fact that "others" are controlling [redacted] and keeping her from doing what is right (getting together with [redacted]. As a result, [redacted] blame these other persons and threatens them accordingly.

[redacted] advised that he was not present when [redacted] was arrested on June 22, 1992, for trespassing on the JACKSON family property in Encino, California. At the time, he was in the Oakland, California, area on location with [redacted]

Investigation on 7/24/92 at Malibu, California File # 9A-LA-142276 -26

by SA SA [redacted] /RGP/rc Date dictated 7/24/92 b6 b7C

This document contains neither recommendations nor conclusions of the FBI. It is the property of the FBI and is loaned to your agency; it and its contents are not to be distributed outside your agency.

FD-302a (Rev. 11-15-83)

9A-LA-142276

b6
b7C

Continuation of FD-302 of [redacted], On 7/24/92, Page 2

However, [redacted] was well known to the security detail due in large part to a program developed by [redacted] (Potential Dangerous Person) in which [redacted] had already been profiled as an extremely dangerous risk to his client and those around her.

[redacted] stated that he has read every letter that [redacted] has sent to [redacted] beginning with the letter dated February 5, 1992. He noted that there was a steady escalation or progression of a threat factor which first manifested itself in April, 1992. At that point, the letters began in earnest to threaten people [redacted] While there was no explicit threat to [redacted] the letters taken in their totality constitute a threat [redacted]

[redacted] explained that [redacted] the perceived threat potential he represents, his ability to get close to [redacted] and the frequency of his contacts (letters), all make [redacted] a high risk and trigger the highest alert as far as his security detail is concerned.

[redacted] advised that the letters currently in possession of the FBI do not constitute all of the letters sent by [redacted] He has several more which were not given to the city attorney's office simply because no threat was contained in them. Nevertheless, he offered to provide the letters to the FBI as they will serve to show the gradual increase in tone and threat level.

[redacted] advised that he will be on vacation starting this date. However, he provided his home telephone as [redacted] and his Skypager number as [redacted]

Memorandum

To : SAC, LOS ANGELES (9A-LA-142276) (C-1) (P)

Date 7/25/92

From : SA [redacted]

Subject: [redacted], AKA;
[redacted] VICTIM;
MICHAEL JACKSON - VICTIM;
[redacted] VICTIM;
[redacted] VICTIM;
THREATENING LETTERS;
OO: LOS ANGELES

b6
b7C

For information, on 7/23/92, subject [redacted] had his initial appearance before U.S. Magistrate CHARLES F. EICK, Los Angeles, on the charge of violation of Title 18, U.S. Code, Section 876, Mailing Threatening Letters. [redacted] was represented by Public Defender [redacted] The government was represented by AUSA GREGORY JESSNER. After advising [redacted] of his rights and confirming that [redacted] was aware of the charge filed against him, U.S. Magistrate EICK granted the government's request for detention and ordered [redacted] remanded to the custody of the U.S. Marshal.

2 - Los Angeles

RGP/rc

9A-LA-142276-23

SERIALIZED FILED

FBI — LOS ANGELES

b6
b7C

FD-515 (Rev. 7-19-91)
Accomplishment Report
(Submit within 30 days from date of accomplishment)

TO: Director, FBI

Date 7/28/92

FROM: SAC, Los Angeles
[redacted] aka
[redacted]-Victim;
Michael Jackson-Victim;
[redacted]Victim;
[redacted]-Victim;
Mailing Threatening Letters;
OO: Los Angeles

Bureau File Number: [blank]

Field Office File Number: 9A-LA-142276

Squad or RA Number: 0009

Agent's Social Security No.: [redacted]

☐ X if a joint operation with: ________ (identity of other agency)

☐ X if case involves corruption of a public official (Federal, State or Local).

Investigative Assistance or Technique Used

Rate each Investigative Assistance or Technique used in connection with the accomplishment being claimed.
1 = Used, but did not help
2 = Helped, but only minimally
3 = Helped, substantially
4 = Absolutely essential

	Rating		Rating		Rating		Rating
1. Acctg Tech Assistance		8. Eng. Sect. Tape Exams		15. Photographic Coverage		22. Telephone Toll Recs	
2. Aircraft Assistance		9. Hypnosis Assistance		16. Polygraph Assistance		23. UCO Group I	
3. Computer Assistance		10. Ident Div Assistance		17. Search Warrants Executed		24. UCO Group II	
4. Consensual Monitoring		11. Informant Information		18. Show Money Usage		25. UCO Other	
5. ELSUR FISC		12. Lab Div Exams		19. Surveil Sqd (SOG) Asst		26. NCAVC/ VI-CAP	
6. ELSUR Title III		13. Lab Div Field Support		20. SWAT Team Action		27. Visual Invest - Analysis (VIA)	
7. Eng. Sect. Field Support		14. Pen Registers		21. Tech. Agt. or Tech Equip			

A. Preliminary Judicial Process (Number of subjects)	Complaints	Informations	Indictments
	1		

B. Arrests, Locates, Summonses or Subpoenas Served (No. of Subjects)

	Subject Priority* A	B	C
FBI Arrests -			
FBI Locates -			
Local Arrests -			

Subpoenas Served____
Criminal Summons____
Local Crim. Summons____
FBI Subj. Resisted____; Armed____

C. Release of Hostages or Children Located: (Number of Hostages or Children Located)

Hostages Held By Terrorists:____ All Other Hostage Situations:____
Missing or Kidnaped Children Located:____

D. Recoveries, Restitutions, or Potential Economic Loss Prevented (PELP) (Explain valuation in remarks)

Property Type Code*	Recoveries	Restitutions	PELP Type Code*	Potential Economic Loss Prevented
	$	$		$
	$	$		$
	$	$		$

E. Civil Matters

		Government Defendant	Government Plaintiff
RICO-Civil Convictions	Civil Suits Amount of Suit	$	$
No. of Subj.	Settlement of Award	$	$

Enter AFA Payment Here

F. Administrative Sanctions

Subject 1 ____ Subject Description Code* -
☐ Suspension ☐ Debarment Time Frame - Years: ____ Months: ____ ☐ Permanent

G. Final Judicial Process: Judicial District ____ District ____ State ____ Conviction or Pretrial Div. Date ____ Sentence Date ____ No. of Subjects ____ Acquitted ____ Dismissed ____

Subject 1 ____ Subject Description Code* -

	Conviction Title	Section	Counts	In-Jail Yrs.	Mos.	Suspended Yrs.	Mos.	Probation Yrs.	Mos.
☐ Felony									
☐ Misdemeanor									
☐ Parole Revocation									
☐ Probation Revocation				Total Fines $					
☐ Plea ☐ Trial									
☐ Pretrial Diversion									

Subject 2 ____ Subject Description Code* -

	Conviction Title	Section	Counts	In-Jail Yrs.	Mos.	Suspended Yrs.	Mos.	Probation Yrs.	Mos.
☐ Felony									
☐ Misdemeanor									
☐ Parole Revocation									
☐ Probation Revocation				Total Fines $					
☐ Plea ☐ Trial									
☐ Pretrial Diversion									

Add consecutive sentences together. Enter longest single concurrent sentence. Do not add concurrent sentences together. Sentence 10 yrs.- 8 yrs susp. = 2 yrs. In-Jail.

Attach additional forms if reporting final judicial process on more than two subjects, and submit a final disposition form (R-84) for each subject.

H. Identifying Data: For every subject reported in Sections A, B, E, F, or G above, provide the following: *Attach additional forms for more than four subjects.*

Name	Date of Birth	Race*	Sex	Place of birth (if available)	Social Security Number (if available)
[redacted]		B	M	[redacted]	

b6
b7C

Explanation of accomplishment claimed:

On 7/21/92, an authorized Complaint was filed charging [redacted] with violation of Title 18, U.S. Code, Section 876, Mailing Threatening Letters, before U.S. Magistrate Charles F. Eick, Los Angeles, Central District of California.

SEARCHED ____
INDEXED ____
SERIALIZED ____

1-Admin Stat File
1-9A-LA-142276
1-C-1 Supervisor
1-P/F SA [redacted]

4
2 - Bureau
- Field Office
* See codes on reverse side.

9A-LA-142276-28

FD-515 (Rev. 7-19-91)
Accomplishment Report
(Submit within 30 days from date of accomplishment)

TO: Director, FBI
FROM: SAC, Los Angeles
SUBJECT:

[redacted] aka [redacted] Victim;
Michael Jackson-Victim;
[redacted] Victim;
[redacted] Victim;
Mailing Threatening Letters;
OO: Los Angeles

Bureau File Number: 9A-LA-142276
Field Office File Number: 0009
Squad or RA Number: [redacted]
Agent's Social Security No.

☐ X if a joint operation with: ______ (identity of other agency)

☐ X if case involves corruption of a public official (Federal, State or Local).

Date 7/28/92 b6 b7C

Investigative Assistance or Technique Used

Rate each Investigative Assistance or Technique used in connection with the accomplishment being claimed.
1 = Used, but did not help 3 = Helped, substantially
2 = Helped, but only minimally 4 = Absolutely essential

Technique	Rating	Technique	Rating	Technique	Rating	Technique	Rating
1. Acctg Tech Assistance		8. Eng. Sect. Tape Exams		15. Photographic Coverage		22. Telephone Toll Recs	
2. Aircraft Assistance		9. Hypnosis Assistance		16. Polygraph Assistance		23. UCO Group I	
3. Computer Assistance		10. Ident Div Assistance		17. Search Warrants Executed		24. UCO Group II	
4. Consensual Monitoring		11. Informant Information		18. Show Money Usage		25. UCO Other	
5. ELSUR FISC		12. Lab Div Exams		19. Surveil Sqd (SOG) Asst		26. NCAVC/ VI-CAP	
6. ELSUR Title III		13. Lab Div Field Support		20. SWAT Team Action		27. Visual Invest - Analysis (VIA)	
7. Eng. Sect. Field Support		14. Pen Registers		21. Tech. Agt. or Tech Equip			

A. Preliminary Judicial Process (Number of subjects): Complaints ___ Informations ___ Indictments ___

B. Arrests, Locates, Summonses or Subpoenas Served (No. of Subjects)

	Subject Priority A	B	C
FBI Arrests -	1		
FBI Locates -			
Local Arrests -			

FBI Subj. Resisted ___; Armed ___
Subpoenas Served ___ Criminal Summons ___ Local Crim. Summons ___

C. Release of Hostages or Children Located: (Number of Hostages or Children Located)
Hostages Held By Terrorists: ___ All Other Hostage Situations: ___
Missing or Kidnaped Children Located: ___

D. Recoveries, Restitutions, or Potential Economic Loss Prevented (PELP) (Explain valuation in remarks)

Property Type Code*	Recoveries	Restitutions	PELP Type Code*	Potential Economic Loss Prevented
	$	$		$
	$	$		$
	$	$		$

E. Civil Matters: RICO-Civil Convictions; No. of Subj.; Civil Suits Amount of Suit; Settlement of Award — Government Defendant $ / Government Plaintiff $; Enter AFA Payment Here

F. Administrative Sanctions: Subject 1 ___ Subject Description Code* - ___
☐ Suspension ☐ Debarment Time Frame - Years: ___ Months: ___ ☐ Permanent

G. Final Judicial Process: Judicial District ___ District State; Conviction or Pretrial Div. Date; Sentence Date; No. of Subjects; Acquitted; Dismissed

Subject 1 / Subject 2 — Subject Description Code* -
☐ Felony ☐ Misdemeanor ☐ Parole Revocation ☐ Probation Revocation ☐ Plea ☐ Trial ☐ Pretrial Diversion
Conviction: Title, Section, Counts; Combined Sentence: In-Jail Yrs. Mos., Suspended Yrs. Mos., Probation Yrs. Mos.; Total Fines $
Add consecutive sentences together. Enter longest single concurrent sentence. Do not add concurrent sentences together. Sentence 10 yrs.- 8 yrs susp. = 2 yrs. In-Jail.

Attach additional forms if reporting final judicial process on more than two subjects, and submit a final disposition form (R-84) for each subject.

H. Identifying Data: For every subject reported in Sections A, B, E, F, or G above, provide the following: *Attach additional forms for more than four subjects.*

Name	Date of Birth	Race*	Sex	Place of birth (if available)	Social Security Number (if available)
[redacted]		B	M	[redacted]	

b6 b7C

Explanation of accomplishment claimed:

On 7/23/92, Subject [redacted] was taken into federal custody by agents of the FBI in Los Angeles, California. [redacted] was arrested on charges of violation of Title 18, U.S.C., Section 876, Mailing Threatening Letters.

SEARCHED
INDEXED

1-Admin Stat File 1-P/F SA [redacted]
1-9A-LA-142276 1-P/F SA
1-C-1 Supervisor

2 - Bureau
5 ● - Field Office
* See codes on reverse side.

9A-LA-142276-29

FD-302 (Rev. 3-10-82)

FEDERAL BUREAU OF INVESTIGATION

Date of transcription 7/31/92

b6
b7C

On July 28, 1992, [redacted] was interviewed by Special Agent (SA) [redacted] of the Federal Bureau of Investigation (FBI) Los Angeles Field Office. After identifying himself through a show of credentials, SA [redacted] explained to [redacted] that he was being interviewed regarding his knowledge of the events leading up to the arrest of [redacted] by Los Angeles Police Department (LAPD) officers on June 22, 1992. The interview took place on the grounds of the JACKSON family estate, 4641 Hayvenhurst Avenue, Encino, California. The above arrest took place here. [redacted] works as a security guard at the residence and has been so employed for the past five years by MICHAEL JACKSON Productions.

Present during this interview was [redacted] attorney, representing [redacted]

Regarding the events of June 22, 1992, [redacted] advised that he was on duty at the front gate [redacted] [redacted] Sometime around 9:00am, as [redacted] [redacted] was sweeping the driveway with the gate opened, [redacted] observed trough the TV monitor the person later identified as [redacted] approaching [redacted] and the gate. [redacted] proceeded down the driveway. As he got closer, he immediately recognized the individual as [redacted] based on the photograph of [redacted] kept in the Potential Dangerous Person (PDP) manual provided by the JACKSON security detail. [redacted] described it as an "alert book" which identifies all those individuals believed to pose a risk or threat to the JACKSON family as a result of their celebrity status.

[redacted] stated that he told [redacted] "Sir, this is private property - wait on the other side of the street". [redacted] started asking for [redacted] and [redacted] [redacted] advised that neither was at home. Then [redacted] asked to speak to [redacted] Again, [redacted] told him she was not there either. All the while, the gate, which is on a timer, was closing until [redacted] was on one side of the gate, still

Investigation on 7/28/92 at Encino, California File # 9A-LA-142276-30

by SA [redacted] rc Date dictated 7/28/93

b6
b7C

FD-302a (Rev. 11-15-83)

9A-LA-142276

b6
b7C

Continuation of FD-302 of ______, On 7/28/92, Page 2

speaking to [redacted] who was on the other (street) side of the gate. At this time, responding to [redacted] questions of who he was and what he wanted [redacted] stated that he was JOHN GOTTI's son and also [redacted] husband. [redacted] also stated that he was trying to find out why [redacted] and why he kept thinking that he was [redacted] husband. [redacted] also stated words to the effect that if he "couldn't find out why, he would either kill himself or...". The implication, according to [redacted] was that he would kill someone else. Besides insisting that he has to find a "conclusion" to his problems [redacted] told [redacted] that he had threatened the President and that he had been arrested on the White House Grounds in Washington. [redacted] stated that [redacted] kept repeating the same things over and over again. When asked who he was, [redacted] identified himself as [redacted]

[redacted] concluded that [redacted] and returned to his guard shack to call the police, telling [redacted] that he had to go check on something. At the guard shack, he advised [redacted] and [redacted] both of whom happened to be in the immediate area, of the problem. He told [redacted] to get inside the house and told [redacted] that the individual at the gate was [redacted] of the PDP book. While he could see [redacted] via the TV monitor sitting on the sidewalk in front of the gate, [redacted] once again asked him through the intercom to identify himself. When [redacted] confirmed his identity, [redacted] called the police. In fact, [redacted] stated that four calls were made before the police responded with four patrol cars. In the meantime, [redacted] observed [redacted] via the TV monitor. Knowing that [redacted] was potentially dangerous, [redacted] did not want to force [redacted] to move.

When the patrol cars arrived, [redacted] walked out to meet them. He could hear [redacted] repeat the same statements to the officers that he had made to him. The statement that he recalls most vividly is [redacted] saying that if he [redacted] didn't find out why he was this way, he [redacted] was going to have to come to a conclusion and he was "going to have to make his own conclusion". At this point, [redacted] was taken into custody by LAPD.

[redacted] was asked if [redacted] made any specific threats to [redacted] advised that he did not recall hearing [redacted] mention [redacted] However, he

FD-302a (Rev. 11-15-83)

9A-LA-142276

Continuation of FD-302 of [redacted], On 7/28/92, Page 3

recalled that at one point [redacted] did threaten to kill [redacted] but he could not remember the exact words. [redacted] appeared confused and was rambling a he spoke to [redacted] but [redacted] also noted that [redacted] seemed to make a distinction between [redacted]

b6
b7C

At the end of the interview, [redacted] was shown a copy of a two page JACKSON Incident Report dated June 22, 1992, and prepared by [redacted] acknowledged that it was his report and admitted that it was not as detailed as perhaps it should have been.

The following descriptive data was obtained for [redacted]

Name
Race
Sex
Date of Birth
Place of Birth
Height
Weight
Hair
Eyes
California Driver's
License Number
Social Security
Account Number
Residence

Telephone

FD-302 (Rev. 3-10-82)

- 1 -

FEDERAL BUREAU OF INVESTIGATION

Date of transcription 7/31/92

On July 28, 1992, by way of a conference call at approximately 4:00pm, [redacted] was telephonically interviewed by Special Agent (SA) [redacted] of the Federal Bureau of Investigation (FBI) Los Angeles Field Office. [redacted] was joined in the call by [redacted] [redacted] and [redacted] [redacted] Also participating in the interview was Assistant United States Attorney (AUSA) GREGORY JESSNER, Los Angeles. b6 b7C b7D

At the outset, SA [redacted] introduced himself to [redacted] [redacted] and explained the reason for the interview, namely, to determine [redacted] regarding one [redacted] [redacted] who has written threatening letters [redacted] and threatening persons [redacted] [redacted] Persons threatened include [redacted] [redacted] and [redacted] President GEORGE BUSH is also threatened in one of the letters [redacted]

Investigation on 7/28/92 at Los Angeles, California File # 9A-LA-142276 -31

by SA [redacted] rc Date dictated 7/28/92 b6 b7C

This document contains neither recommendations nor conclusions of the FBI. It is the property of the FBI and is loaned to your agency; it and its contents are not to be distributed outside your agency.

FD-302a (Rev. 11-15-83)

9A-LA-142276

b6
b7C
b7D

Continuation of FD-302 of [redacted], On 7/28/92, Page 2

At this point, SA [redacted] explained to [redacted] the federal judicial process which has been set in motion by the arrest of [redacted] by the FBI. It was further explained [redacted] [redacted]

[redacted] asked how many counts [redacted] would be charged with and AUSA JESSNER advised that that determination had not been made as of yet.

Since [redacted] had no questions regarding the interview, the interview was terminated at approximately 4:25pm.

[redacted] The following descriptive date was obtained for

Name
Sex
Race
Date of Birth
Place of Birth
California Driver's
License Number
Social Security
Account Number
Residence

TTY-01
Computerized Record Request Form
(Revised July,1990)

TO: TELETYPE ROOM RETURN TO: SA [redacted] C-1

DATE: 7/30/92 FILE NUMBER: 9A-LA-142276

Driver's License ☐ Data (L1)
Driver's License ☐ Photograph
Registered ☐ Vehicle Data
Los Angeles ☐ County Wants
CA State/NCIC ☐ Wants
CA State Criminal ☒ History (CII)*
NCIC Criminal ☒ History (III)*
10-28/Vehicle ☐ Registration
* RAP SHEET *

b6
b7C

Name of Subject: [redacted]

Alias(es):

Address:

Previous Address:

Driver's License Number: [redacted]

Date of Birth (or approximate age): [redacted]

Vehicle License Number and State:

Sex: ☒ Male ☐ Female

Social Security Number:

Height/Weight/Hair/Eyes: 6 200 BLK BRN

Other Identifying Information (Specify): FBI # [redacted]

Reason*: TRIAL PREPARATION (SUBJECT IN CUSTODY)

Comments:

- DMV CHECK DID NOT MATCH (DIFFERENT MIDDLE NAME) VBF
- NO WANTS/WARRANTS
- FBI & NY & FL CRIM. RAP SHEETS ATTACHED.

VBF

Thank You

9A-LA-142276-32

SEARCHED / SERIALIZED / INDEXED / FILED

FBI — LOS ANGELES

*Per DOJ, a reason for the request and a file number are mandatory.

12.20.0 (R.3/87)

LOS ANGELES POLICE DEPARTMENT

ANALYZED EVIDENCE REPORT

DATE	TYPE OF INVESTIGATION	DATE & TIME OF OCCURRENCE	DR NO. Q.D. No. 347 / AREA OF OCCURRENCE
7/24/92	Nuisance Letters	--------------	------------

ANALYSIS REQUESTED: Handwriting

EVIDENCE BOOKED TO: [redacted] ☒ ARRESTEE ☐ VICTIM ☐ OTHER

LOCATION EVID BOOKED: --------------

OFFICER REQUESTING	SERIAL NO.	DIVISION	PHONE NO.	EXT.	CORONER NO.
Holly Beckner, DDA		D/A Office	(818)902-2182		--------b6 ---- b7C

— SID USE ONLY —

I, the undersigned, am prepared to testify that I am a Senior Examiner of Questioned Documents, employed by the Los Angeles Police Department; that I did on the 23rd. day of JUly, 1992 obtain from DDA Holly Beckner, Office of District Attorney evidence consisting of:

Item #1-EXEMPLAR: 2-LAPD 5.7 Cards w/7-Yellow Sheets bearing request writing prepared by [redacted] on July 6, 1992.

Item #2-QUESTIONED: 11-Handprinted Letters dated 2/5/92(4-Pages), 2/12/92(1-Pg), 2/29/92(12-Pgs.), 3/1/92(2-Pgs.), 3/21/92(5-Pgs.), 4-5-92(2pgs), 4/6/92(2-Pgs.), 5/30/92(3-Pgs.), 4/24/92(1-Pg.), 6/7/92(2-Pgs.)(P), and 6-11-92(1-Pg.)(P);

- 5-Typed Letters dated 5/21/92(1-Pg.)(P), 6/7/92(2-Pgs.)(P), 6/9/92(2-Pgs.)(P), 6/10/92(1-Pg.)(P), and 6/11/92(2-Pgs)(P)

- 9-Envelopes date stamped 2/6/92, 2/13/92, 3/2/92, 3/23/92, 4/6/92, 6/2/92, 6/8/92, 6/11/92, and 6/12/92;

- 1-Card(For the Woman I Love);

- 2-Photographs bearing writing on back side)

That I did make an examination and analysis of this evidence and in my opinion: Exemplar Writer [redacted] (Item #1) wrote questioned hand printing on 11-Letters, 9-Envelopes, 1-Card, and 2-Photos(Item #2). The same person also wrote the questioned [redacted] signatures on the five typed letters(Item #2)(P).

9A-LA-142276-33

SEARCHED ___ INDEXED ___ SERIALIZED ___ FILED ___

FBI — LOS ANGELES

DATE ANALYSIS COMPLETE: 7/27/92

DISPOSITION OF EVIDENCE:

SUPERVISOR APPROVING: [redacted]

Memorandum

To : SAC, LOS ANGELES (9A-LA-142276) (C-1) (P)

Date 8/5/92

From : SA [redacted]

Subject: [redacted] AKA [redacted]
[redacted] - VICTIM;
MICHAEL JACKSON - VICTIM;
[redacted] - VICTIM;
[redacted] - VICTIM;
MAILING THREATENING LETTERS;
OO: LOS ANGELES

b6
b7C

For information, on 8/4/92, a Federal Grand Jury, Los Angeles, Central District of California, handed down a True Bill, indicting subject [redacted] on four (4) counts of violation of Title 18, U.S. Code, Section 876, Mailing Threatening letters.

[redacted] taken into federal custody by the FBI on 7/23/92, is currently incarcerated at the Metropolitan Detention Center (MDC), Los Angeles, California.

2 - Los Angeles

RGP/rc

9A-LA-142276-34
INDEXED
FILED
1992
FBI — LOS ANGELES

Accomplishment Report
(Submit within 30 days from date of accomplishment)

TO: Director, FBI

Date 8/6/92

FROM: SAC, Los Angeles

SUBJECT: [redacted] aka [redacted]

[redacted]-Victim;
Michael Jackson-Victim;
[redacted]-Victim;
[redacted]-Victim;
Mailing Threatening Letters
OO: Los Angeles

Bureau File Number: 9A-LA-142276

Field Office File Number: 0009

Squad or RA Number: [redacted]

Agent's Social Security No.

☐ X if a joint operation with: (Identity of other agency)

☐ X if case involves corruption of a public official (Federal, State or Local)

b6
b7C

Investigative Assistance or Technique Used
Rate each Investigative Assistance or Technique used in connection with the accomplishment being claimed:
1 = Used, but did not help; 2 = Helped, but only minimally; 3 = Helped, substantially; 4 = Absolutely essential

	Rating		Rating		Rating		Rating
1. Acctg Tech Assistance		8. Eng. Sect. Tape Exams		15. Photographic Coverage		22. Telephone Toll Recs	
2. Aircraft Assistance		9. Hypnosis Assistance		16. Polygraph Assistance		23. UCO Group I	
3. Computer Assistance		10. Ident Div Assistance		17. Search Warrants Executed		24. UCO Group II	
4. Consensual Monitoring		11. Informant Information		18. Show Money Usage		25. UCO Other	
5. ELSUR FISC		12. Lab Div Exams		19. Surveil Squad (SOG) Asst		26. NCAVC/ VI-CAP	
6. ELSUR Title III		13. Lab Div Field Support		20. SWAT Team Action		27. Visual Invest. Analysis (VIA)	
7. Eng. Sect. Field Support		14. Pen Registers		21. Tech. Agt. or Tech Equip.			

A. Preliminary Judicial Process (Number of subjects)

Complaints	Informations	Indictments
		1

B. Arrests, Locates, Summonses or Subpoenas Served (No. of Subjects)

	Subject Priority A	B	C
FBI Arrests			
FBI Locates			
Local Arrests			

Subpoenas Served ___ Criminal Summons ___ Local Crim. Summons ___

FBI Subj. Resisted ___ Armed ___

C. Release of Hostages or Children Located: (Number of Hostages or Children Located)

Hostages Held By Terrorists ___ All Other Hostage Situations ___

Missing or Kidnaped Children Located ___

D. Recoveries, Restitutions, or Potential Economic Loss Prevented (PELP) (Explain valuation in remarks)

Property Type Code*	Recoveries	Restitutions	PELP Type Code*	Potential Economic Loss Prevented
	$	$		$
	$	$		$
	$	$		$

E. Civil Matters

		Government Defendant	Government Plaintiff
RICO -Civil Convictions	Civil Suits - Amount of Suit	$	$
No. of Subj.	Settlement of Award	$	$ Enter AFA Payment Here

F. Administrative Sanctions

Subject 1 ___ Subject Description Code* ___

☐ Suspension ☐ Debarment Time Frame: Years: ___ Months: ___ ☐ Permanent

G. Final Judicial Process:* Judicial District: ___ District ___ State ___ Conviction or Pretrial Div. Date ___ Sentence Date ___ No. of Subjects ___ Acquitted ___ Dismissed ___

Subject 1 ___ Subject Description Code* ___ / Subject 2 ___ Subject Description Code* ___

☐ Felony ☐ Misde-meanor ☐ Parole Revocation ☐ Probation Revocation ☐ Plea ☐ Trial ☐ Pretrial Diversion

Conviction: Title, Section, Counts — Combined Sentence: In-Jail Yrs. Mos., Suspended Yrs. Mos., Probation Yrs. Mos. — Total Fines $

Add consecutive sentences together. Enter longest single concurrent sentence. Do not add concurrent sentences together. Sentence 10 yrs.- 8 yrs susp. = 2 yrs. In-Jail.

Attach additional forms if reporting final judicial process on more than two subjects, and submit a final disposition form (R-84) for each subject.

H. Identifying Data: For every subject reported in Sections A, B, E, F, or G above, provide the following: *Attach additional forms for more than four subjects.*

Name	Date of Birth	Race*	Sex	Place of birth (if available)	Social Security Number (if available)
[redacted]	[redacted]	B	M	[redacted]	[redacted]

b6
b7C

Explanation of accomplishment claimed:

On 8/4/92, a Federal Grand Jury, sitting in Los Angeles, Central District of California, handed down a True Bill, indicting [redacted] [redacted] on four (4) counts of violation of Title 18, U.S. Code, Section 876, Mailing Threatening Letters.

SEARCHED ___
INDEXED ___
SERIALIZED ___
FILED ___

1-Admin Stat File
1-9A-LA-142276

1-C-1 Supervisor
1-P/F SA [redacted]

2 - Bureau
4 - Field Office
* See codes on reverse side.

9A-LA-142276-35
OFFICE COPY

FD-302 (Rev. 3-10-82)

- 1 -

FEDERAL BUREAU OF INVESTIGATION

Date of transcription 8/12/92

On August 12, 1992, [redacted] was interviewed at the JACKSON Family Estate, 4641 Hayvenhurst Avenue, Encino, California by Special Agent (SA) [redacted] of the Federal Bureau of Investigation (FBI) Los Angeles Field Office. Present for this interview was [redacted] b6 b7C b7D

At the outset, after identifying himself through a show of credentials, SA [redacted] explained to [redacted] that she was being interviewed with regard to her knowledge of the events which took place at the estate on June 22, 1992. Namely, she would be questioned concerning the detention and arrest of [redacted] who had mailed several threatening letters to [redacted] It was further explained to [redacted] that the United States Attorney's Office was prosecuting the case and as such, the FBI was tasked with collecting all evidence pertinent to this case. [redacted] necessitated this interview.

[redacted] the interview of [redacted] took place.

Investigation on 8/12/92 at Encino, California File # 9A-LA-142276-36

by SA [redacted] /rc Date dictated 8/12/92 b6 b7C

This document contains neither recommendations nor conclusions of the FBI. It is the property of the FBI and is loaned to your agency; it and its contents are not to be distributed outside your agency.

FD-302a (Rev. 11-15-83)

9A-LA-142276

b6
b7C
b7D

Continuation of FD-302 of [redacted], On 8/12/92, Page 2

[redacted] recognized the individual at the front gate as [redacted]

[redacted] started remarking that he needed to talk to [redacted] and about needing to "get his life straight". [redacted] stated that he did not know who he was anymore. [redacted]

[redacted] made reference to the fact that he had sent several letters and had received no response. He was upset and stated that "this has gone on long enough". At one point, according to [redacted] said words to the effect, "I tried to kill the president of the United States and I'm going to kill that [redacted] guy, too!" [redacted] was calling the police [redacted]

He identified himself first as [redacted] and then as [redacted] He further identified himself as JOHN GOTTI's son and cautioned the police not to ask him anything about what the Mafia is doing. [redacted] also repeated to the police the fact that he was there to see his wife, [redacted], and to get his life in order. At this

FD-302a (Rev. 11-15-83)

9A-LA-142276

b6
b7C
b7D

Continuation of FD-302 of [redacted], On 8/12/92, Page 3

[redacted] had no other information of value to provide regarding this matter.

It should be noted that [redacted] refused to provide interviewing agent with any biographical data other than [redacted] stating that the FBI did not need to know [redacted]

COPY

UNITED STATES DISTRICT COURT

FOR THE CENTRAL DISTRICT OF CALIFORNIA

June 1992 Grand Jury

UNITED STATES OF AMERICA, Plaintiff, v. [redacted] Defendant.	)	CR 92-________ **INDICTMENT** [18 U.S.C. § 876: Mailing Threatening Communications]

The Grand Jury charges:

b6
b7C

COUNT ONE

[18 U.S.C. § 876]

On or about March 23, 1992, in Los Angeles County, within the Central District of California, defendant [redacted] knowingly caused to be delivered by the Postal Service, according to the directions thereon, a written communication dated March 21, 1992, addressed to [redacted] at Sherman Oaks, California, and containing a threat to injure [redacted]

GWJ:gwj

9A-LA-142276-37

COUNT TWO

[18 U.S.C. § 876]

On or about April 6, 1992, in Los Angeles County, within the Central District of California, defendant [redacted] knowingly caused to be delivered by the Postal Service, according to the directions thereon, a written communication dated April 5, 1992, addressed to [redacted] at Sherman Oaks, California, and containing a threat to injure [redacted]

b6
b7C

2

COUNT THREE

[18 U.S.C. § 876]

On or about June 8, 1992, in Los Angeles County, within the Central District of California, defendant [redacted] knowingly caused to be delivered by the Postal Service, according to the directions thereon, a written communication dated June 7, 1992, addressed to [redacted] at Sherman Oaks, California, and containing a threat to injure [redacted] [redacted]

b6
b7C

3

COUNT FOUR

[18 U.S.C. § 876]

b6
b7C

On or about June 12, 1992, in Los Angeles County, within the Central District of California, defendant [redacted] knowingly caused to be delivered by the Postal Service, according to the directions thereon, a written communication dated June 12, 1992, addressed to [redacted] at Sherman Oaks, California, and containing a threat to injure [redacted] [redacted]

A TRUE BILL

____
Foreperson

LOURDES G. BAIRD
United States Attorney

ROBERT L. BROSIO
Assistant United States Attorney
Chief, Criminal Division

THOMAS H. BIENERT, JR.
Assistant United States Attorney
Chief, Criminal Complaints

4

FD-302 (Rev. 3-10-82)

- 1 -

FEDERAL BUREAU OF INVESTIGATION

Date of transcription 8/10/92

On August 10, 1992, [redacted] at his request, was interviewed telephonically by Special Agent (SA) [redacted] of the Federal Bureau of Investigation (FBI) Los Angeles Field Office. The interview concerned his knowledge of the threatening letter sent to [redacted] by one [redacted] [redacted] in which [redacted] threatened to kill [redacted] The letter in question was dated June 7, 1992, and addressed to [redacted] The letter made reference to [redacted] [redacted]

b6
b7C
b7D

[redacted] was asked if he was aware of the letter containing the threat, if he knew anything about [redacted] [redacted]

According to [redacted] the name [redacted] meant nothing to him as he had never met anyone by that name. He was however, aware of the threatening letter, having been made aware of it by [redacted] [redacted] He was aware of the contents of the letter, having read a copy provided by [redacted] sometime in July, 1992. He confirmed that [redacted] [redacted] [redacted] had no idea as to why [redacted] would threaten [redacted] [redacted]

[redacted] was curious as to the status of [redacted] [redacted] He appeared relieved upon hearing that [redacted] was currently in custody but made it a point to ask that he be advised should [redacted] be released from jail. [redacted] [redacted] It was explained to [redacted] that the possibility did exist that this matter would go to trial. It was also explained that he

Investigation on 8/10/92 at Los Angeles, California File # 9A-LA-142276 - 38

by SA [redacted] Date dictated 8/10/92

b6
b7C

FD-302a (Rev. 11-15-83)

9A-LA-142276

Continuation of FD-302 of [redacted], On 8/10/92, Page 2

The following descriptive date is set forth for [redacted] [redacted]

b6
b7C
b7D

Name
Sex
Race
Date of Birth
Place of birth
California Driver's
License Number
Height
Weight
Hair
Eyes
Mailing Address

Telephone

Memorandum

To : SAC, LOS ANGELES (9A-LA-142276) (C-1) (P)

Date 10/6/92

From : SA [redacted]

Subject: [redacted] AKA;
[redacted] - VICTIM;
MICHAEL JACKSON - VICTIM;
[redacted] - VICTIM;
[redacted] - VICTIM;
MAILING THREATENING LETTERS;
OO: LOS ANGELES

b6
b7C

For information, on 10/5/92, Assistant United States Attorney (AUSA) GREG JESSNER advised that the competency hearing scheduled for this date for subject [redacted] in U.S. District Court had been continued due to the unavailability of [redacted] defense counsel. The hearing to determine if [redacted] is mentally competent to stand trial with regard to captioned matter was rescheduled for next Tuesday, 10/13/92, at 1:30pm.

b6
b7C

2 - Los Angeles

RGP/rc

9A-LA-142276-39

OCT [illegible]

ROUTING SLIP

TO:

______SAC

______ASAC I (ADMIN)

______ASAC II (WCC)

______ASAC III (WCC)

______ASAC IV (DRUGS/OC)

______ASAC V (VCMOP)

______ASAC VI (FCI/CT, CR, APPS)

______SQUAD

✓ SA [redacted] C-1

______FILE # ______

______MEDIA ______

b6
b7C

ATTACHED PRESS CLIPPING SENT TO:

______BUREAU ______

______SAC ______

______ASAC I (ADMIN)______

______ASAC II (WCC)______

______ASAC III (WCC)______

______ASAC IV (DRUGS/OC______

______ASAC V (VCMOP)______

______ASAC VI (FCI/CT, CR, APPS)______

______SQUAD______

______SA______

______FILE #______

______QUANTICO______

______MEDIA______

FD-350 (Rev. 5-8-81)

(Mount Clipping in Space Below)

(Indicate page, name of newspaper, city and state.)
DAILY NEWS
SAN FERNANDO, CA

Date: WED., 10-14-92
Edition: SAN FERNANDO VALLEY
PG. 3

Title: MAN RULED INCOMPETENT
FOR TRIAL IN DEATH THREATS

Character:
or
Classification:
Submitting Office:
LOS ANGELES

Indexing:

Man ruled incompetent for trial in death threats

By Karen Nikos
Daily News Staff Writer

A federal judge ruled Tuesday that a New York man is incompetent to stand trial on charges he threatened to kill President Bush and entertainer Michael Jackson to get the attention of singer Janet Jackson.

U.S. District Judge A. Andrew Hauk said Frank Paul Jones may be suffering from a mental illness, and he ordered that Jones be evaluated by psychiatrists and placed in the custody of a mental hospital, said Assistant U.S. Attorney Gregory W. Jessner.

Hauk issued his ruling in Los Angeles after a competency hearing requested by federal Deputy Public Defender Myra Sun.

Jones, 33, was arrested June 22 on the grounds of the Jacksons' parents' home in Encino.

Misdemeanor stalking and trespassing charges were dismissed in Van Nuys Municipal Court so federal prosecutors could proceed with a charge of mailing threatening communications, which carries higher penalties.

One month before his Encino arrest, Jones was arrested by White House police for attempting to enter White House grounds in what appeared to be an effort to get Janet Jackson's attention, according to an affidavit filed in support of the federal charge.

The incident came a day after Jones wrote a letter threatening to kill Bush, according to the affidavit.

"Since no one is taking me serious, and I can't handle my state of mind, then I am going to Washington, D.C., to threaten to kill the President of the United States, George Bush," the letter said.

"If they do not arrest me or solve my problem, I'm gonna attempt to kill President Bush," he wrote. "No answer from Janet is is the only wrong answer and I will not accept it."

The affidavit said Jones also threatened to kill entertainer Michael Jackson to get the attention of his sister, Janet Jackson.

In his written ruling, Hauk said Jones is "presently suffering from a mental disease or defect rendering him mentally incompetent to the extent that he is unable to understand the nature and consequences of the proceedings against him or to assist properly in his defense."

9A-LA-142276-40

SEARCHED ___ INDEXED ___
SERIALIZED ___ FILED ___
OCT 15
FBI — LOS ANGELES

FBI/DOJ

Memorandum

To : SAC, LOS ANGELES (9A-LA-142276 (C-1) (P)

Date 10/15/92

From : SA [redacted]

b6
b7C

Subject: [redacted], AKA;
[redacted] VICTIM;
MICHAEL JACKSON - VICTIM;
[redacted] VICTIM;
[redacted] - VICTIM;
MAILING THREATENING LETTERS;
OO: LOS ANGELES

For information, on 10/13/92, subject [redacted] was deemed incompetent to stand trial on charges stemming from captioned matter. U.S. District Judge A. ANDREW HAUK stated that [redacted] may be suffering from a mental illness and was not able to understand the nature and consequence of the proceedings against him. [redacted] was ordered evaluated by psychiatrists and placed in the custody of a federal mental hospital. b6 b7C

On 10/15/92, Assistant United States Attorney (AUSA) GREGORY JESSNER advised that in all likelihood, [redacted] In effect, all legal proceedings now stop until such time as [redacted] is found to be competent to stand trial. If that determination is not made, then [redacted] will remain in custody indefinitely or until he is no longer considered to be a danger to himself or others. b6 b7C

On this same date, the office of [redacted] was notified of the above developments. At that time, writer was advised that [redacted] was no longer with the company and as such, did not have to be notified. b6 b7C

2 - Los Angeles

RGP/rc

9A-LA-142276-41

SEARCHED ____ INDEXED ____
SERIALIZED ____ FILED ____
OCT 19 1992
FBI — LOS ANGELES

Memorandum

To : SAC, LOS ANGELES (9A-LA-142276) (C-1) (P)

Date 11/19/92

From : SA [redacted]

b6
b7C

Subject: [redacted] AKA;
[redacted] VICTIM;
MICHAEL JACKSON - VICTIM;
[redacted] - VICTIM;
[redacted] - VICTIM;
MAILING THREATENING LETTERS;
OO: LOS ANGELES

For information, on 11/19/92, writer contacted AUSA GREGORY JESSNER for an update concerning captioned subject. AUSA JESSNER indicated that subject [redacted] is still undergoing court-ordered psychiatric evaluation. It was unknown whether or not [redacted] was in [redacted] Nevertheless, AUSA JESSNER stated that he would receive a copy of the evaluation report whenever it was completed and he would advise writer upon receipt of said report. All legal proceedings continue to be held in abeyance, pending the completion of the evaluation.

b6
b7C

2 - Los Angeles

RGP/rc

9A-LA-142276-42

Memorandum

To : SAC, LOS ANGELES (9A-LA-142276) (C-1) (P)

Date 12/7/92

From : SA [redacted]

b6
b7C

Subject: [redacted] AKA;
[redacted] - VICTIM;
MICHAEL JACKSON - VICTIM;
[redacted] VICTIM;
[redacted] - VICTIM;
MAILING THREATENING LETTERS;
OO: LOS ANGELES

For information, on 12/3/92, at the request of Assistant United States Attorney (AUSA) GREG JESSNER, Los Angeles, (213) 894-0511, writer made inquiries to determine the exact location where subject [redacted] is currently incarcerated and undergoing court-ordered psychiatric evaluation. b6 b7C

Subject [redacted] is currently [redacted]

2 - Los Angeles

RGP/rc

9A-LA-142276-43

INDEXED FILED

DEC 08 1992

FBI — LOS ANGELES

Memorandum

To : SAC, LOS ANGELES (9A-LA-142276) (C-1) (P)

Date 2/25/93

From : SA [redacted]

Subject: [redacted], AKA;
[redacted] - VICTIM;
MICHAEL JACKSON - VICTIM;
[redacted] VICTIM;
[redacted] - VICTIM;
MAILING THREATENING LETTERS;
OO: LOS ANGELES

b6
b7C

For information, on 2/22/93, Assistant United States Attorney (AUSA) GREGORY JESSNER, Los Angeles, (213) 894-0511, advised writer that [redacted] This report was presented to the judge presiding over the case, Judge HAUK, last week. The judge apparently took exception to the report and has ordered additional evaluation.

b6
b7C

At this point, AUSA JESSNER knows that another competency hearing is scheduled for 4/6/93. It is his belief that if [redacted] is found to be mentally competent, he will enter a plea of guilty to count four (4) of the indictment against him arising from captioned matter.

b6
b7C

AUSA JESSNER advised that [redacted] has been relocated back to the Metropolitan Detention Center (MDC) in Los Angeles. He stated that he would keep writer apprised of any new developments should they arise.

2 - Los Angeles

RGP/rc

9A LA 142276-44

b6
b7C

Memorandum

To : SAC, LOS ANGELES (9A-LA-142276) (C-1) (P)

Date 4/20/93

From : SA [redacted]

Subject: [redacted] AKA;
[redacted] - VICTIM;
MICHAEL JACKSON - VICTIM;
[redacted] - VICTIM;
[redacted] - VICTIM;
MAILING THREATENING LETTERS;
OO: LOS ANGELES

b6
b7C

For information, on 4/20/93, Assistant United States Attorney (AUSA) GREGORY JESSNER, Los Angeles, (213) 894-0511, advised writer that on 4/12/93, subject [redacted] pleaded guilty to count four of the Federal Indictment against him pursuant to captioned matter. The guilty plea was entered before U.S. District Judge A. ANDREW HAUK who scheduled [redacted] sentencing for 6/21/93, at 2:00pm.

b6
b7C

According to AUSA JESSNER, [redacted] is currently [redacted] incarcerated [redacted] and presents the image of someone who is no longer a threat to anyone. JESSNER felt that these might be factors at sentencing which would determine whether or not [redacted] will be given additional prison time to what he has already served.

b6
b7C

2 - Los Angeles

RGP/rc

9A-LA-142276-45

SEARCHED ___ INDEXED ___
SERIALIZED ___ FILED ___

APR 21 1993

FBI — LOS ANGELES

4/22/93

Memorandum

To : SAC, LOS ANGELES (9A-LA-142276) (C-1) (P)

Date . 6/24/93

From : SA [redacted]

b6
b7C

Subject: [redacted] AKA [redacted] - VICTIM;
MICHAEL JACKSON - VICTIM;
[redacted] VICTIM;
[redacted] - VICTIM;
MAILING THREATENING LETTERS;
OO: LOS ANGELES

On 6/24/93, SA [redacted] of the FBI Los Angeles Field Office was advised by AUSA GREGORY JESSNER, (213) 894-0511, that the sentencing scheduled for subject [redacted] on 6/21/93 had been continued. According to JESSNER, the defense requested the delay in order to have their psychiatrist make a statement prior to sentencing. Apparently, the psychiatrist was unavailable on the scheduled date. Sentencing was rescheduled before U.S. District Judge ANDREW HAUK on 7/12/93 at 2:00pm.

b6
b7C

On this same date, at AUSA JESSNER's request, writer contacted [redacted] and advised him of the above. Also, at AUSA JESSNER's request [redacted] was told that if they so desire [redacted] and/or [redacted] could speak at the sentencing to make it known to the court the mental anguish they had gone through as a result of [redacted] actions.

b6
b7C

2 - Los Angeles

RGP/rc

9a-la-142276-46

SEARCHED ___ INDEXED ___
SERIALIZED ___ FILED ___
JUL 1 1993
FBI — LOS ANGELES

FD-350 (Rev. 5-8-8?)

(Mount Clipping in Space Below)

(Indicate page, name of newspaper, city and state.)

L.A. TIMES
LOS ANGELES, CA

Date: TUE., 7-13-93
Edition: METRO, B-2

Title: OBSSESSED FAN GETS TWO YEARS FOR THREATS TO POP SINGER

Character: or Classification:

Submitting Office: LOS ANGELES, C-1

Indexing:

LOS ANGELES

Obsessed Fan Gets 2 Years for Threats to Pop Singer

A New York man who was obsessed with pop singer Janet Jackson and believed he was married to her was sentenced Monday to two years in prison on one count of mailing a threatening communication.

Frank Paul Jones, 34, initially was charged with four counts of sending threatening letters, including two to Jackson, one to her boyfriend, Rene Elizondo, and another to director John Singleton, who worked with her on the soon-to-be-released film "Poetic Justice."

Jones pleaded guilty to one count involving a threat to Elizondo, said Assistant U.S. Atty. Gregory Jessner. Jones was charged last summer, but found incompetent to stand trial. He was treated in a federal correctional institution in North Carolina until doctors determined that he had recovered enough to return to court, Jessner said.

9a-la-142276-47

FBI/DOJ

(Mount Clipping in Space Below)

(Indicate page, name of newspaper, city and state.)

L.A. DAILY NEWS
WOODLAND HILLS, CALIF.

Date: TUE., 7-13-93

Edition: NEWS, PG. 4

Title: MAN GETS PRISON FOR JACKSON THREATS

Character: or Classification:

Submitting Office: LOS ANGELES, C-1

Indexing:

Man gets prison for Jackson threats

A New York man who was obsessed with pop singer Janet Jackson and believed he was married to her was sentenced Monday to two years in prison on one count of mailing a threatening communication.

Frank Paul Jones, 34, was charged last summer, but found incompetent to stand trial. He was treated in a Federal Correction Institution in North Carolina until doctors determined he had recovered enough to return to court, said Assistant U.S. Attorney Gregory Jessner.

During his sentencing, Jones said he had suffered a nervous breakdown, but that he could control his condition with medication.

— City News Service

9a-LA-142276-48

FD-515 (Rev.1-1-93)

Accomplishment Report

(Submit within 30 days from date of accomplishment)

Report Date: 7/15/93

From: SAC, Los Angeles

Does Accomplishment Involve: (check all that apply)	
Drugs	☐
A Fugitive	☐
Bankruptcy Fraud	☐
Computer Fraud/Abuse	☐
Corruption of Public Officials	☐
Forfeiture Assets	☐

File Number: 9A-LA-142276

Stat Agent Soc. Sec. No.

RA	Squad
HQ	C-1

Task Force

Assisting Agents Soc. Sec. No.×
1. _ _
2. _ _

Assisting Joint Agencies ×•
1.
2.

[pl] Squad Supervisor approval (please initial)

Investigative Assistance or Technique Used

1 = Used, but did not help; 2 = Helped, minimally; 3 = Helped, substantially; 4 = Absolutely essential

b6 b7C

Rating	IAT	Rating	IAT	Rating	IAT
	Financ. Analyst Asst.		Informant Info.		Tech. Agnt. or Equip.
	Aircraft Assistance		Lav. Div. Exams		Telephone Toll Recs.
	Computer Assistance		Lab. Div. Field Supt.		UCO - Group I
	Consensual Monitor		Pen Registers		UCO - Group II
	ELSUR / FISC		Photograph Coverage		UCO - Other
	ELSUR / Title III		Polygraph Assistance		NCAVC / VI - CAP
	Eng. Sect. Field Supt.		Search Warrants Exec.		Visual Invest. Anal.
	Eng. Sect. Tape Exams		Show Money Usage		Crisis Neg. - Fed.
	Hypnosis Assistance		SOG Assistance		Crisis Neg. - Local
	Ident Div. Assistance		Swat Team Action		

Accomplishment type •	Accomplishment Date	Serial No. of FD-515
CONVICTION	7/12/93	

A. Complaint / Information / Indictment
Also Complete Section I
Serial number ________
Check if Civil / Rico Complaint ☐

B. Arrest / Locate / Summons
Arrest
☐ Federal ☐ Local ♦
Subject Priority: ☐A ☐B ☐C
☐ Subject Resisted
☐ Subject was Armed
Locate
Subject Priority: ☐A ☐B ☐C
Summons
☐ Federal ☐ Local ♦

C. Hostage(s) Released
Released by: ☐ Terrorists ☐ Other
Number of Hostages: ________

D. Recovery / Restitution / Potential Economic Loss Prevented (PELP) × ♦
Recovery
☐ Federal ☐ Local
Restitution
☐ Court Ordered
☐ Pretrial Agreement

Code •	Amount	Code •	Amount
	$		$
	$		$
	$		$

E. Civil / Rico Matters
Also Complete Section I
Date of Complaint: __/__/__
Judgment____ •
Judicial Outcome ____ × •
Fines: $________
Suspension: Years | Months

F. AFA Payment
Amount: $________

G. Administrative Sanctions
Type: ☐ Suspension ☐ Debarment ☐ Injunction
Length: ☐ Permanent ☐ Years | Months
Subject Description Code: ____ •

H. Final Judicial Process
Conviction
Also Complete Section I
Date of Complaint, Information or Indictment: 7/21/92
Date of Conviction: 4/12/93
Date of Sentence: 7/12/93
Subject Description Code: 8A •
Judicial State: CA District: CENTRAL
Sentence type: JS × •
Sentence Term:

☑ Federal ☐ Local ♦
☑ Felony ☐ Misdemeanor
☑ Plea ☐ Trial

In-Jail Years	In-Jail Months	Suspended Years	Suspended Months	Probation Years	Probation Months
2				3	

Fines: $ ________

I. U.S. Code Violations

Title	Section	Counts	Title	Section	Counts
18	876	1			

Required for Sections A, E, and H (Conviction)
Optional for Section B (arrest)

Acquittal / Dismissal / Pretrial Diversion
Date of Indictment or Information: __/__
Subject Description Code: ____ •

SEARCHED ____ INDEXED ____ SERIALIZED ____ FILED ____ b6 b7C

J. Subject Information (Required for Sections A, B, D (Restitution), E, F, G, and H)

Name	Date of Birth	Race •	Sex	Place of Birth (if available)	Social Security No. (if available)
		B	M		

☐ Subject Related to an LCN, Asian Organized Crime (AOC), or Italian Organized Crime (IOC) Group. (If checked, also submit form FD-515a)

× Additional information may be added by attaching another form or a plain sheet of paper for additional entries.
♦ Requires that a written explanation on plain paper be attached. (Court Ordered Restitution does not require a written explanation)
• See codes on reverse side.

9A-LA-142276-49 7-15-93

ACCOMPLISHMENT TYPES

Complaint
Information
Indictment
Arrest
Locate
Summons
Hostage(s) Released
Child Locate
Recovery
Restitution
PELP
Civil/RICO
AFA Payment
Admin. Sanction
Conviction
Pretrial Diversion
Acquittal
Dismissal

PELP CODES

22 Counterfeit Stocks/Bonds/Currency/ Negotiable Instruments
23 Counterfeit/Pirated Sound Recordings or Motion Pictures
24 Bank Theft Scheme Aborted
25 Ransom, Extortion or Bribe Demand Aborted
26 Theft From or Fraud Against Government Scheme Aborted
27 Commercial or Industrial Theft Scheme Aborted
30 All Other

PROPERTY CODES

01 Cash
02 Stocks, Bonds or Negotiable Instruments
03 General Retail Merchandise
04 Vehicles
05 Heavy Machinery & Equipment
06 Aircraft
07 Jewelry
08 Vessels
09 Art, Antiques or Rare Collections
11 Real Property
20 All Other

JOINT AGENCY CODES

BATF Bureau of Alcohol, Tobacco and Firearms
DEA Drug Enforcement Administration
DOI Department of Interior
FAA Federal Aviation Administration
INS Immigration and Naturalization Service
IRS Internal Revenue Service
NBIS National NARC Border Interdiction
RCMP Royal Canadian Mounted Police
USBP U.S. Border Patrol
USCS U.S. Customs Service
USDS U.S. Department of State
USTR U.S. Treasury
ST State
LOC Local
OTHR Other

SENTENCE TYPES

CP Capital Punishment
JS Jail Sentence
LS Life Sentence
NS No Sentence (Subject Died or is Fugitive)
PB Probation
SJ Suspension of Jail Sentence
YC Youth Correction Act

JUDGMENT CODES

CJ Consent Judgment
CO Court Ordered Settlement
DF Default Judgment
DI Dismissal
JN Judgment Notwithstanding
MV Mixed Verdict
SJ Summary Judgment
VD Verdict for Defendant
VP Verdict for Plaintiff

JUDICIAL OUTCOME

AG Agreement
BR Barred/Removed
CC Civil Contempt
DC Disciplinary Charges
FI Fine
PI Preliminary Injunction
PR Temporary Restraining Order
RN Restitution
SP Suspension
VR Voluntary Resignation
OT Other

RACE CODES

B Black
C Chinese
I Indian/American
J Japanese
O Other
U Unknown
W White

For Further Instructions See: MAOP, Part II, Section 3.3-5.

SUBJECT DESCRIPTION CODES

ORGANIZED CRIME SUBJECTS

1F Boss
1G Underboss
1H Consigliere
1J Acting Boss
1K Capodecina
1L Soldier

KNOWN CRIMINALS

2A Top Ten or I.O. Fugitive
2B Top Thief
2C Top Con Man

FOREIGN NATIONALS

3A Legal Alien
3B Illegal Alien
3C Foreign Official W/out Diplomatic Immunity
3D U.N. Employee W/out Diplomatic Immunity
3E Foreign Student
3F All Others

OTHERS

8A All Other Subjects
8B Company or Corporation

TERRORISTS

4A Known Member of a Terrorist Organization
4B Possible Terrorist Member or Sympathizer

UNION MEMBERS

5D President
5E Vice-President
5F Treasurer
5G Secretary/Treasurer
5H Executive Board Member
5I Business Agent
5J Representative
5K Organizer
5L Business Manager
5M Financial Secretary
5N Recording Secretary
5P Office Manager
5Q Clerk
5R Shop Steward
5S Member
5T Trustee
5U Other

GOVERMENT SUBJECTS

6A Presidential Appointee
6B U.S. Senator/Staff
6C U.S. Representative/Staff
6D Federal Judge/Magistrate
6E Federal Prosecutor
6F Federal Law Enforcement Officer
6G Federal Employee - GS 13 & Above
6H Federal Employee - GS 12 & Below
6J Governor
6K Lt. Governor
6L State Legislator
6M State Judge/Magistrate
6N State Prosecutor
6P State Law Enforcement Officer
6Q State - All Others
6R Mayor
6S Local Legislator
6T Local Judge/Magistrate
6U Local Prosecutor
6V Local Law Enforcement Officer
6W Local - All Others
6X County Commissioner
6Y City Councilman

BANK EMPLOYEES

7A Bank Officer
7B Bank Employee

☆ U.S. GOVERNMENT PRINTING OFFICE: 1993 342-484/72323

R-84 (Rev. 5-14-80)

FINAL DISPOSITION REPORT

Leave Blank

Note: This vital report must be prepared on each individual whose arrest fingerprints have been forwarded to the FBI Identification Division without final disposition noted thereon. If no final disposition is available to arresting agency, also obtain subject's right four finger impressions on this form, complete left side and forward the form when case referred to prosecutor and/or courts. Agency on notice as to final disposition should complete this form and submit to: **Director, FBI, Washington, D.C. 20537, Attention: Identification Division.**
(See instuctions on reverse side)

b6
b7C

FBI No.

Name on Fingerprint Card Submitted to FBI
Last First Middle

Date of Birth Sex Male

Henry Fingerprint Classification From FBI 1-B Response

State Bureau No. (SID)

Social Security No. (SOC)

Contributor of Fingerprints (Include complete name and location of agency, together with ORI number.)

FEDERAL BUREAU OF INVESTIGATION
LOS ANGELES, CALIFORNIA

Arrest No. (OCA)

Date Arrested or Received
7/23/92

Offenses Charged at Arrest

Title 18, U.S.C. 876
(Mailing Threatening Letters)

If additional space is needed, check ☐ and continue on reverse side of this f

Final Disposition & Date
(If convicted or subject pleaded guilty to lesser charge, include this modification with dispostion.)

Plead guilty to one (1) count on 4/12/93; sentenced in U.S. District Court on 7/12/93 to two (2) years in prison and three (3) years supervised probation

This Form Submitted By:
(Name, Title, Agency, ORI No., City & State)

Charlie J. Parsons
Special Agent in Charge
FBI
Los Angeles, California

Charlie J Parsons 7/16/93
Signature Date

Title

☐ COURT ORDERED EXPUNGEMENT:
Return Arrest Fingerprint Card to Contributing Agency;
Certified or Authenticated Copy of Court Order Attached.

9A-LA-142276-50

SEARCHED ___ INDEXED ___
SERIALIZED ___ FILED ___
JUL 1 ? 1993
FBI — LOS ANGELES

Memorandum

To : SAC, LOS ANGELES (9A-LA-142276) (C-1) (C)   Date 7/16/93

From : SA [redacted]

Subject: [redacted] AKA;
[redacted] - VICTIM;
MICHAEL JACKSON - VICTIM;
[redacted] - VICTIM;
[redacted] - VICTIM;
MAILING THREATENING LETTERS;
OO: LOS ANGELES

b6
b7C

Re memo of SA [redacted] dated 6/24/93.

b6
b7C

On 7/13/93, Assistant United States Attorney (AUSA) GREGORY JESSNER, Los Angeles, (213) 894-0511, advised that subject [redacted] had been sentenced the previous day, 7/12/93, in U.S. District Court. U.S. District Judge ANDREW HAUK sentenced [redacted] to two (2) years in federal prison and three (3) years supervised probation based on his guilty plea to one count of threatening [redacted] Judge HAUK also ordered that [redacted]

AUSA JESSNER expressed satisfaction with the sentencing and was of the opinion that it would serve as a deterrent to others bent on stalking or threatening celebrities.

In view of subject's sentencing, the fact that subject [redacted] set of major case prints as well as form R-84 (Final Disposition Report) have been sent to FBIHQ Identification Division, all logical investigation has been conducted and no leads remain outstanding, it is recommended that this case be closed administratively.

b6
b7C

1 - Los Angeles

RGP/rc

7/22/93

9A-LA-142276-57

JUL 21 1993

FEDERAL BUREAU OF INVESTIGATION
FOIPA
DELETED PAGE INFORMATION SHEET

No Duplication Fees are charged for Deleted Page Information Sheet(s).

Total Deleted Page(s) ~ 111
Page 15 ~ b6, b7C, b7D
Page 33 ~ b6, b7C
Page 75 ~ b6, b7C
Page 77 ~ b6, b7C
Page 79 ~ b6, b7C
Page 81 ~ b6, b7C
Page 83 ~ b6, b7C
Page 85 ~ b6, b7C
Page 87 ~ b6, b7C
Page 89 ~ b6, b7C
Page 91 ~ b6, b7C
Page 93 ~ b6, b7C
Page 95 ~ b6, b7C
Page 107 ~ b6, b7C
Page 108 ~ b6, b7C
Page 109 ~ b6, b7C
Page 110 ~ b6, b7C
Page 111 ~ b6, b7C
Page 112 ~ b6, b7C
Page 113 ~ b6, b7C
Page 114 ~ b6, b7C
Page 115 ~ b6, b7C
Page 116 ~ b6, b7C
Page 117 ~ b6, b7C
Page 118 ~ b6, b7C
Page 119 ~ b6, b7C
Page 120 ~ b6, b7C
Page 121 ~ b6, b7C
Page 122 ~ b6, b7C
Page 123 ~ Duplicate
Page 124 ~ Duplicate
Page 128 ~ b6, b7C
Page 129 ~ b6, b7C
Page 130 ~ b6, b7C
Page 131 ~ b6, b7C
Page 143 ~ b6, b7C
Page 144 ~ b6, b7C
Page 157 ~ Duplicate
Page 158 ~ Duplicate
Page 159 ~ Duplicate
Page 160 ~ Duplicate
Page 176 ~ b6, b7C
Page 183 ~ Duplicate
Page 184 ~ Duplicate

Page 188 ~ Duplicate
Page 189 ~ Duplicate
Page 190 ~ Duplicate
Page 192 ~ Duplicate
Page 195 ~ Duplicate
Page 197 ~ Duplicate
Page 201 ~ Duplicate
Page 203 ~ Duplicate
Page 209 ~ Duplicate
Page 210 ~ Duplicate
Page 211 ~ b6, b7C
Page 212 ~ b6, b7C
Page 214 ~ Duplicate
Page 215 ~ Duplicate
Page 216 ~ Duplicate
Page 217 ~ Duplicate
Page 218 ~ Duplicate
Page 223 ~ Duplicate
Page 225 ~ Duplicate
Page 226 ~ Duplicate
Page 227 ~ Duplicate
Page 228 ~ Duplicate
Page 231 ~ Duplicate
Page 232 ~ Duplicate
Page 233 ~ Duplicate
Page 234 ~ Duplicate
Page 246 ~ Duplicate
Page 249 ~ Duplicate
Page 250 ~ Duplicate
Page 251 ~ Duplicate
Page 255 ~ Duplicate
Page 256 ~ Duplicate
Page 257 ~ Duplicate
Page 259 ~ Duplicate
Page 260 ~ Duplicate
Page 267 ~ Duplicate
Page 268 ~ Duplicate
Page 269 ~ Duplicate
Page 270 ~ Duplicate
Page 273 ~ b6, b7C
Page 274 ~ b6, b7C
Page 275 ~ b6, b7C
Page 276 ~ b6, b7C
Page 279 ~ b6, b7C
Page 290 ~ b6, b7C
Page 315 ~ b6, b7C
Page 316 ~ b6, b7C
Page 317 ~ b6, b7C
Page 318 ~ b6, b7C
Page 319 ~ b6, b7C
Page 320 ~ b6, b7C

Page 321 ~ b6, b7C
Page 322 ~ b6, b7C
Page 323 ~ b6, b7C
Page 324 ~ b6, b7C
Page 325 ~ b6, b7C
Page 326 ~ b6, b7C
Page 327 ~ b6, b7C
Page 328 ~ b6, b7C
Page 329 ~ b6, b7C
Page 330 ~ b6, b7C
Page 331 ~ b6, b7C
Page 366 ~ Referral/Direct
Page 367 ~ Referral/Direct
Page 368 ~ Referral/Direct
Page 369 ~ Referral/Direct
Page 370 ~ Referral/Direct

Chapter Seven - Failed Mann Act

OUTCOMES

Outcomes

On 14 September 2004, a request was made to open a caption file.

Following an interview in New York on 09 December 2004, a further request was made to **close the file**.

> *"There are no outstanding leads or evidence items."*

Outcome: **Caption case closed.**

(Rev. 01-31-2003)

FEDERAL BUREAU OF INVESTIGATION

Precedence: ROUTINE **Date:** 09/14/2004

To: Los Angeles

From: Los Angeles
Santa Maria RA
Contact: SA [redacted] b2 b6 b7C

Approved By: [redacted]

Drafted By: [redacted] b6 b7C

Case ID #: 305B-LA-239204 (Pending) - 1

Title: MICHAEL JOE JACKSON;
[redacted] (MINOR) - VICTIM
IINI - TRAVELERS/ENTICEMENT

Synopsis: Case opening.

Details: Writer request a case be opened for captioned investigation. In June 2004, Santa Barbara Assistant District Attorneys (SBADAs) Ron Zonen and Gordon Auchincloss met with Behavior Analysis Unit (BAU) at Quantico. After hearing the facts about the captioned victim, the BAU informed the SBADAs that a Federal case could still be pursued.

On 08/30/2004, a conference call was held to discuss various details of the potential case. As a result of call, it was agreed that the Santa Maria RA open a case for captioned victim.

9/14/04 O+Assign SA 9/14/04 b6 b7C

♦♦
257dfw01.04

S-06
CPI-NONE

305B-LA-239204-1

(Rev. 01-31-2003)

FEDERAL BUREAU OF INVESTIGATION

Precedence: ROUTINE **Date:** 09/23/2004

To: New York **Attn:** SA [redacted] C-20 b6 b7C

From: Los Angeles
Santa Maria RA
Contact: SA [redacted] b2 b6 b7C

Approved By: [redacted]

Drafted By: [redacted] b6 b7C

Case ID #: 305B-LA-239204 (Pending) -2

Title: Michael Joe Jackson;
[redacted] (MINOR) - VICTIM
IINI - Travelers/ Enticement

Synopsis: Travel to New York division to interview victim.

Details: In June 2004, the Santa Barbara District Attorneys office (SBDA) met with Behavior Analysis Unit (BAU) at Quantico. After hearing the facts about the captioned victim, the BAU informed the SBDA that a Federal case could still be pursued. As a result, Los Angeles opened captioned investigation.

The writer plans to interview [redacted] with SA [redacted] C-20 on Tuesday, September 28, 2004 at 1:00 p.m at a hotel in New York City. A second interview later in the week is expected. b6 b7C

Writer requests permission to travel to New York on Monday, September 27, 2004, division to meet with [redacted]

To: New York From: Los Angeles
Re: 305B-LA-239204, 09/23/2004

LEAD(s):

Set Lead 1: (FYI)

NEW YORK

AT NEW YORK, NEW YORK

Los Angeles assumes travel is approved unless otherwise advised.

266fdw01.04
♦♦

2

(Rev. 01-31-2003)

FEDERAL BUREAU OF INVESTIGATION

Precedence: ROUTINE **Date:** 10/15/2004

To: Los Angeles

From: Los Angeles
Santa Maria RA
Contact: SA [redacted] b2 b6 b7C

Approved By: [redacted]

Drafted By: [redacted]

Case ID #: 305B-LA-239204 (Pending) -3 b6 b7C

Title: Michael Joe Jackson;
[redacted] (MINOR) - VICTIM
IINI - Travelers/ Enticement

Synopsis: Meeting with [redacted]

Details: On September 28, 2004, SAs [redacted] and [redacted] [redacted] met with [redacted] to discuss captioned matter. During the meeting [redacted] advised the agents that he had no interest in testifying against Jackson. [redacted] advised that he would legally fight any attempt to do so. [redacted] believed that he had done his part [redacted] [redacted] b6 b7C

[redacted] b6 b7C

♦♦

288dfw02.04

(Rev. 01-31-2003)

FEDERAL BUREAU OF INVESTIGATION

Precedence: ROUTINE **Date:** 12/09/2004

To: Los Angeles

From: Los Angeles
Santa Maria RA
Contact: SA [redacted] b2 b6 b7C

Approved By: [redacted]

Drafted By: [redacted] DFW

Case ID #: 305B-LA-239204 (Closed) - 4 b6 b7C

Title: MICHAEL JOE JACKSON;
[redacted] (MINOR) - VICTIM
IINI - TRAVELERS/ENTICEMENT

Synopsis: Close case.

Details: Writer requests that captioned matter be closed. There are no outstanding leads or evidence items.

♦♦
343dfw01.04

12/14/04
C-4
12/13/04

305B-LA-239204-4

Summary

Press Cuttings:
Computers: NO EVIDENCE Found.
Mann Act:
VHS Tape: Physical & Electronic examination - NO EVIDENCE
09 DEC 2004: NO OUTSTANDING LEADS OR EVIDENCE ITEMS.
Task Force Investigations in the Philippines, Canada, Mexico and New York: NO EVIDENCE.
Files Closed.
199 pages: extortion + threats

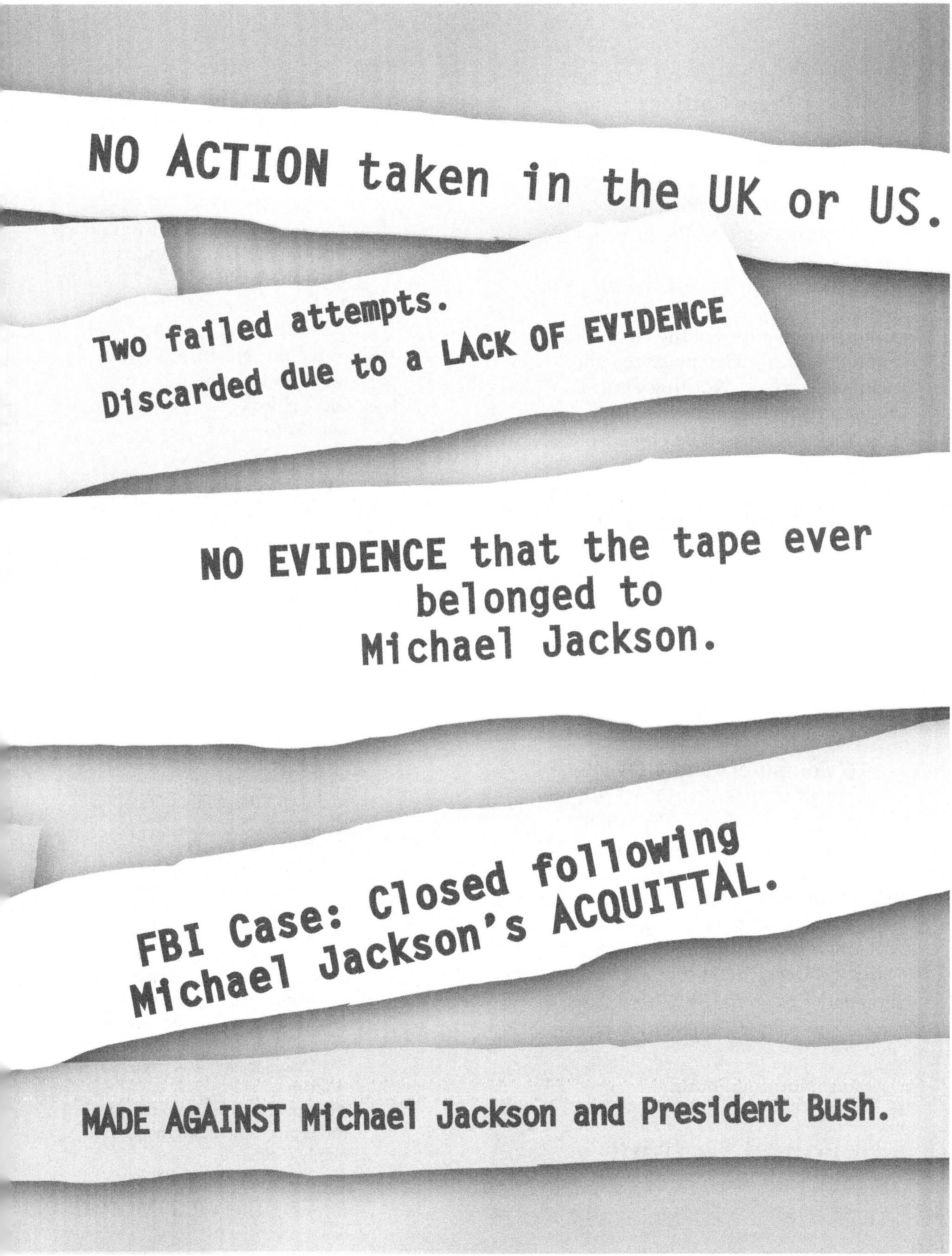
NO ACTION taken in the UK or US.
Two failed attempts.
Discarded due to a LACK OF EVIDENCE
NO EVIDENCE that the tape ever belonged to Michael Jackson.
FBI Case: Closed following Michael Jackson's ACQUITTAL.
MADE AGAINST Michael Jackson and President Bush.

Press Cuttings

- Legat, London sent Los Angeles SAC in September 1993, Press Cuttings - **No action** taken by the UK or the USA law enforcement agencies. Produced for *"information only"*.
- Unsubstantiated telephone allegations
- Further enquiries of the New York Supreme Court - Computerized and manual searches - **Nothing Found**.
- No outstanding leads for the Los Angeles Office - **File closed.**

Found Nothing

Random VHS Tape

- **No evidence** that the VHS ever belonged to Michael Jackson.
- VHS tape was sent to the FBI by the United States Customs Service
- The VHS was a multiple generation tape, poor quality
- Result: **Nothing Found** on the VHS tape.

No evidence that the tape ever belonged to Michael Jackson.

Found Nothing

16 Computers and 4 DVD's

- Review of string search /keyboard hits
- Santa Barbara Sheriff's Department requested assistance from the FBI on 15 January 2004. The FBI investigation was undertaken at the Santa Barbara Laboratory and under the supervision of the local enforcement team.
- Sheriff's Department sent a letter of commendation to the FBI, *"their assistance in this matter was greatly appreciated"*.
- Result: **Nothing Found.**

Found Nothing

199 Pages

- 199 pages - nothing to do with the child molestation allegations.
- A man sent letters which included threats to kill President George Bush and Michael Jackson.
- The man wrote, *"Michael I will personally attempt to kill if he doesn't pay me my money"*.
- Threats extend to committing *"mass murder at a Michael Jackson concert"*.
- Michael Jackson was cited as the **'Victim'**.
- The man was arrested outside the White House and the Jackson family residence.

Michael Jackson
the **VICTIM**

Agencies and Requests mentioned in the FBI Files

- FBI: Engineering Research Facility Regional Computer Forensics (RCFL)
- FBI: Investigative Technology Division
- Los Angeles Police Department
- Legat London
- FBI: Video Analysis
- FBI: Forensic Audio Video Image Analysis Unit (FAVIAU)
- FBI advice on Prosecutive Strategies
- FBI advice on Interview Strategies
- FBI advice on Expert Testimony
- FBI a request for Forensic Guidance
- National Centre for the Analysis of Violent Crime (NCAVC)
- Behavioral Analysis Unit-3
- Behavioral Sciences Unit
- Computer and Analysis and Response (CART)
- Technical Surveillance Countermeasures (TSCM)
- FBI (Ventura)
- Crimes Against Children's Unit (CACU)
- Victim Witness Unit
- FBI Lab
- Department of Child Exploitation and Obscenity Section (CEOS)
- Critical Incident Response Group (CIRG)
- FBI - Automated Case Management System (ASC)
- FBI: Privacy Impact Assessment
- FBI: Los Angeles Division - Consideration of Potential Federal Allegations
- FBI: New York and Miami Divisions
- Santa Barbara County Sheriff's Department (SBSD)
- Santa Barbara Sheriff's Office Laboratory
- Sheriff's Department, Santa Barbara County, Criminal Investigations - Sheriff/ coroner
- Santa Barbara County District Attorney's Office
- Santa Barbara County Investigation and Prosecution Teams

Found Nothing

Summary

Threats and Extortion:
The bulk of the Michael Jackson FBI files cited Michael Jackson as the 'VICTIM' of death threats and extortion.

Approximately two-thirds of the released files, contained threats made **against** Michael Jackson and President Bush.

A man was apprehended outside the White House and later arrested at the Jackson family compound.

Date 7/30/92
Title and Character of Case
[redacted] aka
[redacted]-Victim;
Michael Jackson-Victim;
[redacted] Victim;
[redacted]-Victim;
Mailing Threatening Letters;
9A-LA-142276-1a
b6
b7C
Date Property Acquired 7/27/92
Source From Which Property Acquired Holly Beckner, Asst. City Atty, Los Angeles
Location of Property or Bulky Exhibit
Reason for Retention of Property and Efforts Made to Dispose of Same

[FBI file: image crop with red highlight.]

The balance of the files, related to the FBI's investigations at the behest of the domestic authorities,

Press Cuttings:
The FBI considered historical press cuttings sent from Legat London. The press cuttings were provided for *information only.*

Legat London took *no further action.*

VHS Tape:
US Customs asked the FBI to investigate a VHS tape. It was examined and found to be a multi-generational copied tape. The tape was not worn, but it was a poor quality reproduction.

No child pornography when found on the tape.

There was **no evidence** that the VHS tape ever belonged to Michael Jackson.

Worldwide Task Force:
Task Force Teams investigated disgruntled former employee claims in the Philippines. **Lead closed.**

Task Force to Ottawa, Canada, investigated a claim a by a social worker. **Lead closed.**

Mexican Boys:
A writer made a claim to the FBI that Michael Jackson had been investigated in relation to an allegation that he had molested two boys in Mexico.

On investigation **no records were found. No action.**

New York:
A telephone caller claimed that a restraining order had been made against Michael Jackson. Enquires were made at the New York Supreme Court both manual and electronic, and **nothing was found.**

Seized Computers and Media:
The FBI were requested to investigated sixteen seized computers and media. Their report stated that ***nothing* was found.**

A letter of commendation was sent from the Santa Barbara County Sheriff's Department to the Senior Resident Agent in Los Angeles dated 27 April 2004.

> ***"...Your staff are truly experts at what they do, Their assistance in this matter was greatly appreciated."***

Mann Act:
Two attempts were made to prosecute Michael Jackson under the Mann Act. Both attempts were discarded in the early stages due to a **lack of evidence.**

First Attempt: On 07 September 1993, an agent contacted AUSA Patricia Donahue inviting her to attend a meeting. The following day AUSA Donahue had advised that a decision had been made that,

> *"...The United States Attorney was not interested in prosecuting Michael Jackson for a[n alleged] violation of the Mann Act..."*

During a meeting on 10 September 1993, the FBI agreed to offer assistance in pursing leads. These leads proved fruitless and the caption **files were closed.**

Second Attempt: In June 2004, the Santa Barbara District Attorneys Office (SBDA) met with the Behavior Analysis Unit (BAU) at their headquarters in Quantico.

The record states that after hearing information about an alleged victim, the BAU informed the SBDA that a Federal case could still be pursued. A file was opened.

The agents visited the alleged victim on 28 September 2004. The alleged victim was not interested in testifying against Michael Jackson and indicated that they would use legal means to prevent their attempts.

On 09 December 2004 a routine request was made to **close the file.**

"There are no outstanding leads or evidence items".

Two attempts were made to pursue Michael Jackson under the Mann Act and both **attempts failed** due to a lack of evidence.

In conclusion, Michael Jackson was thoroughly investigated by social services, the police, the DAs office, the FBI and several other agencies.

Public requests were made at the initial press conference in November 2003 for leads and information.

The media produced wall to wall coverage of the case from commencement to acquittal.

After Michael Jackson's death, a Freedom Information Request was made and in December 2009, 333 pages of the FBI files were released.

The majority of the pages cited Michael Jackson as the caption **'VICTIM'.**

The balance of the pages documented **closed leads.**

The FBI found nothing.

Mock up of a possibly more accurate account of the FBI Files.
Photo: screengrab.

"The truth (however sometimes late) will at last prevail"

[15]
"Some people may think, that such an accomplishment as this, can be of no great use to the owner, or his party, after it has been often practised and is become notorious; but they are widely mistaken. Few lies carry the inventor's mark, and the most prostitute enemy to truth, may spread a thousand without being known for the author: besides, as the vilest writer has his readers, so the greatest liar has his believers: and it often happens, that if a lie be believed only for an hour, it has done its work, and there is no farther occasion for it. Falshood flies, and truth comes limping after it; so that when men come to be undeceived, it is too late; the jest is over, and the tale has had its effect: like a man, who has thought of a good repartee, when the discourse is changed, or the company parted; or like a physician, who has found out an infallible medicine, after the patient is dead.

"Considering that natural disposition in many men to lie, and in multitudes to believe, I have been perplexed what to do with that maxim so frequent in every body's mouth; that truth will at last prevail.

[16]
"... wherein I shall endeavour to undeceive, or discover, those deluded, or deluding persons, who hope or pretend, it is only a short madness in the vulgar, from which they may soon recover; whereas, I believe, it will appear to be very different in its causes, its symptoms, and its consequences; and prove a great example to illustrate the maxim I lately mentioned; that truth (however sometimes late) will at last prevail."

THURSDAY, NOVEMBER 9, 1710.
The Examiner, Number 14
Rev. Jonathan Swift

Verdict Day - 13 June 2005

Not Guilty
Not Guilty
Not Guilty
Not Guilty
Verdict
Not Guilty
Not Guilty
Not Guilty

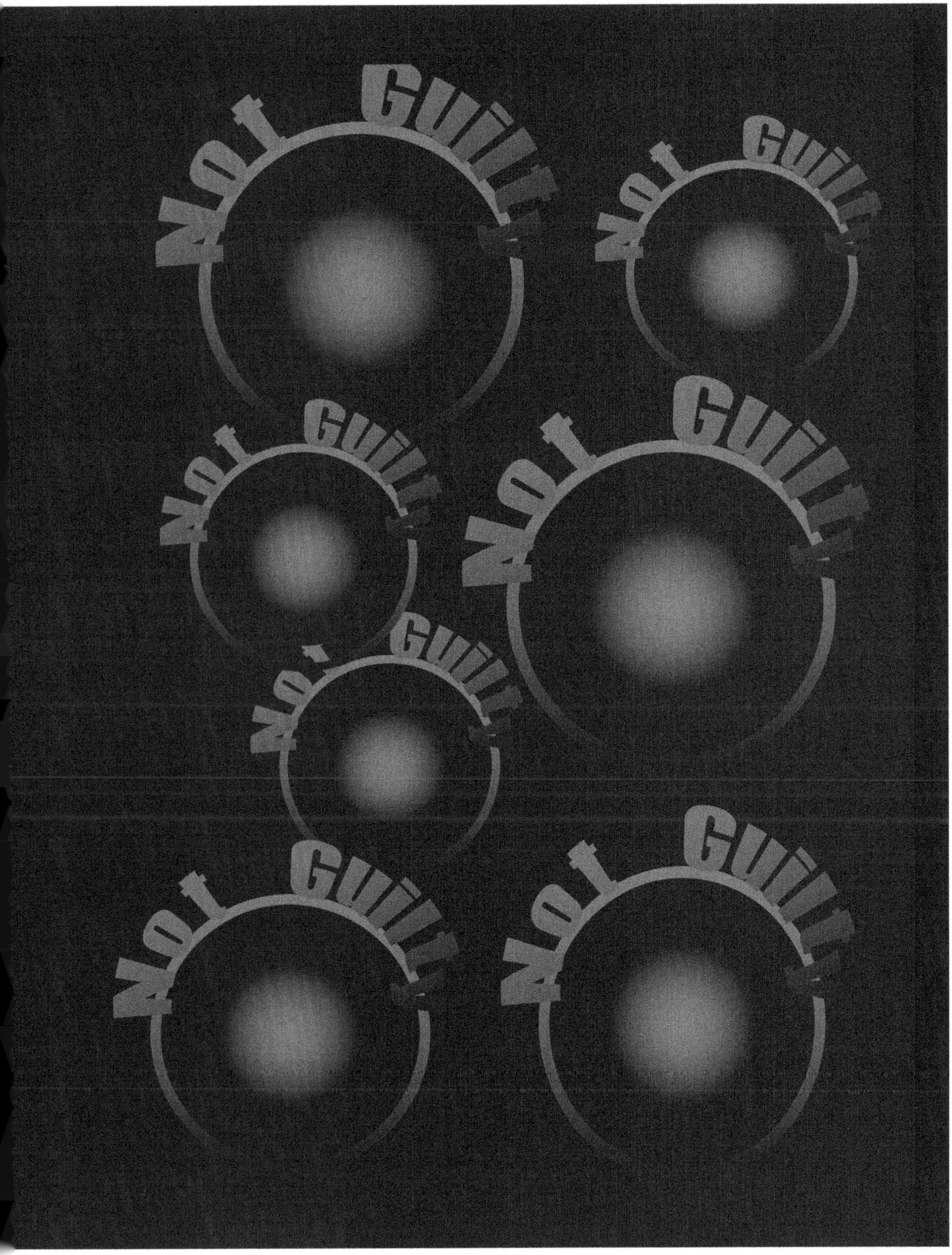
Not Guilty
Not Guilty
Not Guilty
Not Guilty
Not Guilty
Not Guilty
Not Guilty

THE CLERK:
"Superior Court of the State of California for the County of Santa Barbara, Santa Maria Division.

The People of the State of California, Plaintiff,
versus Michael Joe Jackson, Defendant,
Case No. 1133603.

"COUNT 1, verdict: We, the jury, in the above-entitled case, find the Defendant NOT GUILTY of Conspiracy as charged in Count 1 of the Indictment.
Dated: June 13th, 2005. Foreperson: No. 80.

"COUNT 2, verdict: We, the jury, in the above-entitled case, find the Defendant NOT GUILTY of a Lewd Act Upon a Minor Child as charged in Count 2 of the Indictment.
Dated: June 13th, 2005. Foreperson: No. 80.

"COUNT 3, verdict: We, the jury, in the above-entitled case, find the Defendant NOT GUILTY of a Lewd Act Upon a Minor Child as charged in Count 3 of the Indictment.
Dated: June 13th, 2005. Foreperson: No. 80.

"COUNT 4, verdict: We, the jury, in the above-entitled case, find the Defendant NOT GUILTY of a Lewd Act Upon a Minor child as charged in Count 4 of the Indictment.
Dated: June 10th, 2005. Foreperson: No. 80.

"COUNT 5, verdict: We, the jury, in the above-entitled case, find the Defendant NOT GUILTY of a Lewd Act Upon a Minor Child as charged in Count 5 of the Indictment.
Dated: June 10th, 2005. Foreperson: No. 80.

"COUNT 6, verdict: We, the jury, in the above-entitled case, find the Defendant NOT GUILTY of Attempting to Commit a Lewd Act Upon a Minor Child, as charged in Count 6 of the Indictment.

Dated: June 13th, 2005. Foreperson: No. 80.

"**COUNT 7**, verdict: We, the jury, in the above-entitled case, find the Defendant **NOT GUILTY** of Administering an Intoxicating Agent to Assist in the Commission of a Felony as charged in Count 7 of the Indictment.
Dated: June 13th, 2005. Foreperson: No. 80.

"**COUNT 7**, verdict, lesser offense: We, the jury, in the above-entitled case, find the Defendant **NOT GUILTY** of Providing Alcoholic Beverages to Persons Under the Age of 21, a lesser-included offense of that charged in Count 7 of the Indictment.
Dated: June 13th, 2005. Foreperson: No. 80.

"**COUNT 8**, verdict: We, the jury, in the above-entitled case, find the Defendant NOT GUILTY of Administering an Intoxicating Agent to Assist in the Commission of a Felony as charged in Count 8 of the Indictment.
Dated: June 13th, 2005. Foreperson: No. 80.

"**COUNT 8**, verdict, lesser offense: We, the jury, in the above-entitled case, find the defendant **NOT GUILTY** of Providing Alcoholic Beverages to Persons Under the Age of 21, a lesser-included offense of that charged in Count 8 of the Indictment.
Dated: June 13th, 2005. Foreperson: No. 80.

"**COUNT 9**, verdict: We, the jury, in the above-entitled case, find the Defendant **NOT GUILTY** of Administering an Intoxicating Agent to Assist in the Commission of a Felony as charged in Count 9 of the Indictment.
Dated: June 10th, 2005. Foreperson: No. 80.

"**COUNT 9**, verdict, lesser offense: We, the jury, in the above-entitled case, find the Defendant **NOT GUILTY** of Providing Alcoholic Beverages to Persons Under the Age of 21, a lesser-included offense of that charged in Count 9 of the Indictment.

Dated June 10th, 2005. Foreperson: No. 80.

"**COUNT 10**, verdict: We, the jury, in the above-entitled case, find the Defendant **NOT GUILTY** of Administering an Intoxicating Agent to Assist in the Commission of a Felony as charged in Count 10 of the Indictment.
Dated: June 10th, 2005. Foreperson: No. 80.

"**COUNT 10**, verdict, lesser offense: We, the jury, in the above-entitled case, find the Defendant **NOT GUILTY** of Providing Alcoholic Beverages to Persons Under the Age of 21, a lesser-included offense of that charged in Count 10 of the Indictment.
Dated: June 10th, 2005. Foreperson: No. 80."

13 JUNE 2005

Picture: screengrab from CNN news coverage - via youtube

BREAKING NEWS
LIVE
MICHAEL JACKSON VERDICT
NOT GUILTY
ON ALL TEN COUNTS
CNN
JACKSON ACQUITTED
MEXICO ▲ 84.99
BREAKING NEWS

Mixed compiled news:screengrabs

TIMES
NOT GUILTY
ON ALL COUNTS
SCOTTISH DAILY
Mirror
FREE £2 BET AT ROYAL ASCOT
NOT GUILTY
Trial sensation as Jacko cleared of ALL TEN charges
TIMES
NOT GUILTY
ON ALL COUNT
MICHAEL JACKSON ACQUITTED OF 10 FELONY
STAR
THE JACKSON VERDICT
Not guilty
on all counts
ACQUITTED!!!
DAILY NEWS
RELIEF FOR JACKO AS HE'S FOUND NOT GUILTY OF 10 COUNTS IN CHILD SEX-ABUSE CASE
BOY, OH BOY!
MJ child molestation trial
NOT GUILTY
Jury clears Michael Jackson of all 10
Puts Agenda on the Ballot
Jackson Acquitted

Remember this date

Photo: screengrab
Source: mjjsource.com

for it is a part of ***HIS*tory**

The TRUTH

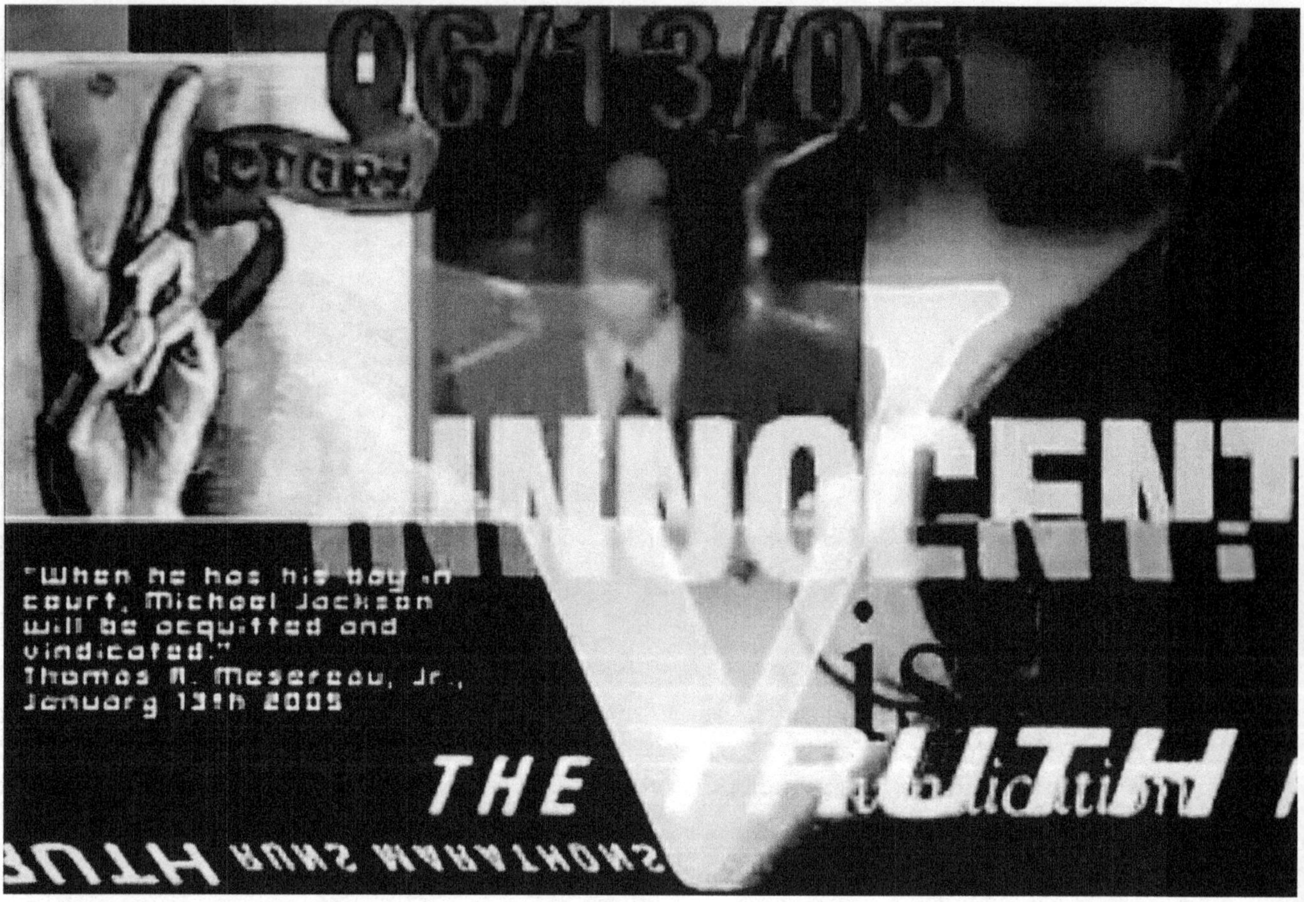

Photo: screengrab
Source: mjjsource.com

Runs Marathons

Victory

Photo: screengrab
Source: mjjsource.com

Thank you to my family, friends and fans
for all your love and support.
I will never forget.
I love you all .

Michael.

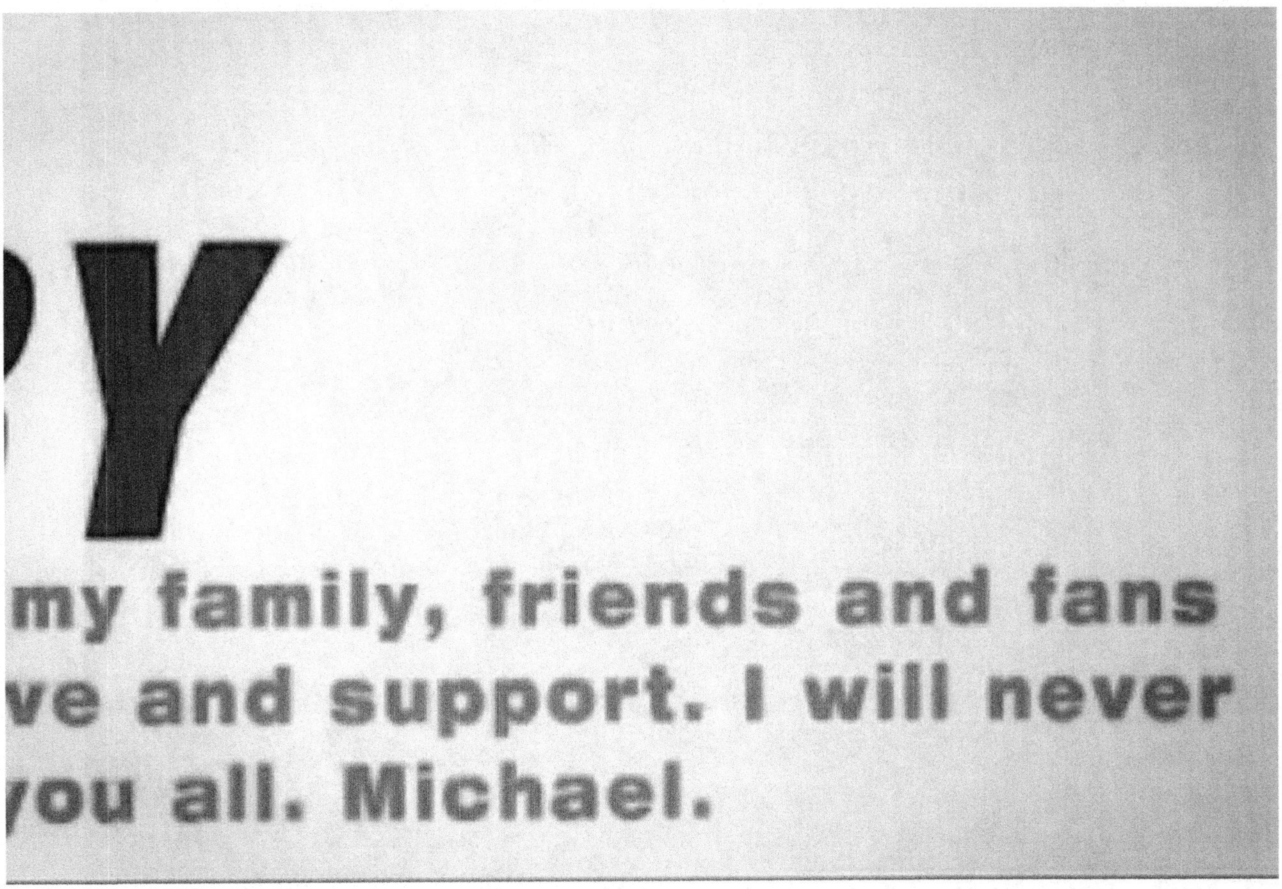

Statement of Michael Jackson: A Message For My Fans

Created Sunday, 26 June 2005

Without God, my children, my family and you, my fans, I could not have made it through.

Your love, support and loyalty made it all possible.

You were there when I really needed you. I will never forget you. Your ever present love held, dried my tears, and carried me through.

I will treasure your devotion and support forever. You are my inspiration.

Love,

Michael Jackson

Source: mjjsource.com

Comments

He was not a criminal and he was not a paedophile.

The fact that so many agencies investigated him and couldn't find anything proves he was completely innocent.

Mr Tom Mesereau
Lead Counsel for Michael Jackson.
December 2009.

> If you really looked at the evidence in this case. They had nothing.
>
> They had absolutely nothing.

Mr Tom Mesereau
Lead Counsel for Michael Jackson.
14 June 2005.

To Debra Opri, response?

Nancy Grace
CNNHN
13 June 2005

Well , this is a bitter pill you're going to have to swallow, Nancy. This is the reality, not the reality you have created for the last year.

Michael Jackson is not guilty.
Let him live his life in peace and stop trying to retry the case, and that's what you're doing.

Debra Opri
Attorney to
Michael Jackson's Parents
13 June 2005

You know what? You're right. So I guess I don't need to hear from the defense, either, and that would be you!

What are you doing? Don't you think you're doing a little rehash yourself, Miss Opri?

Nancy Grace
CNNHN
13 June 2005

No, I just want the world to know that our system works. We had a trial. We had a jury acquit him, and he is innocent.

He walked out of that courtroom. To use Mesereau's words, 'Justice was served'.

Debra Opri
Attorney to
Michael Jackson's Parents
13 June 2005

Sneddon said, 'I accept the jury verdict'.

Why don't you, Nancy?

Debra Opri
Attorney to
Michael Jackson's Parents
13 June 2005

Well, you know, there was a jury that took its job extremely seriously.

There was no smoking gun, said one of the jurors at the news conference. And I really think it summed it up, that yes, the mother was a huge problem for them.

And they did their job because they looked at the law and they considered that there was reasonable doubt on all these 10 charges. And that's why they found Michael Jackson not guilty. I think much respect to every single member of this jury.

Peter Bowes
BBC Correspondent
13 June 2005

Sources

Sources

Credit / Source

Michael Jackson

FBI Vault

Michael Jackson's Speeches Transcribed from Video Footage on Youtube

NAACP

Jasmine Guy

Debbie Allen

Michael Jackson's videographer

Michael Jackson Trial Transcripts

Reuters

LA Times

Various media oulets mentioned

Youtube and Youtubers

Zilk Media

MJJSource

The Examiner / Rev. Swift

Pictures

Screengrabs

Google

Royalty Free Images

Author's Logo

Graphic Design: Authors

MJJSource (Website credit to Zilk Media)

CNN and the BBC

Printed Newspapers as seen in book

Gratitude to:

Michael Jackson

The Jackson Family

Michael Jackson's videographer

Michael Jackson's Legal Team

Debra Opri

Peter Bowes

The Court Transcribers

FBI

Zilk Media

Michael Jackson Fans

Ms Watson

The Family

Theo Jones

Other Titles

Other Titles

Michael Jackson Innocent

David Bowie: Love from Brixton

The First 100 Days -
The 45th President of the United States of America
(Part 1)

The First 100 Days -
The 45th President of the United States of America
(Part 2)

TRU

Lies runs sprints,
but the truth runs marathons.
H
The truth will win this
marathon in court.

Made in the USA
Monee, IL
13 September 2026

63023694R00260